Eve Tuck, K. Wayne Yang, and Jade Nixon have curated a gorgeous and essential collection of first-person accounts by researchers dedicated to approaching the study of race and inequality with Black and Indigenous youth with care, respect, and imagination. The volume unveils the transformative power of using transdisciplinary and co-constructed theories and methods, inspiring readers to challenge traditional frameworks and forge new paths in research to reduce inequality.

Fabienne Doucet, *Executive Director, NYU Metropolitan Center for Research on Equity and the Transformation of Schools*

We cannot dismantle racism if we do not understand its depths, dynamics, and reinventions. In ways both vulnerable and courageous, the authors offer their intimate stories to produce stronger theories of racism, racialization, and settler colonialism. This volume is a source of inspiration for all those seeking to advance social justice.

Vivian Tseng, *President and CEO, Foundation for Child Development*

This critical and timely book promises to change your life and the world.

Michelle M. Jacob (Yakama)

This book makes an essential and timely contribution to scholarship on theoretical commitments to researching racial and settler colonial marginalization with young people. Grounded in an ethos of refusing deficit-centered and universalizing theories of marginalized youth, the book powerfully narrates possibilities for storying theory alongside young people in ways that are relational, anticolonial, and that carefully attend to the significance of place in making theory.

Dr. Fikile Nxumalo, *Associate Professor and Director of The Childhood Place Pedagogy Lab, OISE, University of Toronto, Author of* Decolonizing Place in Early Childhood Education

Too often in the social sciences, arid conceptions of racial inequality result in poorly-informed efforts to respond, and weak interpretations of research findings. Breaking new ground in conceptualizing Blackness, Indigeneity, and racialization, this innovative collection promises to inspire deeper and more theoretically grounded studies that will be better positioned than those of the past to improve the lives of those who continue to be harmed by racial oppression.

Adam Gamoran, *President, William T. Grant Foundation*

NEW APPROACHES TO INEQUALITY RESEARCH WITH YOUTH

Those engaging in research to reduce youth inequality know that robust and resonant theories are needed alongside strong methods to study racialization, racism, and the consequences of racial categorization. This edited volume shares contributors' first-person narrations of some of the hard-fought learnings and challenges of breaking from the traditions of their disciplinary fields and finding new and reclaimed ways to think about race. Featuring contributors' narrations of how they came to engage with compelling theories of Blackness, Indigeneity, and/or racialization, and how such theories inform the social science research they do with young people, this timely and consequential text tells a multi-disciplinary story about the careful reading and co-theorizing that is required to refuse universal theories of Blackness, Indigeneity, and racialization.

Eve Tuck is a professor of Critical Race and Indigenous Studies, and Canada Research Chair of Indigenous Methodologies with Youth and Communities at the Ontario Institute for Studies in Education, University of Toronto, Canada.

K. Wayne Yang is a professor of Ethnic Studies and Provost of John Muir College at the University of California, San Diego, USA.

Jade Nixon is a Ph.D. candidate at the Women & Gender Studies Institute at the University of Toronto, Canada.

NEW APPROACHES TO INEQUALITY RESEARCH WITH YOUTH

Theorizing Race Beyond the Traditions of Our Disciplines

Edited by Eve Tuck, K. Wayne Yang, and Jade Nixon

Routledge
Taylor & Francis Group

NEW YORK AND LONDON

Designed cover image: Donald E. Hall / Getty Images

First published 2024
by Routledge
605 Third Avenue, New York, NY 10158

and by Routledge
4 Park Square, Milton Park, Abingdon, Oxon, OX14 4RN

Routledge is an imprint of the Taylor & Francis Group, an informa business

Library of Congress Cataloging-in-Publication Data
Names: Tuck, Eve, editor. | Yang, K. Wayne, editor. | Nixon, Jade, editor.
Title: New approaches to inequality research with youth : theorizing race beyond
the traditions of our disciplines / Eve Tuck, K. Wayne Yang and Jade Nixon.
Description: New York : Routledge, 2024. | Includes bibliographical references
and index.
Identifiers: LCCN 2023031292 | ISBN 9781032283982 (hbk) | ISBN
9781032301853 (pbk) | ISBN 9781003303800 (ebk)
Subjects: LCSH: Equality--Research. | Minority youth--Research.
Classification: LCC HM821 .N468 2024 | DDC 305.23--dc23/eng/20231016
LC record available at https://lccn.loc.gov/2023031292

ISBN: 978-1-032-28398-2 (hbk)
ISBN: 978-1-032-30185-3 (pbk)
ISBN: 978-1-003-30380-0 (ebk)

DOI: 10.4324/9781003303800

Typeset in Galliard
by MPS Limited, Dehradun

CONTENTS

PART IV
Our stories are the heart of theory   **151**
Joanna L. Williams

PREFACE

This book had many potential names. One of our early favorites for the book title was inspired by Dani Ahuicapahtzin Cornejo's chapter, which actually became the title of one of the sections in the book, "Our stories are the heart of theory." This idea, that our storied paths are the soul of theory, is reflected in the cover image that we selected for this book. It also respects the land as a storyteller, and we hope it beckons your own path as a theorist.

Another title idea that we deeply considered included the phrase, "Moving against the tides of our disciplines," or "moving against the currents of our disciplines." This was a favored possibility for a long time in the project. Those with more knowledge about search engine results suggested that this title wouldn't necessarily help this book to find its readers. Even more compellingly, we moved away from this idea because of the kind intervention of a Quw'utsun graduate student, Ella Martindale, who works in the Tkaronto CIRCLE Lab. Ella pushed us to think differently about how we might inadvertently be attributing our disciplines with an overstated level of authority and permanence by giving them tidal qualities. We didn't really want to think of ourselves as in opposition to tidal waters, and of academic disciplines as empowered and agentic as waters. Instead, we want to think of *our* work, *our* projects, *our* senses of futurity, and the need for justice for communities as actually being the tides with which our theories are aligned. This intervention helped us to let go of the framing of working against the supposed tides of our disciplines, and working within the tides of justice.

In our dedicated naming time within our Tkaronto CIRCLE Lab meetings, we felt like every configuration of the words young people, research, disciplines, storytelling, and meaning-making was under consideration in this brainstorming, and that is how we arrived at the title that is now on the cover of this book. It has been such an expansive project that it has been important to find the name that would bring readers into relation with authors—all of us who are thinking through these ideas.

There are several social science disciplines that are notably absent from this book, even though we were in conversations with scholars from those disciplines to encourage their participation. In all instances, the potential authors had so much to say about what they would change in their disciplines, but were stretched thin in terms of time and other demands on them.

Indeed some disciplines need to transform, and others may need to be so shifted by the tides that they erode away entirely. When asked how certain disciplines with white supremacist origins can change, Eve has sometimes quipped that not every discipline is going to make it through the revolution. Revolution is being referred to in an imprecise way here, but marks instead the thinking that there will be a time in which the world we will be living in is different than the one we are living in now, and that academic knowledge production, and learning, and writing within the university has been transformed. Our imagination is that, in the future, many of our disciplines that are the homes of authors in this book (and not in this book) will need new formations to meet the tides of the next generations of scholars and learners. Threaded throughout this book is an invitation to everyone to consider our connection to disciplines, and question why some disciplines make some questions and theorizations possible, and others close down particular ways of knowing, thinking, and dreaming. We affirm that there are disciplines, including Indigenous studies, Black studies, queer and trans studies, that have long histories in the theories that are storied in this text. Our encouragement is to attend to these disciplines—including how they have emerged and struggled with and against institutionalization—as disciplines that enact responsibility. This is a responsibility to Black and Indigenous life, to the lives of communities of color, to the lives of young people, in cities, in rural areas, and lives shaped by ongoing occupation, and premature death. Our theories are in relation, in obligation to those youth and communities.

1

LEARNING TO THEORIZE MEANINGFULLY ABOUT RACE, RACIALIZATION, AND RACISM IS HUMBLING

Eve Tuck, K. Wayne Yang, and Jade Nixon

For many scholars wanting to do research on reducing inequality in youth outcomes, there might be a moment, years after the completion of our scholarly degrees, in which we realize that our preparation to research and write about important matters of Blackness, Indigeneity, and racialization has been insufficient. We notice that our preparation to research and write about the people and communities we care most about is … incomplete. We realize that we are out of our depths without more meaningful, respectful, and resonant theories of race and racism.

Sometimes scholars realize this while they are still in graduate school, and form study groups or other kinds of undercommons (Harney & Moten, 2013) to provide for themselves what their curriculum is missing. Sometimes the absence of meaningful, respectful, resonant theories of Blackness, Indigeneity, or racialization isn't clear until sometime after, when we stumble to address the complexity of the lived lives of young people and their communities.

Many of us have indeed received miseducation and mistraining that have proffered flawed, deeply problematic, and racist logics. In these instances, scholars might choose to embark on an individual journey to educate themselves so that they may be more prepared to adequately contend with their research questions and to support their students. In some cases, scholars have had to engage in the daunting task of working to undo their previous training and the consequences for their scholarly thinking and teaching. Sometimes these realizations may be prompted by their students or mentees. In other cases, especially during graduate school, students may not have the support or access to the theories of race and racism that are a

DOI: 10.4324/9781003303800-1

match with their experiences in the world. Notably, disciplinary and institutional culture may actually *discourage* scholars from seriously engaging with Critical Studies, making the journey to access and engage with this scholarship all the more challenging.

Nevertheless, those of us engaging in research to reduce youth inequality know that alongside strong methods, we also need strong theorizing about racialization, racism, and racial categorization. Graduate school might have been a place where some of us learned methods that can be utilized to reveal deep set systems of racism in our society. However, many of us had to learn to *theorize* racialization and racism in less formal ways, including through participation in social movements, collaborations outside our comfort zones, peer-to-peer mentoring, discussions with students, or self-guided reading outside of our discipline. Across these less formal settings, many of us extended the theories of racialization and racism we had already learned in our communities long before our arrival at the university, bringing shared language to something already deeply known.

Certainly, learning to theorize meaningfully about race, racialization, and racism is humbling. The goal is not to arrive as an expert at a final destination, but instead, to understand our thinking as always a work-in-progress.

In much research on young people's experiences of racism—especially research that seeks to reduce racism and anti-Blackness—scant attention is paid to rigorous theories of Blackness, Indigeneity, and racialization; any researchers working to reduce inequality may problematically treat race as a biological, static or naturalized category. Research, levers of inequality, and measures of youth outcomes related to racism may rely on racial categories and racial schemas that go uninterrogated. One of the more obvious ways that this can happen is when people casually swap their uses of the words race and racism. They may say that they are studying the impacts of race, whereas what their studies are really doing (or perhaps should really be doing) is tracing the impacts of racism as experienced by specific communities within specific places and power structures.

At the same time, in fields such as Indigenous Studies, Black Studies, Latinx Studies, and Asian American Studies, there is explicit theorizing about the invention of race and the ongoing consequences of racial stratification. These fields draw upon theories of race, Blackness, and Indigeneity in order to understand how such categories are socially constructed. Such theories undergird our understanding of how Blackness, Indigeneity, racialization, and racism matter for social science research on these topics, and how research findings can be applied. The theories of Blackness, Indigeneity, and racialization that scholars rely upon in social science research toward a more just society is an important preoccupation of this edited volume.

Excavating compelling theories of Blackness, Indigeneity, and racialization

This book shares first-person narrations of authors working across many disciplines, on their own learning and unlearning curves, and some of the challenges and disappointments of breaking from the traditions of their fields, and finding another way. Drawing together narrations of how scholars across fields came to engage with compelling theories of Blackness, Indigeneity, and/or racialization, and how such theories inform the social science research they do with young people, this edited volume tells a multi-disciplinary story about the careful study and assessment that is required to refuse universal theories of Blackness, Indigeneity, and racialization.

The terms and habits of referring to racialized groups are often disciplinary and reveal more about what various disciplines believe about race rather than how communities understand themselves to be racialized. Decisions about how racialized groups are defined, combined, collapsed, and not counted in statistical data, and about the terms researchers use to refer to people's experiences of being racialized and experiencing racism have consequences for youth and communities.

There are several innovative features that set this edited volume apart from other books on theories of race and racialization.

Storytelling approach. In every chapter, authors reflect upon and tell a story about how they grow in their learning and understanding around Blackness, Indigeneity, and racialization. More specifically, chapter authors share the teachers, books, places, and lived experiences that intimately shaped how they learned to theorize about Blackness, Indigeneity, and racialization and share how such learning informs their current research with youth. This collection of stories narrating the twists and turns, contradictions, dilemmas and shifts in authors' learning around theories of Blackness, Indigeneity, and racialization, invites readers to critically reflect on their own understandings of race and to consider what this means for the research they do with young people, and the consequences that such understandings of race and racism can have on young people.

Addressing theories of Blackness, Indigeneity and racialization. Chapters in this volume excavate the compelling theories that inform contributors' understandings of Blackness, Indigeneity and racialization in youth research, and engage policy and practice that impact youth. The theories of Blackness, Indigeneity, and racialization that contributing authors reflect upon, call often unaddressed racial hierarchies into question in their research to reduce inequality for Black and Indigenous youth and youth of color. Addressing theories of Blackness, Indigeneity, and racialization in this way offers scholars doing research on reducing inequality in youth outcomes a moment of pause to consider how their own understandings of race have serious implications for the research they do with Black and Indigenous youth and youth of color.

Discussion of social science research with young people. A primary focus of all of the chapters is social science research on reducing inequality in youth outcomes. Chapter authors reflect on theories of Blackness, Indigeneity, and racialization that pay detailed attention to the systems of anti-Blackness and settler colonialism that intimately shape the lives of Black and Indigenous youth and youth of color, and their communities. By grappling with such theories, contributors prioritize the often unaddressed consequences that being racialized and experiencing racism has on Black and Indigenous youth and youth of color in their research.

A book across many disciplines (and beyond them)

The reflections that contributors share about moving against the grain of their disciplines and towards their current approaches to youth research are major interventions of this edited volume. Because of the many theories, communities, disciplines, places, and theories of change herein, the chapters do not cohere into a universal theory that can just be simply applied—having different epistemological and ontological roots will mean that the theories do not necessarily fit together easily. The goal of this volume is not to assert a grand theory of race and racialization that can be generalized to every youth context. Rather, the volume as a whole is a gathering place of stories that encourage vulnerable and theoretically reflexive conversations about theories of Blackness, Indigeneity, and racialization among a community of scholars who are committed to reducing inequality in the lives of young people. These collections of stories offer various models for how we can make our way to more meaningful theories of race, racialization, and racism beyond our disciplines. As a storied book across many disciplines (and beyond them), you may opt to read the chapters in any order, flipping through to find the ones that speak directly to your field. We are fortunate to have a generous offering of chapters from researchers in the fields of Education, Black Studies, Indigenous Feminism, Sociology, History, Literary Studies, Chicanx Feminism, Public Health, and Multicultural and Equity Studies. Perhaps you will find a story that you would like to share with a colleague or a student in or beyond your discipline.

At the same time, the chapters within each section are also in conversation with one another. To write their chapters, authors and section editors met at a virtual writing retreat, read their earlier drafts aloud, and thoroughly contemplated one another's work. We encourage you to join in these conversations and to imagine or even curate your own dialogues with colleagues in other fields about your stories of (un)learning theories of racialization. Our stories of (un)learning are important to share with one another.

How this book came to be

The initial idea for this book came from a post-retreat workshop for people in the William T Grant Foundation Scholars Program, organized by Eve Tuck, Leah Doane, and Laura Tach, with support from Vivian Tseng. The workshop was an exciting opportunity for participating scholars to reflect on the theories behind the theories of their work as they related to studying race and racism in the lives of young people. Vivian Tseng, then Vice-President and Senior Program Officer of the William T Grant Foundation encouraged Eve and others to create further opportunities to consider these ideas and practices. Perhaps this could have been a conference, but instead, Eve turned to K. Wayne Yang and Jade Nixon, both dear collaborators, and we created what would become the William T Grant Foundation Writing Fellows Initiative.

Nearly 70 people applied to this one-time initiative, and we ultimately selected 21 Writing Fellows to participate in the creation of two edited volumes. Those selected would have the opportunity to participate in occasional writing sessions and a two-day virtual writing retreat with one-of-a-kind writing workshops with Alexis Pauline Gumbs and Michelle Jacob. Writing Fellows also met with the senior program team of the William T Grant Foundation.

All Writing Fellows participated in a webinar about their chapters. We hope that readers will also view, share, and teach the companion webinars based on each section, available at https://wtgrantfoundation.org/theorizing-blackness-indigeneity-racialization and the Tkaronto CIRCLE LAB Youtube Channel at https://www.youtube.com/@tkarontocirclelab6308. In each webinar, facilitated by the section editors, you can hear and see authors read from their work, discuss their stories in additional detail, and talk with one another about the lasting impacts of working to theorize differently than they had been taught to do.

As noted above, this edited volume emerged with and alongside the edited volume, *Conceptualizations of Blackness in Education,* also published by Routledge/Taylor and Francis. Both volumes are in chorus, and share stories of the winding paths scholars embarked on to make their way to the places, people, communities, and ideas that shape their theories of Blackness, Indigeneity, and racialization.

Organization of this book

There are four parts to this volume: "Our theories takes place", edited by Jade Nixon; "Racialization is an ongoing (settler) process", edited by Leah Doane; "Refusing to speak against ourselves and our communities", edited by Eve Tuck and K. Wayne Yang, and "Our stories are the heart of theory", edited by Joanna Williams. Arguably all knowledge is place-based knowledge, all theory is specific to the where, when, and who of land and peoples. Thus, the book opens with "Our theories takes place" in which Indigenous, Black, and Latinx authors describe how places and peoples are often our first teachers who—as much as researchers may be theorizing/racializing our communities—theorize back. The second section reminds us that racialization is a product of colonization. Because settler colonialism is ongoing, shapeshifting through capitalism's many adaptations, racism is constantly being reinvented. In "Racialization is an ongoing (settler) process", contributors describe contemporary forms of colonial racialization in the politics of civic education and Islamophobia. Section three, "Refusing to speak against ourselves and our communities", excavates insidious disciplinary racializations that are so naturalized within well-intended, ostensibly anti-racist paradigms of examining inequality, that we struggle to even refuse them. Authors offer storied critiques of social work, quantitative methods, and restorative justice. In the final section, "Our stories are the heart of theory", contributors resist grand theories of race—themselves forms of racialization—in order to transcend the limits placed upon dreaming theories of liberation. Together, all of these sections reflect the ways that learning to do this work can be humbling, but entirely worthwhile.

Writing as a way of knowing

This edited volume, and the William T Grant Foundation-funded Writing Fellows initiative as a whole, are meant to enliven understandings of Blackness, Indigeneity, and racialization that are at work in social science research intended to reduce inequality in youth outcomes. At the heart of the stories told here are stories of transformation, observation, and curiosity about one's own growth and learning, and a vulnerability in sharing that story of transformation with others, even while it is still unfolding. Growing out of something is awkward, made all the more awkward by doing it in front of others. For these reasons, our encouragement as editors has been toward embracing the practice of writing as a way of knowing.

Writing as a way of knowing has been a core part of Eve's writing and mentoring practices since graduate school, and being a student of Composition and Rhetoric scholar Sondra Perl (see Perl, 1980; 2004). Writing as a way of knowing and writing as a way of telling is a framework first introduced in an NCTE lecture by McCrimmon (1970). In writing as a way of knowing we are truly using the process of bringing a pen to the page, bringing our hands to a keyboard, or doing dictation into a document in order to process—through that writing—what we know about something. This is writing that begins in one place, and then goes to another place. Writing as a way of knowing is for us as the writer. Our main concern is not for an audience; oftentimes, this writing is private and won't be seen by anybody else. Writing as a way of knowing is not concerned with what the writing looks like to somebody else, but instead what it feels like, and what it does in relation to our thinking and understanding, of ourselves.

Writing as a way of telling is an audience-oriented form of writing. It is deliberately pedagogical in terms of bringing a reader through the paces of our ideas, and our understanding of a topic. Writing as a way of telling is very intentional about creating an introduction, moving from that introduction into a discussion, playing that discussion out until it is satisfactorily, thoroughly addressed, and then moving into a deliberate closing. There is an organized arc to writing as a way of telling and that organization is based on our anticipation of the reader's needs. Writing as a way of telling, when it is at its best, is a pedagogical practice. We are considering in our organization of that work, what would be the best way to bring that set of ideas to the reader.

In academia, the form of writing that is almost exclusively promoted is writing as a way of telling. In academia, it's not even clear that writing is meant to meet a reader's needs. So, presumably, even though writing in academia is writing as a way of telling, academic publications often miss the mark in being generous with a reader, or telling in a way that anticipates the questions that a reader will have. Instead writing as a way of telling in academia is often a defensive telling. It is often a stingy telling, a telling that is meant to *occlude* understanding or to keep further questions at bay. So, we are left with a genre of writing as a way of *not telling*.

Writing as a way of knowing is writing that starts somewhere and ends somewhere else, a dropping into somewhere interior within ourselves to learn what we know, and what needs to be said. Writing as a way of telling is writing designed to be generous to a reader, anticipating that they will be learning from our work. To say we need both in our practice is not to double our work as scholars, but to say that it is so hard to be generous with readers when we have not taken the time to be generous with ourselves. Without writing as a way of knowing, we can be superficial about why our research matters, and who needs to hear what we have to say. Knowing and telling are not oppositional forms of writing. They are dialectical, informing each other. Both are needed to move beyond flimsy theories of change and urgencies in writing that are not ours.

A reminder to carry

If anything, we hope that in trying to enliven these discussions in the chapters, the webinars, and the gatherings we made to create these works, can serve as a reminder that our stories are indeed the heart of theory, that we cannot be made to speak against ourselves, and that our work matters for the futures we are already dreaming, even if the terms need to be discarded along the way. We are living in the mismatches between what inquiry could be, and what it is, for now. We use our stories to fill those gaps between what it is, and what we know is possible. Don't feel that you are alone in feeling like you are stretching to fill that gap. Balancing the discourse of our disciplines with the needs of our communities is worthy of our time and attention. Tell us your story as you do it, and we will be there with you.

Acknowledgments

For their cherished contributions to this volume and to the William T Grant Foundation Writing Fellows Initiative, everlasting thanks to Vivian Tseng, Jenny Irons, Noelle Hurd, Adam Gamoran, Lenore Neier, Billy Hunter, Tiffany Hill, Milen Negash, Ella Martindale, Sefanit Habtom, Megan Femi-Cole, Education Commons at the Ontario Institute for Studies in Education at the University of Toronto, Desmond Wong, Alexis Pauline Gumbs, Michelle M. Jacob, and Jennifer Sylvester. Qagasaakung to Tkaronto CIRCLE Lab member Razan Samara for careful and thoughtful copy-editing of chapters in this book.

References

Harney, S., & Moten, F. (2013). *The undercommons: Fugitive planning and Black study*. Autonomedia.

McCrimmon, J. M. (1970). Writing as a way of knowing [paper presentation]. In L. W. Moffett (Ed.), *The promise of English: Distinguished lectures from the 1970 national convention of the national council of teachers of English, Denver, Colorado* (pp. 32–43). National Council of Teachers of English.

Perl, S. (1980). Understanding composing. *College Composition and Communication*, *31*(4), 363–369.

Perl, S. (2004). *Felt sense: Writing with the body*. Portsmouth, NH: Boynton/Cook Heinemann.

PART I

Our theories take place

Jade Nixon

The collection of writing in this opening section carefully attends to what Black feminist geographer Katherine McKittrick identifies as "where we know from" (McKittrick, 2021, p. 29). Across these pages, authors Beardall, Henry, and Puente tell stories about the places that taught them much of what they know about themselves as Indigenous, Black, and Latinx people, their communities, and later, their academic disciplines. In this section, the authors draw our attention to the highway border patrol near the Manzanita Kumeyaay Reservation, Mawmaw's front porch steps in New Orleans, and the rural agricultural fields in San Joaquin Valley as the specific places where they know from.

As you read through this section, you will notice that place is not just a "neutral backdrop, or … a bounded and antiquated concept, or as only physical landscape" in social science research (Tuck and McKenzie, 2014, p. 18). Instead, authors emphasize place as central to their theorizations of Indigeneity, Blackness, and racialization. All three authors foreground place and their communities, as first teachers, as holding wisdom, and as compasses helping them make their way to other ideas, stories, and people beyond their disciplines. "Our theories take place" illuminates the places where rich theorizations of Indigeneity, Blackness, and racialization have always been happening.

In the opening chapter of this section, Chapter 2, Theresa Rocha Beardall pushes our thinking of place "Toward a sociology of Indigenous placemaking". Beardall's conceptualization of Indigenous placemaking is shaped by the story she tells of her and her sister being stopped by a white Border Patrol Officer at the border patrol highway checkpoint near to

DOI: 10.4324/9781003303800-2

where her sister lives on the Manzanita Kumeyaay Reservation in San Diego, California. For Beardall and her sister, this checkpoint is one they cross through regularly. Yet, it is this particular encounter with border patrol that revealed to Beardall that the disciplinary training she was receiving as a PhD student in Sociology did not account for what she was experiencing at the checkpoint. She realized that Indigenous ways of knowing were obscured and did not count in the field of Sociology. Thinking with her experiences at the highway checkpoint, and the field of Indigenous Studies, Beardall brings attention to what she conceptualizes as Indigenous placemaking. Indigenous place-making has three main considerations: 1) It is a tribally specific engagement with a "system of reciprocal relations and obligations" (Coulthard, 2014, p. 13). 2) It understands that land is a relative and teacher. 3) It is a practice of resistance and refusal against ongoing settler colonialism. Beardall's conceptualizations of Indigenous placemaking intervene in sociological conceptions of place by centering Indigenous worldviews and Indigenous land. Beardall encourages readers, especially those studying inequality and racialization, to learn from Indigenous placemaking. This shift in focus, she suggests, can work against settler colonialism structuring the border patrol highway checkpoints, and the discipline of Sociology.

In Kevin Lawrence Henry Jr.'s chapter titled, "They are here with me: (Critical Race) Theories from my flesh", his grandmother and community in New Orleans, and Hurricane Katrina offer him lessons on love and heartbreak. The time Henry spends with his grandmother, Gertrude Edwards, whom he calls Mawmaw, in her car, at the Seafood market, or on her front steps taught him about love, care, and joy. These teachings would also stay with Henry through the heartbreak of Hurricane Katrina, which brought forth its own set of lessons. During Hurricane Katrina and the "policy disaster" (p. 1) that followed, Henry learned about structured vulnerability, state-sanctioned poverty, and divestment. He would also learn about neoliberal restructuring in his teacher education program where he witnessed the takeover of public education, the mass firing of Black educators, and high rates of suspension and expulsion of Black children identified as the problem in real-time. Henry's early lessons on care made him especially aware of how little charter schools cared about Black children.

It is Critical Race Theory (CRT) that offered Henry precise language to express that "shit aint right" (p. 6). Henry refers to CRT as the Blues Epistemology that makes room for stories of pain at the same time that it heals Black people, and affirms Black life. Henry's research draws upon the CRT and the Black Radical Tradition to understand the relationship between post-Katrina neoliberal educational restructuring, the takeover of public education, and how Black people engage as well as contest it.

Henry's work is also shaped by the "place [he] call[s] home" in New Orleans with his Mawmaw, her friends, Ms. Delores and Mr. Gene, and his aunts, Aunt Bernice, and Aunt Zenobia as the people in New Orleans where he first learned of Black study.

In the final chapter of this section, Chapter 5, "'Central California's completely different': Theorizing racialization in the San Joaquin Valley through a rural Latinx epistemology" Mayra Puente narrates her earliest memories of racialization that took place on the agricultural fields in San Joaquin Valley, California. As an 8-year-old girl, Puente learned early that exploitation, racism, xenophobia, and white supremacy were happening on the rural farms where her parents and many other Latinx im/migrants worked. She witnessed how Latinx im/migrants were treated as racialized low-waged and disposable workers, and what consequences this had for her family and community.

Puente's understanding of racialization deepened when she moved away from her rural Latinx farm community to attend University in the urban city of Los Angeles. During her undergraduate degree, Puente began noticing that the academic fields of Political Science, Chicana/o Studies, and Education were centered on the urban contexts and left people like her from rural farm communities out. To intervene in these sets of absences, Puente began developing, what she describes as, a rural Latina epistemology. She names her mentor, Daniel (Danny) G. Solórzano, a Chicano Studies scholar, as a scholar who nurtured her interests in race and the rural and invited her to think across the fields of Critical Race Theory (CRT), Latino Critical Race Theory (LatCrit), and Chicana feminism. The rural agricultural fields in East Portville helped her find her way to the people, and fields of study that brought her back to what she always knew. The rural agricultural fields also shaped her educational research with rural Latinx young people living in San Joaquin Valley. In her research, Puente turned to young people as experts who already had an analysis of their own racialization in the rural agricultural regions where they lived. Like her 8-year-old self, the young people in Puente's research knew a lot about how exploitation, racism, xenophobia, and white supremacy was happening on the farm, and where they lived. In this chapter, Puente shines a light on her rural community in San Joaquin Valley as the place informing her rural Latina epistemological intervention and a place where rural Latinx young people theorize from.

All three chapters in this section offer robust examples of how to meaningfully engage a place in theorizations of Indigeneity, Blackness, racialization, and racism. If this writing had been available to me at the beginning stages of my graduate studies, it would have been clearer that all of the lessons I learned in place and in my community were significant and always right there with me. I hope that these chapters find you right on time. My hope especially for Black, Indigenous, and racialized graduate students is that this section affirms what you already know, and have learned from place, land, and waters. As you read through these chapters one by one or out of sequence, I invite readers to deeply reflect on what place has taught you, the wisdom place holds, and how place has been guiding your thinking all along.

References

Coulthard, G. S. (2014). *Red skin, white masks: Rejecting the colonial politics of recognition*. Minneapolis: Minnesota.

McKittrick, K. (2020). *Dear science and other stories*. Duke University Press.

Tuck, E., & McKenzie, M. (2014). *Place in research: Theory, methodology, and methods*. Routledge.

2

TOWARD A SOCIOLOGY OF INDIGENOUS PLACEMAKING

Theresa Rocha Beardall

"Ma'am, please pull to the right and make your way over to secondary," said a white, middle-aged United States border patrol officer with a gruff voice. The officer waved his hand to the side of the highway, shifting his gaze away from us and onto the next car, a fluid motion that felt both robotic and condescending. "Why is that officer? Is there something wrong?" I pipe up to ask from the passenger seat. My big sister shoots me a look, the kind that connects family in a way that says, "Just shut it, okay? Let me do this."

We were two siblings making our way from my sister's home on the Manzanita Kumeyaay Reservation to a day in "town," known to most as San Diego, California. To get there, we must travel through the soaring Ekwiiyemak mountain range and a border patrol checkpoint that has been a part of our lives for as long as either of us can remember. Although my sister and I are separated in age by only three years, our current lives brought us to this dusty highway moment from very different circumstances. As an adult, my sister moved from San Diego back to the reservation that welcomed our Oneida and Sault Ste. Marie family a half-century ago when they arrived from Wisconsin. My sister started a family there, we buried our mother there, and she nourishes a sense of purpose by raising her firstborn in her Kumeyaay traditions. In my sister's life, this checkpoint is a daily reminder of belonging, exclusion, and the potential for removal. This checkpoint is also a physical barrier between my sister's small home and her material needs, a space she must navigate en route to the grocery store, pharmacy, and post office. This dusty little post office is extra special to our relationship because this is where we send and receive lovely care packages each year for our birthday.

DOI: 10.4324/9781003303800-3

In contrast to my sister's journey, I moved away after community college to finish my undergraduate degree and again to attend graduate school. This distance means that I visit San Diego and Manzanita whenever possible, but my education has taken me farther from home than any of us prefer, especially my big sister, who gently reminds me of this each time I am home. We both remember though, that as the last child, this was the educational path our parents and siblings wanted for me. There was a belief that my advanced schooling was our last chance at something different, something more stable and flexible than the circumstances we grew up in. With this distance of time and place, highway checkpoints no longer manage my movement as they once had when I was younger. Indeed, I rarely think of border patrol officers except when I go home. So it is there that my frustration bubbles over because my family still does not have the freedom of movement we expected from adulthood. It is also there, at home, where I am filled with love and possibility about what more this life can be.

At the time of our border patrol encounter, I was living thousands of miles away in New York. Professionally, I was far from home to complete coursework for my Ph.D. in Sociology. More personally, I was away because I hoped to learn new analytical methods and theories to challenge how United States law reproduces intergenerational inequality for families like mine. Sitting on this dusty highway during winter break, I could viscerally feel what I already knew to be true: that the sociological perspective I was learning was too narrow, and it failed to grasp the complexity of the social world that shaped me. This limited sociological theorizing, and the existing literature that accompanied it, could not help me unravel the relationship between racial surveillance and the landscape's sociocultural history along this familiar California mountainscape. As I looked out the truck's windshield and waited for the secondary and more intrusive style of border patrol inspection, this intellectual distance between my doctoral training and the meaning of place and theory unfolding alongside me was so vast but I was encouraged to linger in that distance and figure out what it meant for me.

As we sat, I did my best to explain why I spoke up and why this encounter bothered me so deeply. "It feels like 'Driving While Native' or something like that," I offered to my sister as a gentle invitation for her thoughts. "It's just not right that they always do this. You know, like the problem of 'Driving While Black'," I continued as we stared off at the bright sunshine flooding the dry canyons below. My sister nodded and said, "Yeah, but this just draws attention to us, and I'd rather not. It's not safe with these guys. You already know how they harass me, how my cedar braids and the rezzy decals on my truck are always a reason to pull me out of line. I won't stop being proud of where we come from, but we don't need the extras." I sat back and sighed, the truck idling and humming its own checkpoint song. We both knew she was right.

***

After a week with my sister in the sun-drenched landscape of our youth, I gave her a great big hug and returned to my sociological training in New York. It was still very early in my graduate program, and I spent much of my time learning how the discipline defined itself and its contributions. When friends and family asked what I was learning, I would explain that Sociology is the study of social groups, how they come to be, how they function, and how interactions between group members create change in the society in which they are embedded.

My community was already so proud of my research on race, racism, indigeneity, policing, and inequality. I explained that I was learning a new set of tools and perspectives to empower that work. In response, friends and family would exclaim, "Ah, that's great. You're studying our experiences! What have you found?" Honestly, I never knew how to respond because what I found was that we were missing, erased, and largely cast out of sociological analysis. And when we *were* present, we were a problem, incomplete, or just a footnote in some larger empirical or theoretical intervention.

As my training progressed, I realized that there were many things about the discipline that I could not fully understand. For one, I thought that Sociology's emphasis on studying social problems would provide me with accessible tools to *do* something about the inequalities affecting Native families. Instead, the discipline's investment seemed limited to certain inequalities and only for *particular* social groups.

Secondly, I realized that place as a dynamic social force did not seem to matter in my sociological training. This meant that my coursework paid little attention to people like me with lived experiences at border patrol checkpoints and the spaces between tribal reservations and nearby cities and towns. Instead, place was often construed as a canvas or abstraction upon which social life played out. Understandably then, existing sociological research on place, primarily geographic space, has led to the use of complex statistical methods to uncover neighborhood-level trends and inequalities (e.g., crime, traffic, neighborhood disadvantage, food deserts, and air pollution). This research illuminates a relationship between geography and people's livelihood but does little to shed light on the meaning, relationships, and attachments that people have to place.

Together, these omissions reinforced my determination to build a research agenda that could articulate the relationship between state violence and racialized place-based experiences. This agenda would center on those who endured that violence and thus had the demand, power, and intergenerational knowledge to change it. For this work, new concepts were required.

In the following chapter, I share the concept of Indigenous placemaking to counter sociological erasure and reframe place as an active and dynamic social actor rather than a backdrop to sociality. This Indigenous intellectual practice communicates "felt experiences" as community knowledge (Million, 2008, p. 268), creating a context for a deeper understanding of the social world. Drawing from the rich work of several Indigenous scholars and thinkers, I define Indigenous placemaking in three parts: first it is a tribally specific understanding and engagement with place as a "system of reciprocal relations and obligations" (Coulthard, 2014, p. 13). Second is the recognition that land is a relative and a teacher; it offers vital instructions about upholding responsibilities between peoples, landscapes, and nonhuman kin (Deloria Jr & Wildcat, 2001, p. 144). Third, and most apparent to me in my encounter with my sister, is that Indigenous placemaking is a solidarity practice (Coulthard & Simpson, 2016), that empowers Indigenous peoples to refuse "the permanence of settler colonialism as an unmovable reality" (Simpson, 2014, p. 8). This three-part framing illustrates that sociality is place-based, lived experiences must be centered, and that the land is also a mode of relationality. By foregrounding Indigenous perspectives, sociological research can better analyze how place matters within Indigenous relationality and is imbued with the possibility for interdependent futures (Byrd, 2019). This perspective requires an understanding that Indigenous placemaking predates the arrival of settlers and what we know today as the discipline of Sociology with its tendency toward the settler colonial logics of extraction.

I introduce this concept in hopes of accomplishing three goals: 1) to reckon with the discipline's longstanding investment in Indigenous erasure, 2) to call out the discipline's present denial of Indigenous sovereignty and knowledge production, and 3) to provide a preliminary roadmap for how we might engage Indigenous placemaking in future sociological studies of inequality and racialization, especially that which centers youth and families. To be clear, my intention is not to coin a new phrase for the sake of doing so or to suggest that I have discovered a new way of navigating the social world. Instead, I see my intervention as an opportunity to reveal suppressed knowledge and to introduce others to the reality that "place is infused with multiple meanings: one view emerging from the deeply interwoven relationship of community to location, and another marked by legal contract and ownership" (Coleman, 2005, p. 279).

I also wish to show that Indigenous placemaking is well aligned with disciplinary commitments to take the social and historical context of inequality seriously. It expands this commitment by asking that we also take *place context* seriously, and in a way that makes room for mutual responsibilities between the human and nonhuman world. Engaging these relationships prefigures places as relatives with memories and knowledge that refuse settler erasure. By taking up land as an Indigenous analytic, we can also address the settler logics that drive disciplinary norms about what it means to think sociologically. This is an opportunity for something more.

Past: Reckoning with sociology's investment in Indigenous erasure

Omissions of particular peoples and epistemologies are not accidental and disciplinary avoidance of specific modes of knowing is itself a form of communication. Throughout my training, these persistent omissions led me to wonder: How can one theorize race and place when place is treated as static? How can one theorize place when they are invested in erasing the first peoples, cultures, languages, and songs of that land? And if one cannot (or refuses to) consider the land's totality of relations, how can one meaningfully theorize other social interactions that happen there? Indigenous placemaking's emphasis on land as a site of convergence, reciprocity, and refusal builds out from these limitations in contemporary sociological theory. It illustrates how place "provides the context for understanding social relationships" because place reciprocates with the human and non-human beings that gather there (Coleman, 2005, p. 277).

To investigate this sociological erasure, I turn to Gieryn (2018) and his important contributions within the limited sociological theorizing of place. According to Gieryn, a "place" is a site that is made real by having a location, a material form, and a meaning to a particular set of persons (2018). Gieryn differentiates place from "truth-spots" which are unique locations that lend credibility to beliefs about the world; in time, these beliefs come to be taken as truth among a group of people (2018). Put another way, truth-spots are sites of cultural understanding that confirm people's experiences, memories, and interpretations of the world.

At first glance, these definitions provide me with a language to examine my racialized encounter at the border patrol checkpoint. Upon closer reflection, my experience presents a sociological puzzle involving taken-for-granted assumptions about how social groups encounter, interact with, and navigate place and "truth." For example, Gieryn's definition of place is space-bound and cannot account for the possibility that a place may function as a memoryscape for those displaced or removed from their homelands, such as immigrants, refugees, and Indigenous peoples (Ghanayem, 2023). In this way, Gieryn's operationalization of place and truth-spots fails to acknowledge that land itself brings meaning into the world with and without human interventions and that place and kin build multidimensional meaning about the social world with one another in and through place. Further, Gieryn's definitions do not reflect how settler colonialism and racialization shape social stratification in the United States or how peoples' rights are intertwined with white-centered definitions of place and truth. Thus, it is a *convergence* of social forces that impacts what people believe, where they believe it, why they believe it, and which perspectives and beliefs about the world are deemed credible.

Ultimately, sociological theorizing that privileges a Eurocentric worldview has less to do with Gieryn than with the discipline's longstanding investment in whiteness as a dominant ideology. As a 19th-century intellectual project, Sociology concerned itself with the relationship between society and modernity, the growth of capitalism, class struggle, the division of labor, and how each aspect of social life was intertwined with the secularization of society (Eubanks, 2020). In turn, the transition into the 20th century led many sociologists to consider the impact of rapid social change, including the movement of people from rural to urban life (Wirth, 1938), how individuals made sense of the busy and bright life of urban spaces (Simmel, 2012), and what this population density meant for mutual interdependence (Urry, 2001) and subsequent social (dis)order in families and neighborhoods. These ideas, and their deployment to control and criminalize communities of color for supposedly deviant behavior, shaped who and how the discipline studied social life in the United States.

Contemporary scholars are disrupting presumptions about the value of whiteness by engaging in reclamation work on the relationship between settler and sociological knowledge production (McKay et al., 2020; Steinman, 2021). Critical engagement with settler colonialism, a social process involving the arrival of settlers that take Indigenous lands and resources to create their own homes and societies (Ghanayem, 2023; Glenn, 2015; Rocha Beardall, 2021), necessitates an ongoing analysis of the ideologies and institutions that built and sustain this violence. To this point, McKay et al. (2020) argue that if Sociology cannot acknowledge that the United States is a settler-colonial society, then it lacks a framework to reconcile the existence of subordinated Indigenous nations and the racialized social practices produced by this reality. Likewise, Glenn (2015) argues that Sociology's inattention to settler colonial violence hinders the discipline's understanding of how the white settler state, and its corresponding political economy, structure the racialized and gendered formation of communities of color. Similarly, Go (2018) explains that sociological theories of race alone cannot fully explain how logics of empire and racialized colonial regimes inform the function of racial stratification in the present moment. By drawing attention to the colonial origins of the United States, scholars are challenging the capitalist, patriarchal, anti-Black, and anti-Indigenous values that shape sociological studies and methodologies.

I take up these themes in my research and examine the legal actors that are deputized to continuously enact state violence against Native peoples and other racialized minorities. I focus on social workers and law enforcement officers, including the presence of border patrol agents along my sister's reservation highway, because of their role in protecting settler demands for place as property. Throughout United States history, police have been deployed to protect white interests by monitoring the movement of others, such as who can go where and *when*. This monitoring is inherently racialized, as seen in the forced removal of Indigenous peoples and the enslavement and incarceration of Black people.

I examine these racializing social processes by focusing on their power to destabilize and separate Black and Native families. In addition to measuring the negative consequences of encounters with social workers and police, I analyze how the roots of policing and child welfare in the United States require the othering of select families to legitimize the state's punitive treatment against them (Rocha Beardall & Edwards, 2021). Using a sociology of Indigenous placemaking lens, I also show that families and tribal nations actively refused settler violence, rendering settler intentions to eliminate Indigenous peoples as a failed project. I do so by chronicling how Indigenous kinship networks center care for one another, our homelands, and the non-human kin who sustain us. Thus, Indigenous peoples reinforce their placemaking by engaging with land as much more than a collection of physical properties. They remind us that a place is agentic in the cocreation of relationality and resistance relationships that thrive under, and despite, the auspices of oppression.

Present: Denying Indigenous sovereignty and knowledge production

If Sociology is willing to engage with what cannot be explained through Eurocentric ways of knowing, the discipline can arrive at a more generative place from which to theorize the social world. To facilitate this journey of understanding, I offer three collective goals for consideration: 1) that we unlearn taken-for-granted knowledge in the discipline about inequality and racialization; 2) that we learn to name and engage with indigeneity from the perspective of Indigenous peoples; and 3) that we develop a clear understanding of land as pedagogy by acknowledging the necessity of learning from Indigenous peoples' worldviews, research agendas, and homeland stewardship (Simpson, 2014). To do this work is to grow as both intellectuals and practitioners.

First, sociologists can take deliberate steps to unlearn taken-for-granted knowledge in the discipline by challenging Eurocentric presumptions about truth, belonging, and deservingness. Scholars can do this by engaging with settler colonialism as an ongoing and violent social process, not a remnant of the past. This trajectory shift requires confidence to accept that just because one cannot explain settler-colonial inequality in the discipline's dominant language, it does not mean one cannot learn to reckon with the mechanisms of erasure that made this omission possible. Along the way, this trajectory shift will illuminate the limitations of the Eurocentric perspective and the ways that it hinges on hostility and death and suppresses non-white people's memories, understandings, and construction about the world. One limitation is that Eurocentrism regards place and time as fixed rather than ongoing social relationships informed by socio-historical processes. By integrating Indigenous placemaking and acknowledging the cultural heritage of land, Sociology can stop its "silencing of the past" (Trouillot, 1995) and more accurately theorize race and place.

Second, sociologists can learn to name and engage indigeneity from the perspective of Indigenous peoples. Indigeneity is defined as a land-based historical identity reserved for individuals and communities who existed in a particular place before the arrival of settlers. This identity emphasizes relationships with land, other tribal members, and the responsibilities of kinship more broadly (Tuck & McKenzie, 2015). Thus, when I use the word indigeneity, I am referencing a social relationship to place and not a specific person or group. My Grandmother Theresa, our matriarch and my namesake, taught me to theorize indigeneity as a set of relationships and responsibilities to place, memory, human, and non-human kin networks. She taught me this by describing and embodying her sociocultural connections to her Great Lakes homelands; she could never and would never untether herself from Wisconsin and Upper Michigan, the landscape bordering Lake Superior and Lake Michigan that mapped our family's history. Decades later, I still have such vivid memories of watching her board the Greyhound bus to and from San Diego, California to Green Bay, Wisconsin. She made that journey to care for us *and* to remain rooted and whole no matter the distance.

Informed by my Grandmother's teachings about indigeneity and relationality, I study Indigenous resistance to the possessive surveillance of settler colonialism. I do so by situating indigeneity alongside race, class, and gender as distinct but interrelated social locations that inform the study of state violence (Rocha Beardall, 2016; 2020; 2021; 2022). I follow the tradition of calling attention to the relationship between settler and sociological knowledge production (Glenn, 2015; Go, 2018; Steinman, 2021) and invert and extend that analysis by centering Indigenous placemaking rather than settler epistemologies. For example, mainstream Sociology would likely recount my Grandmother's life using a deficit framing focused on poverty and hardships, obscuring her agency and kinship prerogatives.

Indigenous placemaking counters this limited understanding of agency by centering my Grandmother's reciprocal engagement with, and insistence on, land relationality. A placemaking lens also centers on the kinship responsibilities that compelled her to travel and maintain a sense of herself in her traditional homelands and in the Southwest, where her only child struggled to raise her grandchildren far from family.

A willingness to revise existing sociological perspectives allows scholars to expand our disciplinary toolkit and more fully recognize the power of placemaking among diverse social groups. Likewise, the ability to think with Indigenous placemaking reimagines the sociological study of "social and historical context" into the study of genealogy. A genealogical approach would center the formation of a people, worldview, and the practice of passing down knowledge about how one is meant to live in the world and to whom they are responsible.

My family instilled our place-based genealogy within me despite my being born and raised in California. They made sure that I knew the Great Lakes through routine visits, but perhaps most importantly, because my Grandmother took the time to narrate her regional memoryscape to me. Some memories were filled with deep sorrow, and others with incredible pride for herself and our loved ones; she continuously infused those memories into how she raised me and told me why along the way. I also learned endless Oneida and Ojibwe words and phrases because she took the time to teach them. She told me that even though I would not have many conversation partners in my younger years, I would learn about myself through the language and be ready for the conversation partners I would meet in the years to come.

Likewise, my Grandmother made sure that I knew about the important medicinal properties of many plants. She used to laugh and say that I was not that interested in this learning until she described the importance of strawberries, our Indigenous heart berries. I would sit at the kitchen counter making "strawberry drink" as she explained that this sweet, first berry of the season held healing in their leaves as she boiled them into teas. We were so close that my father would often call me "Theresa la Fresa" (Theresa the Strawberry), blurring my sense of self with my Grandmother and her intergenerational knowledge. I am grateful for this intentionality and her willingness to share how our genealogy was important to our relationship with one another as a family.

Learning to name and engage with indigeneity from the perspective of Indigenous peoples is a complex process because we differ in our approach to Indigenous placemaking, even within the same family. For example, in the story I tell to open this chapter, my sister vividly illustrates that relationality *and* resistance are integral to Indigenous placemaking.

Her place-based awareness and resistance are animated through her presentation of self as a Native woman. She hangs cedar braids from her rearview mirror and adorns her truck with rezzy decals, letting anyone who looks know who she is and where she comes from, including the border patrol officers who staff her local checkpoint. When the officer saw those conspicuous markers, he judged her and selected the truck for a secondary search. Despite the consequences that these markers might activate from the border patrol, she continues to display these dimensions of our identity proudly.

Taken together, the officer's actions and my sister's response illustrate the "possessive surveillance" of settler colonialism, which I describe as the careful observation of the actions of others with the desire to possess their bodies and movement through place, and the subsequent resistance of that surveillance, control, and containment by targeted bodies (Garcia, 2019). My sister's audacious presentation of her Indianness is an explicit form of resistance against possessive surveillance. She resists even when it means that she will not be able to "pass" through this site of racialized state surveillance without suspicion (Garcia, 2019), a personal decision that resonates with me and my understanding of how she moves through both figurative and literal checkpoints.

A third way to stop the denial of Indigenous presence is to invest in a clear understanding of land as pedagogy. As described in "Land as Pedagogy: Nishnaabeg Intelligence and Rebellious Transformation," Simpson (2014) advocates for the reclamation of Indigenous teaching and learning. Simpson (2014) argues that Indigenous peoples are best equipped to understand, engage, and advance our values and worldviews when we have the opportunity "to grow up intimately and strongly connected to our homelands, immersed in our languages and spiritualities, and embodying our traditions of agency, leadership, decision-making and diplomacy" (p. 1). This perspective moves away from the disciplining knowledge production of Western curriculum and toward an educational system that encourages youth and families to learn from and with the land in ways that center Indigenous intelligence (Simpson, 2014, p. 7). This pedagogical framework prioritizes contextually informed theorizing and meaning-making within interpersonal relationships. In this way, Native lands are places and truth-spots in addition to modes of relationality imbued with responsibilities between peoples, landscapes, and intergenerational genealogies that refuse "the permanence of settler colonialism as an unmovable reality" (Simpson, 2014, p. 8). Learning with land as a pedagogy can transform sociological analysis by centering Indigenous peoples and epistemologies as knowledge producers, reorienting our research around new and more generative questions.

Future: Indigenous placemaking in the study of inequality and racialization

This chapter provides a preliminary roadmap for engaging Indigenous placemaking in future sociological studies of inequality and racialization. Although I am still learning how to use this vital map myself, I remain committed to modeling how Sociology might better engage with land as an analytic. In my sociological research, I prioritize engaging and centering territorial awareness and thinking critically about my experiences and relationships with other Native peoples, foodways, language, spiritualities, struggles, joys, and homelands. This engagement is evident in my present research on policing and its exploitative roots in settler colonialism in two ways: 1) by demonstrating how ongoing Indigenous kin relationships with land, place, and peoples jeopardize the settler state's claims to territorial sovereignty, and 2) by centering place-based knowledge in my empirical examination of how state actors such as lawyers, judges, and child welfare workers attempt to destabilize Native families. Both sets of projects illustrate how sociological theories about policing and intersecting inequalities are fundamentally incomplete when detached from the significance of place. They also suggest how we might reflexively theorize the causes and consequences of policing and their effects on children and youth in ways that promote coalition-building among Black and Indigenous communities.

For example, in my publication, "Sovereignty Threat: Loreal Tsingine, Policing, and the Intersectionality of Indigenous Death," I recount the murder of Diné mother Loreal Tsingine by Officer Austin Shipley in Winslow, Arizona in 2016 (Rocha Beardall, 2021). I describe how and why the stories of Ms. Tsingine and many other Native women who have been harmed by the police, as well as tribal intervention on behalf of these community members, are rarely covered by national media (Rocha Beardall, 2021). I locate this intentional erasure within settler assumptions about their credibility to decide what happens on the land and how the land operates within the law. Using an Indigenous placemaking lens, I center a tribally specific engagement with place as a system of reciprocal relations drawn from a series of legal documents filed by the Navajo Nation on behalf of Ms. Tsingine and her family. Through this lens, my study reveals that Ms. Tsingine's death constitutes much more than a case of local law enforcement actualizing their biases. Her death demonstrates the settler state's desire to maintain its fragile claims to territorial sovereignty by controlling the generative power of Native women and their bodies.

In contrast, conventional sociological analysis would center on the "facts" of the case and likely conclude that the murder of Ms. Tsingine is evidence of law enforcement's deep bias and immunity from prosecution for acts of violence against racialized and gendered minorities. These race-gender biases are real and critically important. An Indigenous placemaking lens, however, allows us to draw these conclusions *and* learn to read legal documents as a site of Indigenous knowledge production and worldmaking. This is possible by analyzing archival documents for their settler legal harm *and* the Indigenous meanings about place and land that animate the federal lawsuits and other formal claims-making processes.

In another recent publication, "Abolition, Settler Colonialism, and the Persistent Threat of Indian Child Welfare," my co-author Frank Edwards and I provide a statistical study of Native family separation since the passage of the Indian Child Welfare Act of 1978 (Rocha Beardall & Edwards, 2021). We use administrative and historical data to locate the institutional pathways that funnel Native families into the child welfare system and find that the post-investigation removal decision by child welfare agencies is a key mechanism of inequality in family separation. Using legal and social science research methods, we uncover what the state would prefer remains hidden—that Native children continue to be disconnected from their homelands, families, and sense of self despite the federal government's commitment since 1978 to do otherwise.

A conventional sociological approach would situate our work within a gap or puzzle in the existing literature and build a case for future research from within that intellectual conversation. In contrast, we build our study from the intellectual orientations and practical needs of tribal nations and families. Using an Indigenous placemaking lens in our follow-up qualitative research, for example, we work directly with Native families and advocates to understand how tribes conceptualize and use their sovereignty to protect children from harmful exposure to non-tribal child welfare systems (Rocha Beardall & Edwards, 2021). In this way, we are invested in learning how tribal nations manifest their responsibilities to peoples, landscapes, and nonhuman kin and whether this place-based understanding is reflected in, or *could* be reflected in, their nation-specific kinship welfare practices. With this lens, our focus groups are pushing us to better understand how tribal nations fight to protect their loved ones, especially those living off-reservation, who continue to be at a very high risk of family separation. Much like Simpson's (2014) conceptualization of land as pedagogy, whereby Indigenous learning happens from and with the land, our research prioritizes Indigenous practice and theorizing about what it means to raise our children in immersive, joyful, and positive environments in which they will be trusted, valued, nurtured, and heard (p. 7).

Throughout my learning, I remind myself that theorizing about the social world is a continuous, relational process. And if we are attentive and willing, that process invites each one of us to understand how place is interconnected with the sociohistorical processes unfolding around and within it. In this way, land is not a checkpoint, property, or site of possessive surveillance. Land is a social identity rooted in place and serves as a teacher, classroom, confidant, vessel of knowledge, and site of innovative meaning-making. To continue my learning, I look to other Indigenous methods of Critical Place Inquiry that center land (Tuck & McKenzie, 2015), especially those methods that help me to engage the urban spaces where I grew up and continue to live and conduct research. For those who are interested, this innovative Indigenous-led research includes web-based and digital expressions of place-based issues (Tuck & McKenzie, 2015), urban shell mound work that honors monuments to those who have passed (Gould, 2011), and the use of (re)mapping technologies, a Native feminist method, to explain the role of geographies in organizing place, people, and politics (Goeman, 2013; Tuck & McKenzie, 2015). All of these ways of knowing can guide our theorizing as we collectively learn about how place is interconnected with sociality.

Mindful of my responsibilities to learn *and* do, my research agenda is committed to asking analytical questions that provide empirical support to Native and other racially oppressed families fighting to reduce social inequalities in their communities. I further my responsibilities by directly engaging with policymakers and practitioners about the harmful consequences of policing, family policing, and state violence in the lives of youth of color. I also work continuously with Native families, agencies, and organizations to provide research support as they mobilize against a host of emerging social problems. In this way, I take my work from the page into practice, advocating for Indigenous placemaking in real-time and unsettling Eurocentric assumptions about the meaning of place along the way. Right now, I am most excited to continue my work centering on tribal governments and their visions for child welfare reform. These community-driven efforts leverage place-based knowledge to identify policy shifts that ensure that Native children are loved and cared for within Native family and kinship networks. There is much work to be done but Indigenous placemaking teaches us that this work can be a solidarity practice if it allow it to be.

***

In closing, I encourage sociologists to embrace an understanding of Indigenous placemaking by returning to the material and metaphoric meaning of the liminal space between tribal and non-tribal lands. This return is essential because, for as many years as the United States has existed, checkpoints, borders, and law enforcement agents have restricted the movement of racialized bodies. Today, United States Border Patrol agents pull a couple of sisters into a secondary search lane when the eldest sister's beautiful brown skin and rez vibes are deemed out of place and in need of containment. The secondary search and long wait in the hot sun reinforces the settler state's preferred narrative of Native peoples as other and criminal. This public degradation is staged to invite passersby to see and perhaps unknowingly associate their otherness with a justification for their treatment. By revisiting this encounter through a deep engagement with Indigenous placemaking, sociological inquiry can broaden our understanding of how sociality emerges in place and how land infuses our lives with meaning and purpose.

Reconceptualizing land as a site of unlearning, relearning, and doing invites a more nuanced understanding of the affective dimension of place. It allows the land itself to be instructive, a steward to our ability to think about geography beyond physical space to occupy, use, or extract. Instead, the land holds the stories we are meant to learn about living in good relations with one another, deepening our understanding of meaning-making processes among social groups. The land also holds the memory of how a place came to be and how power relationships are created, maintained, and mobilized. Thus, by foregrounding place in the study of policing and possessive surveillance, we can begin to see how, as a result of their subject position within United States settler society, different minoritized communities such as Black and Native families, are overexposed to *and* resist state violence.

Finally, I hope that the concept of Indigenous placemaking can help sociologists understand how Indigenous peoples move through places differently than other social groups. This way of conceptualizing the world is more expansive than contemporary frameworks by harmonizing the style and strength of my sister existing on that highway in one way, and me in another, and the way we both move together with all of our individual and collective complexity. We are different but interconnected. My sister takes up physical space with her beautiful Native body and conspicuously Native clothing and jewelry, whereas I take up academic space by reading, engaging, and processing our place-based knowledge production alongside my siblings and other Native writers, storytellers, and researchers. Sometimes we merge when I gift her a novel I know speaks to her sense of self and when she gifts me a new pair of earrings that work just right with the way I like to wear my hair. Without a language that can understand the coexistence of these experiences and the dynamics of indigeneity within them, Native peoples are rendered simultaneously invisible and burdened by Sociology's inability to understand how we make meaning together. By centering Indigenous placemaking, sociological inquiry can learn to analyze how Indigenous lands and peoples are always informing the study of social groups, how they come to be, how they function, and how interactions between group members create change in the society in which they are embedded.

References

Byrd, J. A. (2019). Weather with you: Settler colonialism, antiblackness, and the grounded relationalities of resistance. *Critical Ethnic Studies*, 5(1–2), 207–214.

Coleman, C. L. (2005). Framing cinematic Indians within the social construction of place. *American Studies*, 46(3–4), 275–293.

Coulthard, G. S. (2014). *Red skin, white masks: Rejecting the colonial politics of recognition*. Minneapolis: University of Minnesota Press.

Coulthard, G. S., & Simpson, L. B. (2016). Grounded normativity/place-based solidarity. *American Quarterly*, 68(2), 249–255.

Deloria Jr, V., & Wildcat, D. (2001). *Power and place: Indian education in America*. Canada: Fulcrum Publishing.

Eubanks, V. (2020). The sociology of sociology: Whiteness and Eurocentrism in North American sociology. *Ethnic and Racial Studies*, 43(13), 2328–2346.

Garcia, K. T. (2019). Possessive investments in white settler colonialism: Police power, indigenous resistance, and the gendered dangers of recognition. *Social Text*, 37(4), 19–41.

Ghanayem, E. (2023). *Being indigenous and refugee: The duality of Palestinian and American Indian narratives*. UK: Routledge.

Gieryn, T. F. (2018). *Truth-spots*. Chicago: University of Chicago Press.

Go, J. (2018). Postcolonial possibilities for the sociology of race. *Sociology of Race and Ethnicity*, 4(4), 439–451.

Glenn, E. N. (2015). Settler colonialism as structure: A framework for comparative studies of US race and gender formation. *Sociology of Race and Ethnicity*, 1(1), 52–72.

Goeman, M. (2013). *Mark my words: Native women mapping our nations*. Minneapolis: University of Minnesota Press.

Gould, C. (2011, June 22). *Glen cove struggle*. Public lecture. Vallejo Naval & Maritime Museum. Retrieved from https://www.indybay.org/newsitems/2011/07/06/18683990.php

McKay, D. L., Vinyeta, K., & Norgaard, K. M. (2020). Theorizing race and settler colonialism within US sociology. *Sociology Compass*, 14(9), e12821.

Million, D. (2008). Felt theory. *American Quarterly*, 60(2), 267–272.

Rocha Beardall, T. (2016). Adoptive couple v. baby girl: Policing authenticity, implicit racial bias, and continued harm to American Indian families. *American Indian Culture and Research Journal*, 40(1), 119–140.

Rocha Beardall, T. (2020). Social distancing the settler-state: Indigenous peoples in the age of COVID-19. In G. W. Muschert, K. M. Budd, D. C. Lane, & J. A. Smith (Eds.), *Social problems in the age of COVID-19: Global perspectives (vol. 2)* (pp. 39–50). Bristol: Policy Press.

Rocha Beardall, T. (2021). Sovereignty threat: Loreal Tsingine, policing, and the intersectionality of indigenous death. *Nevada Law Journal*, 21, 1025–1060.

Rocha Beardall, T. (2022). Settler simultaneity and anti-indigenous racism at land-grant universities. *Sociology of Race and Ethnicity*, 8(1), 197–212.

Rocha Beardall, T., & Edwards, F. (2021). Abolition, settler colonialism, and the persistent threat of Indian child welfare. *Columbia Journal of Race and Law*, 11(3), 533–574.

Simmel, G. (2012). *The metropolis and mental life*. UK: Routledge.

Simpson, L. B. (2014). Land as pedagogy: Nishnaabeg intelligence and rebellious transformation. *Decolonization: Indigeneity, Education & Society, 3*(3), 1–25.

Steinman, E. W. (2021). Settler colonialism and sociological knowledge: Insights and directions forward. *Theory and Society, 51*(1), 145–176.

Trouillot, M. R. (1995). *Silencing the past: Power and the production of history.* Beacon Press.

Tuck, E., & McKenzie, M. (2015). *Place in research: Theory, methodology, and methods.* UK: Routledge.

Urry, J. (2001). The sociology of space and place. In G. Ritzer (Ed.), *The Blackwell companion to sociology* (pp. 3–15). Wiley-Blackwell.

Wirth, L. (1938). Urbanism as a way of life. *American Journal of Sociology, 44*(1), 1–24.

3

THEY ARE HERE WITH ME

(Critical Race) Theories from my flesh

Kevin Lawrence Henry Jr.

Introduction

Perhaps it is the heart and not the mind where our memories, dreams, and hopes reside. I was a senior in high school when my heart shattered, spilling its contents through my tears. I remember it well. Sitting beside my grandmother, my upper torso leaning against her strong legs. Legs whose strength was later hollowed out by what I believe was the same thing to break my heart: Hurricane Katrina. Or, perhaps, more precisely what the hurricane indexed: living in the wake of disaster, ecological devastation, precarity, racial capitalism, and understanding the "totality of our environment" is anti-Black (Sharpe, 2016, p. 104). We watched as the news showcased the flooding, spoke of bloated cadavers in flood waters, people atop roofs pleading to be rescued, others wading in the water, and then there were Black people who, like our enslaved ancestors, escaped their dire circumstances of (water) captivity, but were described as being in possession of something stolen—fugitives, criminals, looters to be sure—those that violated the property interests of capitalist white supremacy. As nearly twenty of us "refugees" watched in horror at my aunt and uncle's home in Houston, we knew our world would forever be changed. We also knew intimately of the protracted violence of white supremacy and state disinvestment, and how those fatal couplings located us within precincts of vulnerability. While Hurricane Katrina and the resulting policy disaster occurred in 2005, its memory and effects have loitered in my life and the lives of those impacted by the devastation of environmental racism. Saidiya Hartman asks, "[h]ow might we understand mourning, when the event has

DOI: 10.4324/9781003303800-4

yet to end?" (Hartman, 2002, p. 758). Like the mold that covered the walls of homes following the hurricane or the loss of our loved ones and institutions, the residue of the storm remains, in fact, and our mourning has "yet to end." The past and present lives of anti-Blackness still contours much of post-Katrina New Orleans.

In 2005, at 17, I did not have the language to describe the "ghostly matters" of anti-Blackness or of the "afterlife of slavery" that did and continue to shape my life, my family, and those within my community (Gordon, 2008; Hartman, 2007). Like hooks (1991), "I came to theory because I was hurting" (p. 1). And it is the pain of white supremacy and the knowledge of Black persistence and resistance that guides my research on neoliberal educational restructuring and the ways Black people experience, understand, pick up, and contest market-based reforms. My work is shaped by theory specifically grounded in the Black Radical Tradition, in Black Study. I understand such a tradition as an onto-epistemological challenge to symbolic and material orders that govern large-scale structures, processes, and logics that secure white dominance that intersects with and is multiplied by other forms of oppression (Harney & Moten, 2013; Henry, 2019; Kelley, 2002; Weheliye, 2014). At base, these onto-epistemological approaches work to honor the humanity of Black people, Black place, and Black imaginations and desires; the textured and sometimes contradictory performances of Blackness and Black politics; illuminates the "richness of possibility" that animates and grounds Black *life;* and works to subvert, refuse, and dismantle oppression (Spillers, 1987; Quashie, 2021). This necessarily means I approach my research, teaching, and policy advocacy as a political and ethical project, rooted in Black desire, liberation, and care. It also means working in community and centering perspectives, methods, and dissemination venues that exceed traditional European academic norms.

Gloria Ladson-Billings (1995) in one of her germinal texts, "Toward a theory of culturally relevant pedagogy" remarked that one of the challenges of traditional education research is that it has failed to "make explicit its theoretical underpinnings" (p. 469), that in some quarters the work is seen as atheoretical. What is more, Western regimes of truth often obfuscate the role of power and positionality in knowledge "production" and the narratives and stories we tell of ourselves and about others. At base, as Sylvia Wynter reminds us, we are a "storytelling species" and those stories may very well cohere around a set of mythological premises that aid and abet in dispossession; stories that may very well be life-giving, life-sustaining, and dare I say heretical inasmuch as they lay bare and attempt to dethrone the orthodoxy of oppression. As a consequence, our research tells a story and is undergirded by a host of conceptual markings; theoretical tattoos that adorn the body of our work. My theoretical tattooing is *first* informed by the stories and wisdom of my grandmother and community. The texture of this work is also shaped by my own personal experiences. These intimate relations of people and place have a bearing on the *body* of work I've committed and been called to do. It is from these locations—often seen as a nuisance and not a site of nuance in traditional Western scholarship—that I arrive at the page, the program, and the project, understanding and re-membering that the insights and ways of knowing and being from the people and places that have shaped me are, as Williamson (2017) remarks, "as appropriate and necessary a starting place as any other" (p. 16).

This chapter is a humble engagement with the theories/stories of my flesh that were born out of necessity. It illuminates my engagement with thinkers from Black Studies and its impact on my research on and experi-ence with post-Katrina educational reforms. It traces my initial engagement with Critical Race Theory (CRT) and considers how through current conversations that focus on humanism/the figure of man/ontology, I have deepened my understanding of liberalism, political economy, and the conditions of crisis that shape school reform.

A place called home, on New Orleans and mis-education

As a child, Fridays were typically my favorite day of the week. It was not merely because it was the day that preceded Saturday but because generally on Fridays, I spent time with my grandmother (Mawmaw), Gertrude Edwards. Born in 1933 in a world more clearly marked by the colorline, a world before *Brown v. Board of Education of Topeka*, before Obama, and before the Movement for Black Lives, she knew the violence and wreckage of white supremacy, of an American grammar that erased her legibility, while simultaneously parasitically needing her to exist (Bonilla-Silva, 2012; Spillers, 1987). She knew of all those things, but she also knew much more. Mawmaw knew of a Black sociality marked by the laughter of friends and family, of dancing and drinking in juke joints, "cozy spots" and (Black) holes in the wall that did not deny the force and fervor of whiteness, but for those moments in time had no concern for or interest in it. She spent most of her adult life working at Charity Hospital in New Orleans, a hospital originally founded in 1736 for those made to experience poverty in the city. The new, larger Charity Hospital was built three years after my grand-mother's birth, which continued to care for those living in the wake of late capitalism and anti-Blackness; it still stands on Tulane Avenue, weathered by time and hallowed by state-sanctioned disinvestment. Charity Hospital was never reopened after Hurricane Katrina in 2005.

Although I was not born by the time my grandmother retired from Charity Hospital, I do recall the part-time job she took following retirement as a caregiver to an elderly Venezuelan woman, who lived a few blocks from my elementary school. On Fridays, my grandmother would pick me up from school, and this is where the joy began. Moving from the affluent Lakeview neighborhood to the significantly less economically wealthy and undeniably more Black 7th Ward of New Orleans my grandmother and I would stop at the seafood market where she would pick up fish or shrimp to cook. Once home, the sounds of Solomon Burke or Aretha Franklin, and most definitely Al Green's "For the Good Times" hummed around the kitchen, seasoning what was sure to be a divine dinner.

With Hurricane Katrina's landfall on August 29, 2005, and the resulting man-made policy catastrophe that helped to instantiate a neoliberal regime of governance in New Orleans, the home I knew, chock full and reeking of love ceased to exist as I knew it. My grandmother's home was decimated by the Hurricane and the failed levee system. My elementary school, no longer there. The seafood market, a fragment of memory. The hospital, a shell. And yet despite all that has occurred, all the undoing, and redoing the "places are still there … the picture of it—stays … out there, in the world" (Morrison, 1987, p. 43).

The "still there" and "out thereness" of my, my family, and my community's past lingered. As my city was ravaged by disaster, I found no other choice but to remain in New Orleans to aid in what I thought was the rebuilding and "recovery" project. I decided to attend Tulane University in New Orleans. The university was positioned and constructed by the city's elites as one of post-Katrina New Orleans' saving graces. With a commitment to service learning and rebuilding public education, Tulane marshaled its resources, particularly the Cowen Institute for Public Education to help transform public education into a market-based system.

One of the benefits of Tulane was that I spent a generous amount of time in the recently developed charter schools of the city and although I was a political science major with minors in Africana Studies and Gender and Sexuality Studies, I enrolled in the teacher education program, not totally sure if law or education would be my career path. But something was amiss. As I sat in class and worked in schools, there were so many moments of disappointment, of frustration, of anger. Following Hurricane Katrina, the teaching force in New Orleans changed drastically. Many veteran Black educators were fired en masse and replaced with overwhelmingly white teachers from Teach for America and other alternative certification programs. Beyond this being one the largest displacements of Black educators since *Brown v. Board of Education of Topeka*, the schools struggled with a variety of issues from culturally irrelevant pedagogies, to high rates of suspension and expulsion of Black children and a general punitive/carceral logic, limited student services, and the leadership and boards of charters being composed of mostly white people. It seemed to me that the devastation wrought by the storm was increasingly eclipsed by the policy and organizational roulette played on Black children.

This, of course, had me double dutching between the feelings of anger and sadness. I wanted to know what I could do. Why was it that Black children were promised the world after the hurricane, but offered gilded shards? I poorly assumed my education classes could offer guidance, but even in a course organized around "education for a diverse society," I was met with answers that suggested the issue with New Orleans schools specifically and urban education, generally, was that children (read: Black children) have a "low internal locus of control" (Rotter, 1954). Parading in the drag of care, these deficit logics located the problems of education within the child and the communities from which they hailed.

Those children that my colleagues discussed from "broken homes" and "poverty stricken" communities were me. Growing up in New Orleans and coming from a working-class background, I knew all too well the sting of white teachers who held me as a pitied afterthought or worse looked down upon me and my family. Yet despite those things, I also knew of a community that saw my highest potential (Siddle Walker, 1996). Folks who looked into my eyes and saw wonder, possibility, and promise. People who were not interested in pity, but who respected my humanity and in doing so they poured into me their hopes, love, stories, and strength.

My grandmother and her neighbors, particularly Ms. Dolores and Mr. Gene, would often spend the evening together, on the porch, having a drink, smoking cigarettes, and discussing the news, politics, and the everyday happenings of their lives. Being a bit precocious, I would sit with them, "at the feet of the elders," as some would say, taking in all the information and, yes, even asking questions and "interviewing" them for my alternative news station "WKLH." I knew early enough that there was something more incisive about their analysis and discussion of politics than what was portrayed in the mainstream media. They possessed what W.E.B. Du Bois (1968) framed as a "second sight," which allowed them to see the world from their lived experience and beyond the constrictions of an "inverted epistemology" of whiteness that distorts, contorts, and misrepresents (Mills, 1997). They were theorizing by offering counter-narratives, a concept I later connected to Critical Race Theory.

The visceral reactions, or the something "not being right in my spirit," that I felt when in those education classes were indexing the tension between the knowledge of home, of people and place and the calcified, deficit, "official knowledge" of Educational Studies (Apple, 1999). The knowledge that coursed through my body was imprinted long before my arrival at Tulane. It was "front porch knowledge" I attained on the steps of my grandmother's house and this knowledge was not only about the physical place and location of learning, but it was/is a reflection of the places and people we carry in our bodies.

Fortunately, via my Africana Studies and Gender and Sexuality Studies courses, I was introduced to a form of analysis that resonated with the embodied and experiential knowledge I brought with me. One that situated power, stratification, discourse, and social structures of accumulation up for grabs, as necessary sites of analysis and deconstruction. At the core, these fields illuminated that theory was not unnecessary, that it was not simply a luxury, but rather theory could be as hooks (1991) reminds us, "a liberatory practice." Critically I learned, much like there were deficit theories about the Black child, that theory in and of itself was not benign but could be deployed for a host of nefarious purposes—or other purposes. Theory could also be transformative, revealing, discerning, critical, and, yes, healing, but "only when we ask that it do so and direct our theorizing towards this end" (hooks, 1991, p. 2).

During this time, I was briefly introduced to Critical Race Theory by one of my professors. While I spent time grappling with the theory, I was eager to know much more about its application in education, policy, and how I could better understand the New Orleans educational landscape. I later enrolled in graduate school where I was introduced to a host of ideas around race and racism, policy and policy analysis, and theory. These ideas often pushed up against the way I was initially taught about policy, the policy process, and policy analysis. Traditional articulations of policy and the policy process underscore it being a rational, technical, and democratic process. One where policymakers explore multiple solutions to social problems, solutions that are, presumably, in the best interest of the public, and solutions that are propped up by the belief in the legitimacy and authority of those who craft them and the institutions they represent. To understand change or rather how policy attempts to address what Rittel and Webber (1973) refer to as "wicked problems" of the world, one is told to believe in a policy incrementalism (Theodoulou & Kofinis, 2004). Such incrementalism is believed to reflect the reflectiveness and ongoing engagement of policymakers with an analysis that is working to rework the solution, once again, in the interest of democracy (Theodoulou & Kofinis, 2004).

Yet, through a deeper engagement with Critical Race Theory, it became abundantly clear that policy formation, implementation, and analysis remain sites of contestation. Critical Race Theory developed in the legal academy in the late 1970s and 1980s, as an intellectual movement grounded in the lived realities of communities of color (Delgado & Stefancic, 2012). It sought to push against legal theories that ignored or minimized the scope and scale of white supremacy in the law and society and critical theories that argued protracted racial stratification and inequity could best be explained by

Marxian and class-based analysis (Delgado & Stefancic, 2012). Most importantly, what became salient for me was the development of a critical vocabulary that acknowledged and named the unequal, antagonistic, and parasitic relations of white supremacy and dominance that pervade educational policy and practice. Moreover, CRT understood that incremental steps to address racial inequity could be swallowed by a structure of white supremacy intent on saving itself. That is to say, it seems to me, that Critical Race Theory put into theory what most of the Black people I know had already known, "shit ain't right."

Critical Race Theory: A blues epistemology

Jazz and blues singer Alberta Hunter once remarked, "[b]lues means what milk does to a baby. Blues is what the spirit is to the minister. We sing the blues because our hearts have been hurt, our souls have been disturbed." In my estimation, Critical Race Theory is a blues epistemology. CRT aims to illuminate and archive the everyday, mundane and extravagant, realities of Black people, and other people of color, and most specifically to bear witness to and hold space for our pain. Of course, the blues cannot be limited to pain, it may very well embrace pleasure, desire, humor, resistance, and the soul. Similarly, CRT by reckoning with the enduring legacies of organized social and political abandonment, structured vulnerability, erasure, disposability, dehumanization, and oppression—that which gives us the blues—also refuses the aforementioned and works to affirm and preserve the fullness of our existence and being. CRT gave me a critical vocabulary for the front porch theorizing and analyzing my grandmother and her friends embarked.

Central to Critical Race Theory is a set of perspectives that shape the theory. Ladson-Billings (2013) in referencing the work of critical race legal theorists Richard Delgado and Jean Stefancic remarked the central hallmarks of the theory are as follows: (1) "belief that racism is normal or ordinary, not aberrant in US society; (2) interest convergence or material determinism; (3) race as a social construction; (4) intersectionality and anti-essentialism; (5) voice or counter-narrative" (p. 37). Given the space limitations of this chapter, I will only offer a brief articulation of these perspectives, for a more detailed account see Ladson-Billings' (2013) piece, "Critical Race Theory—what it is not!"

Returning to the above tenets, the first of these "racism as normal" suggests that racism is a standard operating procedure in the U.S. society; racism is so ingrained in our policies, institutions, and culture that it exceeds random individual incidences of prejudice, but rather buttresses such prejudices to the structural level. Here racism operates in the past, present, and future tenses; it is micro and macro; intended and "unintended"; in fewer words: ubiquitous.[1] Secondly, the notion of interest convergence argues that racial justice initiatives are constrained and enabled by their alignment with elite white interests. The third element that race is a social construct illuminates that race is a product of social and political thought and relations. According to Delgado and Stefancic (2012) races are "not objective, inherent, or fixed; they correspond to no biological or genetic reality; rather races are categories that society invents, manipulates, or retires when convenient" (p. 8). One can think here of the U.S. racial classification system from the 1800s that used terms like "octoroons" and "quadroons" to sort people into racial categories. These terms no longer formally exist in the U.S. census. Nevertheless, while race is a social construct, racism is a social reality.

We also have the notion of intersectionality in CRT. Intersectionality has been central to the theorizing of women of color feminists long before Kimberlee Crenshaw's coining of the term (cf., Sojourner Truth's speech "Ain't I a Woman?", The Combahee River Collective Statement, or Gloria Anzaldúa's *Borderlands/La Frontera*). Central to Crenshaw's (1989) articulation of intersectionality is an understanding of how multiple, interlocking identities (such as race, sex, class, and sexual orientation) cohere as locations of vulnerability in a society structured in dominance. This strand of intersectionality considers how social forces of oppression such as heteropatriarchy, white supremacy, and capitalism come together to have a bearing on the lived experiences of groups.[2] Lastly, the notion of voice and counternarrative are key in the work of CRT. At base, the counternarrative aims to illuminate and deflate the mythologies of white supremacy that aim to continue the violence of the status quo and the taken-for-granted, by piercing them with the perspectives and stories of folx of color. Counternarrative is not merely about stories from folx of color, but rather advances "larger concerns or help us understand how law or policy is operating" in a white supremacist society (Ladson-Billings, 2013, p. 42). As anthropologist and writer Zora Neale Hurston once remarked, "if you are silent about your pain, they'll kill you and say you enjoyed it." For critical race theorists, counternarrative is all at once an acknowledgment of humanity by asserting our voice, our pain, and reimagining the world as we know it. While there are additional constructs that overlay the theory, which I will briefly discuss later in this essay, these key elements give overarching contouring of Critical Race Theory and have been essential to my understanding of the world and program of research.

As I think back to my younger self, who knew and felt racism and thus was angered by what I experienced and witnessed happening in post-Katrina New Orleans, Critical Race Theory helped me to better understand the relationship between neoliberal restructuring and white supremacy. Similar to when I was a child, the simple, "official" narratives of success I heard on the news and in some academic settings about post-Katrina New Orleans, chafed against the realities of folks in my community and what we knew about the world and specifically experienced after Hurricane Katrina. Those official narratives evaded contending with the "unnatural disaster" of neoliberalism.

Neoliberalism is often understood as a political and economic ideology and an approach to governance that prioritizes the expansion of markets and the accumulation of capital. The role of the state in neoliberal thought is to foster deregulation, competition, individualism, and to lubricate processes of rolling back redistributive policies and institutions and rolling out a boot-straps logic of personal responsibility, the entrepreneurial human, the supremacy of the market, and the normalization of inequity. While this traditional reading of neoliberalism is not inaccurate, it does seem incomplete. The lack of attentiveness in Critical Policy Studies to the racial dynamics of critiques of neoliberalism, did not much help me understand the unfolding of neoliberalism in New Orleans, or even Chicago, or Detroit, or D.C.—all locations with a profound Black presence. How could I better understand the takeover of public education by quasi-private organizations (Dixson et al., 2021; Henry, 2021a)? Or a gaunt pedagogy and curriculum that had no interest in sustaining the cultures and lives of Black students (Henry, 2021b)? The demonization and mass firing of Black educators and the dismembering of the teachers union (Henry, 2016)? Black youth being pushed out of schools following one of the most devastating experiences of their lives (Henry & Warren, 2017)? The removal of affordable housing and limited access to healthcare (Arena, 2012)? The overreliance on policing and incarceration (Gilmore, 2007)? It then seemed to me that neoliberal reform, despite its proclamations of multiculturalism and equality, in fact, makes a mockery of Blackness. Neoliberalism aims to erase the historical residues and present-day manifestations of oppression, not by eradicating or dismantling oppression, but rather by masking its stench.

So for me, the question becomes how does one understand race and racism as already embedded within educational policy and political economy? What are the racial dynamics of neoliberalism? Or put more specifically, how might the second-order disasters of Hurricane Katrina be seen as a logical conclusion of an anti-Black political economy? Quite apropos, Christina Sharpe (2016) reminds us, "the weather is the totality of our environments; the weather is the total climate; and that climate is anti-Black" (p. 104).

Two central constructs in Critical Race Theory have been particularly helpful in considering how one might answer the above questions: a critique of liberalism and whiteness as property. Both constructs attempt to lay bare the ideological skeletons and material realities of whiteness that secure, preserve, and reproduce white supremacy. Vaught and Castagno (2008) remark, "whiteness as property is a concept that reflects the conflation of whiteness with the exclusive rights to freedom, to the enjoyment of certain privileges, and to the ability to draw from these rights" (p. 96). On the other hand, a critique of liberalism focuses on how notions of incrementalism, objectivity, meritocracy, color evasiveness, and neutrality of the law and other institutions facilitate and uphold white dominance.

What conjoins these constructs, particularly as they relate to educational markets, is an understanding that whiteness not only affords white people particular advantages in the market, but more precisely those advantages are baked into the performative limitations of liberalism, which whiteness as property falls within. Said differently, liberalism despite its articulations of equality and liberty for all, in a vulgar bait and switch allows for the ongoing catastrophic disasters of settler colonialism and transatlantic slavery, for the expansion of racial capitalism (Henry, 2022; Losurdo, 2011; Mills, 1997). Returning to Sharpe (2016) who succinctly reminds us, "[t]ransatlantic slavery was and is the disaster. The disaster of Black subjection was and is planned; … The history of capital is inextricable from the history of Atlantic chattel slavery" (p. 5). One is then better able to understand a whole series of issues inaugurated under the project of enslavism, most centrally around the parameters of (hu)man (and property). The former is codified as an ontological being and the latter as anything but. So, the "disaster" of Hurricane Katrina is animated by a disaster that long preceded it. One that relies on an understanding of Blackness as a commodity, as fungible, as abject, as criminal, as site for exploration, as body under-development, as other. This begins to reveal itself in the commodification of Black children, an overreliance on high-stakes testing that limits the brilliance of Black thought and creativity, issues around who controls schools and school funding, the curricular and pedagogic choices made within classrooms, the general logics and practices that privilege the individual over the community, and erasure and displacement of Black people, Black ways of knowing, and Black communities. The constructs of Critical Race Theory help me to name how the "invisible hand of the market" assaults the lives of Black low and no-income folx, specifically, and most Black folx generally. Critical Race Theory offers me space to ground their respective perspectives and experiences in my scholarly work.

Coda

Growing up in New Orleans, it was not lost on me how the realities of racial capitalism, the afterlife of slavery, and disinvestment ravaged the city and haunted many of those I cared for and loved. These processes of parasitism sought to feast on the lives of my community by constantly extracting, sometimes quickly, other times slowly, but extracting nonetheless (Henry, forthcoming). The form of the parasitism shifted, but its trace was there. Gentrification. Low or no wages. Housing Instability. Erasure of Black space. Inequitable Schooling. It seemed the appetite for whiteness was insatiable, and it looked to devour Black communities. Yet despite all those things, what was also deeply palpable was the overwhelming presence of Black love and care. It was a practice. Be it Mr. Gene picking me up from elementary school when my mother or grandmother could not, or my Aunt Bernice cooking what I called as a child "chocolate beans," which were red beans and rice, or my MawMaw telling me stories of the past and indulging my various dreams. While they are now all ancestors, their lives and how they lived it was a testament to the complex and intricate dance of Black survival, Black resistance, Black hope and desire, and Black love. They are here with me. And the lessons I learned from them and my hometown, at the base, are really what animates my intellectual projects. How first insisting upon and honoring our humanity is a necessary starting point of any work we do. In New Orleans, we *see* each other. Be it a head nod on the street, a "hey, baaaby" that lingers in the air, a beat that courses through your body, or a meal that sustains and inspires you. The people and places that shape(d) me provoke in me a consideration of how central care must be to our research and teaching. Importantly, they taught me the necessity of Black interpretive authority. It is as my Aunt Zenobia would remark the ability to see "six on one hand and half a dozen on the other." This interpretive authority is one that holds Black joy, Black desire, Black revelry, and Black futures in tandem with the ability to name and call out the horrors of white supremacy that intimately touch our lives. I carry this with me as I move through these (academic) streets.

The formal training I received in the academy is in relation to the people and place that first loved me. The formal constellation of ideas around white supremacy, anti-Blackness, neoliberalism, and educational policy in which I was trained are partial. They certainly cannot give the precise summing up of Blackness, nor would I want them to. What these sets of ideas have offered me is an additional way to think about and articulate the entrenched ongoing struggle for Black life. They are not an attempt to "negate or dismiss Black people's agency, but rather reframe Black agency as necessarily and always engaging the fundamentally antiblack world as it is" (Vargas & Jung, 2021, p. 9). Even as my grandmother and her friends rejected the assertions of white supremacy, it was also very clear that they had to daily contend and resist it and articulate otherwise. Similarly, these theories focus on the wrong, so that we may try to get to the right. In an era where Critical Race Theory is under attack and those who are against it want to solidify and instantiate a type of historical amnesia, though this is more like déjà vu, my hope is that a continued commitment to documenting and challenging these abuses remains steadfast. Critical Race Theory and the larger Black Radical Tradition, which shapes my work, hold a skepticism toward policy, knowing we must deepen our understanding of oppression, while also marshaling a necessary set of alternatives to it. As geographer Gilmore (2007) suggests, we must aim to engage in non-reformist reforms that work to undo the forms of control and subjugation that "widen the net" of inequity. This work is hard; it is collective; and it is perennial. But, after all, I am reminded by Alice Walker that "the nature of this flower is to bloom."

Notes

1 I've placed quotation marks around unintended to signify what I think is a limitation in language here. First, given the vast amount of scholarship we have on race and racism, as well as adjoining discourses on anti-racist practices, the failure to actively disrupt racism only speaks to its pervasiveness and what many in critical race theory argue is its morphic and consistent permanence (Bell, 1992; Henry, 2022). In other critical traditions, scholars have noted that the persistence of anti-Blackness, is in fact, necessary for the structuration of Western society. Therefore, to remove anti-Blackness would be the end of the world as we know it (Henry & Powell, 2021; Jung & Vargas, 2021; Wilderson, 2010). In such a case, the cost is too high and the incentive is too low among white people. Moreover, a second limitation here involves what some have framed as "intent" vs. "impact." Critically, critical race theorists are less interested in the intent of a policy/action and more interested in the questions of what are the impacts, how might "x approach" reify and reproduce regnant racial disparities and forms of harm? It is less a matter of what was intended to be done and more a matter of what was *actually* done.
2 To be clear, this is one articulation of intersectionality. Other perspectives highlight the differing relations to privilege and oppression one might occupy. It focuses less on vulnerabilities and relations to power and more on the intersection of multiple identities. See Nash's (2018) *Black Feminism Reimagined: After Intersectionality* and Grant and Zwier's (2014) *Intersectionality and Urban Education: Identities, Policies, Spaces and Power* for additional discussions of intersectionality.

References

Apple, M. (1999). *Official knowledge: Democratic education in a conservative age* (2nd Ed.). Routledge.

Arena, J. (2012). *Driven from New Orleans: How nonprofits betray public housing and promote privatization.* University of Minnesota Press.

Bell, D. A. (1992). Racial realism. *Connecticut Law Review, 24,* 363–379.

Bonilla-Silva, E. (2012). The invisible weight of Whiteness: The racial grammar of everyday life in America. *Michigan Sociological Review, 26,* 1–15.

Delgado, R., & Stefancic, J. (2012). *Critical race theory: An introduction.* New York University Press.

Dixson, A. D., Royal, C., & Henry, K. L. Jr, (2013). School reform and school choice. In *Handbook of urban education* (pp. 512–541). Routledge.

Dixson, A. D., Royal, C., & Henry, K. L., Jr. (2021). School reform and school choice. In H. R. Du Bois (Ed.), W.E.B. (1903/2003). *The souls of Black folk.* Barnes and Noble Classics.

Du Bois, W. E. B. 1868-1963. (1968). The souls of black folk; essays and sketches. Chicago, A. G. McClurg, 1903. New York: Johnson Reprint Corp.,

Gilmore, W. R. (2007). *Golden gulag: Prisons, surplus, crisis, and opposition in globalizing California.* University of California Press.

Gordon, A. F. (2008). *Ghostly matters: Haunting and the sociological imagination.* University of Minnesota Press.

Grant, C. A., & Zwier, E. (2014). *Intersectionality and urban education: Identities, policies, spaces, and power.* Information Age Publishing.

Harney, S., & Moten, F. (2013). *The undercommons: Fugitive planning and Black study.* Autonomedia.

Hartman, S. (2002). The time of slavery. *The South Atlantic Quarterly, 101*(4), 757–777.

Hartman, S. (2007). *Lose your mother: A journey along the Atlantic slave route.* Farrar, Straus and Giroux.

Henry, K. L., Jr. (2023). Feasing on Blackness: Educational parasitism, necropolicy, and Black thought. *International Journal of Qualitative Studies in Education.* pp. 1–17.

Henry, K. L., Jr. (2016). Discursive violence and economic retrenchment: Chartering the sacrifice of Black educators in post-Katrina New Orleans. In J. K. Donnor & T. L. Affolter (Eds.), *The charter school solution: Distinguishing fact from rhetoric* (pp. 80–98). Routledge.

Henry, K. L., Jr. (2019). Heretical discourses in post-Katrina charter school applications. *American Educational Research Journal, 56*(6), 2609–2643.

Henry, K. L., Jr. (2021a). "The price of disaster": The charter authorization process in post-Katrina New Orleans. *Educational Policy, 35*(2), 235–258.

Henry, K. L., Jr. (2021b). Zones of nonbeing: Abjection, White accumulation, and neoliberal school reform. *Teachers College Record, 123*(14), 129–149.

Henry, K. L., Jr. (2022). A movement in two acts: Actually existing racism, CRT, and the charter school movement. In M. Lynn & A. D. Dixson (Eds.), *Handbook of critical race theory in education* (pp. 427–439). Routledge.

Henry, K. L., Jr., & Powell, S. (2021). Kissing cousins: Critical race theory's racial realism and Afropessimism's social death. In M. Dumas, A. Woodson, & C. A. Grant (Eds.), *The future is Black: Afro-pessimism, fugitivity, and radical hope in education* (pp. 79–85). Routledge.

Henry, K. L., Jr. & Warren, C. A. (2017). The evidence of things not seen? Race, pedagogies of discipline, and White women teachers. In S. D. Hancock & C. A. Warren (Eds.), *White women's work: Examining the intersectionality of cultural norms, teaching, and identity formation in urban schools* (pp. 173–195). Information Age Publishing.

Hooks, b. (1991). Theory as liberatory practice. *Yale Journal of Law and Feminism, 4*(1), 1–12.

Kelley, R. D. G. (2002). *Freedom dreams: The Black radical imagination.* Beacon Press.

Kimberly, C. (1989). Demarginalizing the intersection of race and sex: A Black feminist critique of antidiscrimination doctrine, feminist theory, and antiracist politics. *University of Chicago Legal Forum, 140*(1), 139–167.

Ladson-Billings, G. (1995). Toward a theory of culturally relevant pedagogy. *American Educational Research Journal, 32*(3), 465–491.

Ladson-Billings, G. (2013). Critical race theory: What it is not! In M. Lynn & A. D. Dixson (Eds.), *Handbook of critical race theory in education* (pp. 34–47). Routledge.

Losurdo, D. (2011). *Liberalism: A counter-history,* trans. Gregory Elliott, London and New York: Verso, p. 1.

Mills, C. W. (1997). *The racial contract.* Cornell University Press.

Morrison, T. (1987). *Beloved: A novel.* New York, NY: Knopf.

Nash, J. C. (2018). *Black feminism reimagined: After intersectionality.* Duke University Press.

Quashie, K. E. (2021). *Black aliveness, or a poetics of being.* Duke University Press.

Rittel, H. W. J., & Webber, M. M. (1973). Dilemmas in a general theory of planning. *Policy Sciences, 4*(2), 155–169.

Rotter, J. B. (1954). *Social learning and clinical psychology.* Englewood Cliffs, NJ: Prentice Hall.

Sharpe, C. (2016). *In the wake: On Blackness and being.* Duke University Press.

Siddle Walker, V. (1996). *Their highest potential: An African American school community in the segregated south.* The University of North Carolina Press.

Spillers, H. J. (1987). Mama's baby, papa's maybe: An American grammar book. *Diacritics, 17*(2), 64–81.

Theodoulou, S. Z., & Kofinis, C. (2004). *The art of the game: Unverstanding American public policy making.* Wadsworth/Thomson Learning.

Vargas, C. J. H., & Jung, M. K. (2021). Antiblackness of the social and the human. In M. K. Jung & J. H. C. Vargas (Eds.), *Antiblackness* (pp. 1–14). Duke University Press.

Vaught, S. E., & Castagno, A. E. (2008). "I don't think I'm a racist": Critical race theory, teacher attitudes, and structural racism. *Race Ethnicity and Education, 11*(2), 95–113.

Weheliye, A. G. (2014). *Habeas viscus: Racializing assemblages, biopolitics, and Black feminist theories of the human.* Duke University Press.

Wilderson, F. B., III. (2010). *Red, White & Black: Cinema and the structure of U.S. antagonisms.* Duke University Press.

Williamson, T. L. (2017). *Scandalize my name: Black feminist practice and the making of Black social life.* Fordham.

4

"CENTRAL CALIFORNIA'S COMPLETELY DIFFERENT"

Theorizing racialization in the San Joaquin Valley through a rural Latinx epistemology

Mayra Puente

I looked up at my amá,[1] noticing the decades of sun damage on her face, and then at my apá,[2] whose chest and brazos[3] poked through the multiple holes in his long-sleeve shirt. My heart palpitated as I struggled to find the words to translate the "take it or leave it" attitude of the white[4] male farm owner to my parents.

The farm owner had just announced to the mass of Latinx[5] im/migrant[6] farm workers huddled in the agricultural fields that he would no longer be paying his promised piece rate[7] for harvesting grapes. The workers, primarily Spanish speakers, stared in confusion as the owner disclosed his unscrupulous intentions in a foreign language and careless tone, then walked away.

With trepidation, I said to my parents, "Dice que nos va pagar menos. Diez centavos en vez de una cora."[8]

Among my family, other farm workers negotiated between staying and working for significantly reduced pay or leaving without pay. We had already lost sleep, time, and money to arrive at the fields. Peering into the crowd of ambivalent farm workers, my 8-year-old self was struck by a harsh reality: Only people who looked like me were here, choosing between laboring or hungering.

This incident is one of many firsthand experiences that taught me about racialization. While I did not have the academic language to name these experiences as "racialization," I knew how racialization felt, whom it affected, and *where* it took place. This chapter centers "the where" (Tuck & McKenzie, 2015) in my growing understanding of racialization. It oscillates between my farm working community's experiences with racialization in

DOI: 10.4324/9781003303800-5

California's San Joaquin Valley and my out-of-place learning about issues of race and racism in ivory towers in urban spaces. I explore the tensions of theorizing about racialization in rural places while being away from home. My (dis)location in urban-based institutions with mentors from urban backgrounds introduced me to systems of knowing like Critical Race Theory, Chicana Feminist Epistemology, and Critical Race Spatial Analysis, which are foundational to how I understand processes of racialization. Yet, it was my community's ongoing experiences with racial oppression and my conversations with rural Latinx youth about our racial realities that taught me about the significance and specificity of place in processes of racialization. This chapter provides insight into those conversations shared with rural Latinx youth and offers reflections about the centrality of place in race-centered educational research.

A rural Latina epistemological intervention into critical race, feminist, and spatial theories in educational research

My formal training in theories of race began when I left the San Joaquin Valley for college. I pursued a bachelor's degree at a university in Los Angeles, three hours away from my home. I quickly learned that my decision to attend a faraway, urban-based institution would complicate my opportunities to learn about issues impacting my community. Even the university's Department of Chicana/o Studies, which was named after a foundational leader of the National Farm Workers Association, César E. Chávez, excluded the experiences of my rural community. We were irrelevant to the LA spatial imagination. To reconcile this erasure, I pursued a transdisciplinary undergraduate education, specializing in fields like political science, Chicana/o Studies, and Education Studies. I pieced together these various disciplines, hoping to learn why students from my community struggled to leave the agricultural fields and puruse higher education.

At the same time that I was beginning my higher education journey, my community back home was experiencing an "exceptional drought" (National Integrated Drought Information System, n.d.). East Porterville was on the news for the first time in my life, recognized by prominent metropolitan newspapers like *The New York Times and Los Angeles Times.* The media reported on the hundreds of wells that ran dry during the exceptional drought period of 2014–2017. For three excruciating years, my community members relied on the temporary and unsustainable solution of using state-sponsored bottled water programs for drinking, bathing, and other necessities. This issue resurfaced with the 2021 drought (Whisnand, 2021). I wondered how youth in my community were supposed to focus and excel in school when they could not access running water. I wondered what other sociospatial[9] conditions were unique to the San Joaquin Valley and how these conditions shaped the educational opportunities of rural Latinxs who lived, labored, and learned in this region.

I sought answers to these questions by participating in undergraduate research programs, which gave me greater authority over my (un)learning about racial and spatial issues affecting my community. As I explored faculty mentors who could support my race- and rural-focused educational research interests, I remembered the work of Daniel (Danny) G. Solórzano, whose scholarship I had read in an Education Studies undergraduate course. His research demonstrated a commitment to justice for Chicanx/Latinx students that I hoped to emulate in my research. Danny was also familiar with the educational experiences of rural Latinx students from the San Joaquin Valley. He served as a professor at California State University, Bakersfield in the late 1980s, an institution an hour away from my home. Danny became an instrumental thought partner in my early theorizing about how place influenced educational access and equity for rural Latinx youth from the Valley.

Although place was central to my thinking about educational equity, there was also a dimension of race that played out in the San Joaquin Valley, such that educational opportunities between Latinx students and white students within this agricultural region were unequal. Danny introduced me to Critical Race Theory (CRT) to further my thinking. I understood CRT not only as a theory but as a movement of lawyers, scholars, and activists who sought an alternative to the color-evasive[10] ideology that emerged following the gains made during the civil rights movement (Bonilla-Silva, 2006). CRT scholars argued that race was a central rather than marginal factor that shaped the experiences of individuals with the law (Russell, 1992). Scholars like Danny, Gloria Ladson-Billings, and William F. Tate extended CRT to the field of educational research to examine how racism and other structures of oppression seeped into the classroom to detrimentally impact the educational experiences and life opportunities of Students of Color.[11] These arguments about the permanence of racism in U.S. society, including in U.S. institutions like the law and the educational system, helped me to understand that our underrepresentation in higher education as rural Latinxs was not inconsequential but deliberate. Our educational opportunities were limited because we served as an endless supply of farm labor to be used for the financial and political gains of white farmers and politicians in the region.

In my exploration of Critical Race Theory (CRT), I was especially drawn to the voice-of-color thesis (Delgado & Stefancic, 2017). This thesis posits that People of Color hold knowledge about how race and racism function because of our firsthand subjugation under these systems of oppression.

Within a CRT in education framework (Solórzano, 1997; 1998), this thesis translates to "the centrality of experiential knowledge of Students of Color" tenet (Solórzano & Yosso, 2001, p. 473). I witnessed Danny practice this principle as he validated the stories I shared with him about my experiences with racial and educational inequities in the San Joaquin Valley. These stories were not mere examples of unreliable anecdotal evidence; instead, they were real-life data that I could use to analyze and challenge larger systems of oppression that manifested in my community (e.g., Bell, 1987; Delgado, 1989; 1993; 1995; Solórzano & Yosso, 2001).

My training with Danny also included an introduction to Latino Critical Race Theory (LatCrit). LatCrit is a branch of CRT that specifically analyzes how Latinxs are impacted by issues of race and racism (Solórzano & Delgado Bernal, 2001; Solórzano & Yosso, 2001). While "Latinx" is not a race, Latinxs in the United States are subject to discriminatory treatment based on their perceived racial differences (Haney López, 1997). The dehumanization experienced by my family and community members in the agricultural fields is a prime example of our racialization as Latinxs. Further, LatCrit recognizes that Latinxs' experiences with racialization will vary depending on the intersection of additional social markers, such as ethnicity, skin color, social class, gender, sexuality, language, accent, and immigration status (Solórzano & Delgado Bernal, 2001). The intersections of these social markers produce particular experiences of racial domination for Latinxs in the United States. Within this framing of intersectionality (Crenshaw 1991), I understood rurality as an additional social and spatial marker that defined our experiences with racialization, including the particular type of racialized labor my parents performed and the lack of college opportunities that were available to us as children of Mexican im/migrant farm workers.

In addition to elements of place and race, I wondered how gender impacted the college opportunities of youth in the Valley. I often felt like a "bad daughter" for resisting certain cultural traditions (e.g., Villenas & Moreno, 2001) to pursue higher education. I was privileged to be in a community with generations of critical race mujeristas[12] in Danny's Research Apprenticeship Course (RAC) (Solórzano, 2023), who studied the intersections between racism, sexism, and education. I was particularly inspired by Delgado Bernal's (1998) conceptualization of a Chicana Feminist Epistemology in educational research. She bridged multiple academic fields of study, such as Education Studies, Ethnic Studies, and Women's Studies, to fashion a framework that (re)located the Chicana scholar "at the center of intellectual discourse" (de la Torre & Pesquera, 1993, p. 1). I frequent Delgado Bernal's scholarship and the writings of foundational Chicana feminists like Gloria Anzaldúa, Cherríe Moraga, and others who remind me that my identities and experiences are worthy of generating new knowledge in the academy, even if the academy fails to recognize its legitimacy (Delgado Bernal & Villalpando, 2002). It is legitimate knowledge because it has been theorized from "the flesh" (Moraga & Anzaldúa, 1981, p. 23) and speaks to an embodied experience that rural Latinxs and I.

As I began identifying Critical Race Theory and Chicana Feminisms as my theoretical homes,[13] the nation was conversely embracing white supremacist ideologies. During his 2015 presidential bid announcement, Donald Trump publicly decried undocumented Mexican im/migrants in the United States as "criminals, drug dealers, and rapists" (Lee, 2015). Latinx Critical Race Theorists defined this form of white supremacy as "racist nativism" (Pérez Huber, 2016; Pérez Huber et al., 2008), arguing that the social constructions of race and "native-ness," which were rooted in whiteness, intersected to exclude Mexican im/migrants from Trump's vision of a "great America." White farmers who identified with Trump's disdain for political elites proudly plastered signs of "Trump for president" and "make America great again" in the agricultural fields where my parents and other Mexican im/migrants labored. They were reminded of their "otherness" daily as they worked tirelessly to feed the nation and the world.

The vast support for Trump throughout the San Joaquin Valley region during the 2016 and 2020 presidential elections reminded me that place was an essential element for the (re)production of racial oppression. In my new urban environment, I was shielded from the racial violence characteristic of my rural community, including pesticide exposure, heat stress, and Immigration and Customs Enforcement (ICE) raids in the agricultural fields. These conditions were specific to the Valley, and I began to understand this more thoroughly the longer and further I was away from home. In retrospect, navigating urban and suburban places as I pursued higher education informed my rural sense of self and deepened my understanding of the Valley's racial and sociopolitical structuring. Urban, suburban, and rural areas are not merely neutral backdrops in our lives. Places are themselves socially constructed to maintain and reinforce racist ideologies (Delaney, 2002), typically for the benefit of people racialized as white.

My understanding of place as interactive and dynamic was theoretically strengthened as I extended my critical race and Chicana feminist training to include critical theories of space. With Danny's guidance, I was introduced to the work of Verónica (Veró) N. Vélez, one of his former doctoral students, who engaged the intersections of race, space, and education in her research. Veró's thinking about these relationships was informed by her prior work with a group of Latina im/migrant mothers who organized for educational reform in a school district in Los Angeles (Vélez, 2012).

The stories of these mothers and Veró's training in CRT led to her developing a Critical Race Spatial Analysis (CRSA) framework in education (Vélez & Solórzano, 2017). This framework is concerned with the structural and institutional factors that shape geographic and social spaces in ways that limit the educational opportunities of Students of Color. Although situated in an urban understanding of space, this framework and ongoing conversations with Veró provided me with a theoretical entryway to articulate the spatial expression of racialization in the San Joaquin Valley and its impact on rural Latinx youth's educational experiences and college opportunities.

I gravitated toward CRSA as a theory of racialized space not only because of its theoretical origins in CRT but also because of its epistemological implications. A principal objective of CRSA is "to build spatial models and understandings of the world from the lived experiences of People of Color" (Vélez & Solórzano, 2017, p. 23). This central purpose shifted my thinking about our marginality as rural Latinxs and farm workers in the San Joaquin Valley. To understand my community members as only acted on by structures of oppression perpetuated a "damage-centered" (Tuck, 2009) view of my community. Our lives and opportunities were not only shaped by the spatial expression of racialization in our communities, but we also made space (Vélez et al., 2021) for ourselves within a socially white, politically conservative, and anti-immigrant rural region. In my evolving articulation of space, rural Latinxs were not peripheral but integral to the San Joaquin Valley's demographic and geographic composition and vitality.

In recent projects with Veró (Puente & Vélez, 2023), we have extended a CRSA framework in educational research by theorizing about space from our particular racialized and gendered subjectivities as Chicanas/Latinas. We developed an epistemological and methodological approach in educational research that drew on the situated knowledge of racialized researchers and collaborators to construct meanings and maps of space. The field of Chicana Feminisms was instrumental in our development of a Platicando y Mapeando[14] methodology that viewed and measured space from an embodied standpoint. We argued that spatial representations of the world are always partial (Pavlovskaya, 2009). Yet, understandings of space from Communities of Color are often overlooked and omitted in grand theories of space. Chicana Feminisms demands that we view embodied, partial, and situated knowledge as legitimate and practice principles of reciprocity, vulnerability, and reflexivity (Fierros & Delgado Bernal, 2016) when we construct knowledge with others. Theorizing about space through a Platicando y Mapeando methodology grew to encompass more than a singular individual's lived experiences. It became about our relationships with each other as racialized peoples and our responsibility to our community and the land, especially as rural Latinxs living and laboring on Indigenous land.

Ironically, my training in the academy made me realize that I may have lacked the theoretical language to name my experiences with racialization at eight years old, but I did not lack the knowledge. The knowledge I searched about racialization in rural spaces across academic disciplines and theoretical perspectives had always shaped me. My lived experiences in the San Joaquin Valley imbued me with a set of knowledge about the role of racism, the social construction of space, and their collective impact on the college opportunities of rural Latinx youth. Critical Race and Chicana/Latina Feminist Theorists have legitimized this way of knowing for me. A way of knowing that is deeply rooted in lived experience, community memory, and ancestral wisdom (Delgado Bernal, 1998).

I also recognized that my inability to see myself and my community in the curriculum and grand theories of race was a temporary reality. The Critical Race and Chicana/Latina Feminists who came before me had purposefully created space for themselves and their ways of knowing in the academy. By fashioning frameworks that honored experiential and bodily knowledge, they seemingly invited emerging racialized scholars like me to partake, extend, and ground academic conversations in our ways of being and knowing. This way of producing knowledge allowed me to be shaped by my rural sense of self and way of life, even as I learned and navigated urban-based spaces of education. To theorize from a rural Latinx epistemological standpoint requires researchers to meaningfully wrestle with three important factors: (a) intersectional, transdisciplinary, and inter-generational knowledge, (b) the centrality of place, especially in under-standings of racial and educational inequities, and (c) our community members' roles in our research projects. The coming together of these various ideas that privilege a rural Latinx way of knowing manifested in a research study that I conducted with rural Latinx youth from California's San Joaquin Valley about their spatialities and college (in)opportunities (Puente, 2022a). In the following section, I provide those outside of my community with privileged insight into the conversations that I shared with rural Latinx youth about our experiences with racialization. The examples that youth provide serve to nuance grand theories of race in educational research that often ignore the centrality of place in shaping our racialized identities and available educational opportunities.

Rural Latinx youth's understanding of their/our racialization in the San Joaquin Valley

The study I conducted included 16 rural Latinx youth from im/migrant farm working backgrounds as "co-constructors of knowledge" (Fierros & Delgado Bernal, 2016). I recruited the students by delivering classroom presentations at my former high school and reaching out to community-based organizations serving rural Latinx students. As I prepared to conduct this study in early 2021, we were again reminded of our disposability. The global COVID-19 pandemic ravaged the San Joaquin Valley (Lin et al., 2020), specifically impacting Latinx im/migrant farm workers who experienced limited protection from the highly contagious virus (Puente, 2023a). I wondered if my project was worthy of being carried out during this time when our communities were experiencing high levels of premature death and immense grief. But I also understood this moment as a significant opportunity to facilitate pláticas[15] (Fierros & Delgado Bernal, 2016) with rural Latinx students about our shared pain, hopes, and dreams for our communities. While these pláticas took place online, we still nurtured trust and warmth with each other. Our shared identities and backgrounds inevitably facilitated these practices of relationality and vulnerability. I also believe the injustices we separately yet collectively navigated during the pandemic and a post-Trump presidency fostered a strong sense of solidarity and community among us.

An immediate concern that was centered by youth in our conversations was Trump's political career and his racist nativist discourses that specifically targeted Mexican im/migrants (Pérez Huber, 2016). The youth suggested that the nation's current anti-im/migrant sentiment was not necessarily specific to time but to place. Students argued that their experiences in Central California had predisposed them to blatant expressions of white supremacy long before Trump and Trump-like candidates had dominated national politics. As children of farm workers in a farm worker-dependent economy, they had inherited knowledge about how whiteness specifically operated in their communities to profit off the racialization of Latinx im/migrants. One student claimed that Central California's economy was "completely different" than other places because it "really relies on the backs of people that are Latinos." She argued that the region's lack of higher education opportunities for rural Latinx youth ensured that the current economic system stayed in place. Another student argued that inscribed into the memory of the San Joaquin Valley was the exploitation of her grandfather and of other Mexican im/migrants who were recruited to labor in the Valley's fields through the infamous Bracero Program. The youth understood their current racialization and college (in)opportunities within a history of place-based violence against farm workers in the agricultural region.

In addition to contextualizing their racialization within a history of farm worker exploitation, the youth pointed to physical markers in their communities that demonstrated their present-day racialization. They argued that deteriorated housing, water wells, unpaved roads, and a lack of sidewalks and street lights defined farm working communities. The bigger houses, picturesque landscaping, and countless grocery stores were reserved for the areas where white folks lived, including their teachers. There was a clear racial and spatial divide between "us" and "them," although no physical barrier separated one side of the community from the other. Yet, most youth could point to where that sociospatial division began. Many of the students did not cross that imagined but real boundary for fear of being policed and outed as not belonging. We discussed how the white folks did cross into our communities for our taqueros, carnicerías, and panaderías,[16] delicacies that could only be found within poor housing conditions and drying water wells. The boundaries were porous for them but fixed for us. The rigidness of the boundaries had real-life consequences for our educational experiences and (in)opportunities. We were defined by low levels of educational attainment, college under-enrollment, and immediate entry into manual labor jobs. The youth critically and quickly related these poor educational outcomes to the sociospatial segregated conditions we navigated. They further emphasized that only *we* faced those conditions because of who we were or who we were perceived to be by the white politicians and farmers who governed our communities and whose ideologies and practices shaped our lives.

Rural Latinx students also referenced how larger structures of dominance seeped into their homes and (re)configured their family dynamics. Our parents' roles as farm workers meant they labored in the fields from sunrise to sunset. The vicious cycle of poverty and monotony that plagued our lives robbed us of creating more joyous, carefree memories with our parents. Our inability to rest and share meaningful time and space with our families was a recurring and disheartening topic of conversation. Worse, our parents were deteriorating right before our eyes. Racialization had physically wounded and scarred their bodies. The youth talked about healing their parents' bodies by practicing home remedies or serving as their parents' advocates in the healthcare system. Students juxtaposed their realities with that of their white classmates, whom they argued did not have to worry about such conditions. As their white peers enjoyed their childhoods and adolescence, rural Latinx youth entered adulthood prematurely. They were caretakers, translators, college counselors, and medical and legal advocates, among many other roles and responsibilities they assumed in their families. The youth were honored to serve in these various capacitites. Still, the painful fact remained that their home lives and family dynamics were severely influenced by their "extenuating circumstances" as racialized people in the Valley.

Racialization had even shaped youth's perceptions of themselves and the opportunities and futures they felt were possible within the Valley. The injustices they witnessed and experienced in their rural communities led to "spirit murder," a form of racism that is psychically obliterating (Williams, 1987, p. 129). The weight of systemic racism had impacted their characterizations of themselves as "not good enough" for college. Their feelings of "unworthiness" were exacerbated by the poor-quality tablets and subpar internet speeds their schools provided them to navigate the college application process during the COVID-19 pandemic (Puente, 2022b). Still, most students applied and enrolled in college because their desires for justice exceeded any confinements placed on them by white supremacy. Youth's decisions to enroll in college were shaped by place. Some students felt forced to leave the Valley because their communities did not have a college nearby. In their spatial imaginations, places like Los Angeles and San Francisco had the most colleges because farm workers did not live and labor in those areas. Those cities, they argued, offered beach views while our communities featured premature death and "damaged" land. Many of the rural Latinx youth hoped to return to their home communities post-college graduation to conceive of possibilities and alternative futures that were absent for people like them under current systems of oppression. The spatial expression of racism in the Valley was not permanent but subject to an impending transformation that would one day include their communities' identities, contributions, and desires.

Lastly, the youth discussed their racialization in relation to land, water, and the environment of the San Joaquin Valley. Their relationship with the land was complicated. The youth felt a deep connection to the farm-working communities where their parents had chosen to settle for agricultural work. They expressed gratitude for the educational opportunities possible within a U.S. context compared to the limited options available to their parents in Mexico and other Latin American countries (Puente, 2023b). At the same time, they lamented their parents forced migration to the Valley and their ongoing subjugation in the agricultural fields. The fields were a paradox, both a place of opportunity and misery for the children of farm workers. The youth and I embraced these contradictions in our conversations, as Chicana Feminisms empowers us to do. We explored how capitalism tried to sever our parents' connection to the land, including their homeland and the land they cared for as farm workers. Our parents resisted this estrangement from the land by growing crops, raising animals, and passing down these land-based teachings to us. Within the context of our homes and families, our relationship with the land was reciprocal. We took care of the land, and the land took care of us. Youth juxtaposed this relationship with the (dis)connection white farmers and the state had with the land. The transactional nature of those relationships resulted in damage to the land and the environment, evidenced by triple-digit temperatures, wildfires, polluted air, pesticide use, and persistent drought in the San

Joaquin Valley. These place-based examples of racialization motivated youth to pursue higher education with hopes of transforming the spatial injustices that shaped their communities.

Centering place in race-centered educational research, policy, and practice

My lived experiences and conversations with rural Latinx youth point to the significance and specificity of place in (de)constructing racialization. The identities, experiences, and college opportunities of youth were shaped by their presence in an agricultural region that was socially, economically, and politically constructed to disadvantage people who looked like them. The critical race, feminist, and spatial theories that I employ in my research provide me with the theoretical validity to assert that our "othering" and marginalization in our rural communities are indicative of the permanence of racism at a systemic level. Yet, it is the centering of place and inclusion of critical race theories of space in my research that help me locate the distinct ways in which we are specifically racialized as rural Latinxs in the San Joaquin Valley. In arguing for the meaningful inclusion and specificity of place in educational and social science research, Tuck and McKenzie (2015) suggest that harm cannot be redressed if place is abandoned in our theorizing. Ignoring place in our research contributes to the preservation of white supremacy because we cannot name "the where" of its expression and therefore cannot address it. Inattention to place also contributes to our essentialism as People of Color because we advance a false understanding that all racialized experiences are equal across all places. Attending to the specificity of place in educational research allows us to more thoroughly address the multiple and particular ways that racialization takes shape to affect the educational experiences and life opportunities of Students of Color, which vary by spatial context and the dynamics of power within those contexts.

The conversations with rural Latinx youth also revealed their profound understanding of place-based racialization. The youth, untrained in theories of race, meticulously and loudly detailed how they experienced racism in their rural communities. Yet, their voices and contributions to knowledge production are largely absent in educational research, policy, and practice. The erasure of rural Latinx knowledge indicates a pervading belief in the social sciences that the mind is separate from the body and the body from the land (Tuck & McKenzie, 2015). The ideological separation of people from place is evident in the researcher's positioning as "all-knowing," regardless of their (dis)connections from the communities and places they study and the participant's diminutive role as the "object" of study. My employment of critical race, feminist, and spatial theories necessitates that

I anchor theorizations of race and racism in the lived experiences of rural Latinx youth and that I further invite them to co-construct knowledge with me about our shared racialized experiences in the San Joaquin Valley. Youth's daily navigation of systems of oppression imbues them with an intimate knowledge of U.S. society and its organizing structure that is inaccessible to outsiders, even those with acquired specialized training and skills. Positioning youth and community members as experts in their lives and needs advances their rights to self-determination and self-preservation. It also (re)sutures a relationship between mind-body-land that western understandings of "place as separate from self" seek to invalidate.

Lastly, I offer a final reflection on my conversations with rural Latinx youth about place. Youth were undeniably spatial experts able to map out the politics of the San Joaquin Valley and their positioning within a racial capitalist system (e.g., Puente & Vélez, 2023). This expertise was nurtured from living and learning in racially and socially segregated rural communities. They continued to develop this knowledge by exchanging conversations with their families and friends and by comparing their realities with the lives of people they deemed "not like us," including white farmers, teachers, and politicians in the region. As I replay the audio recordings of youth and embed their words in my writing, I realize that youth and I could grow in our understanding of place. Many of us were not taught whose land we are on and what the history of the land is. Our knowledge about place, and particularly land, is also impacted by the lack of ethnic studies in K-12 curricula in the Valley and the continued erasure of Indigenous peoples by processes of colonization and settler colonialism. Theories of race that meaningfully engage place must also consciously include Indigenous intellectual contributions, which have always engaged issues of land and place (Tuck & McKenzie, 2015). Our spatial understandings and pursuit of racial justice should reflect deep accountability to Indigenous peoples to whom our liberation is bounded.[17]

This chapter centered "the where" in processes and consequences of racialization to bring awareness to the sociospatial conditions that rural Latinxs in the San Joaquin Valley face. It also highlighted the voices of youth who are attuned to their social location within the racial and economic hierarchy of the region. This chapter invites scholars of race to center "the where" in their theorizing and include community members' voices and knowledge in their explanation of "the where." We cannot theorize about place without the direction and guidance of our community members who live in racially segregated places and have a better understanding of the processes and consequences of racialized places than the knowledge instilled in us by our postsecondary intuitions and degrees. As I continue to theorize about place, the youth in my study remind me that place is more than its physical elements. The agricultural fields provided an entryway to think about racialization in the Valley, but the grapevines were not only physical. The vines also hold our memories, collective experiences and efforts against racialization, and future hopes and dreams for a more just and equitable San Joaquin Valley.

Notes

1 Mother
2 Father
3 Arms, and a reference to the Bracero Program that imported millions of Mexicans to labor in the agricultural fields following the labor shortages in agriculture induced by World War II.
4 Latino Critical Race Theorists (e.g., Lindsay Pérez Huber) who reject the power that capitalization brings to this dominant racialized group.
5 Pelaez López (2018) argued that "Latinx" is a linguistic intervention into the Spanish language put forth by transgender and gender-nonconforming Latin Americans out of survival. To identify with this term and to use this term is to acknowledge the violence faced by LGBTQIA+ Latin Americans within Latinx communities and globally. I use this term purposefully to disrupt the gender binary and to pursue Latinx liberation in my writing and theorizing.
6 I intentionally place a "/" between "im" and "migrant" to disrupt the normalized asymmetrical relationship im/migrants are assumed to have with the United States. Transnational migration is not always one-directional. Im/migrants may migrate back and forth from the United States and their home countries, send remittances to family members outside the United States, and/or disidentify with citizenship structures and efforts to assimilate. To represent these varied and complex realities more accurately, I choose to use "im/migrant" instead of "immigrant" as a grammatical move toward social and racial justice.
7 Piece rate is the payment method that most farm workers are paid. This payment is based on the number of buckets or bags farm workers fill with the crops they harvest (National Farm Worker Ministry, 2022).
8 "He says he's going to pay us less. Ten cents instead of one quarter."
9 Sociospatial refers to geographers' understandings that the social and spatial mutually reinforce each other (Delaney, 2002).
10 I use "color-evasive" instead "color-blind," which is the traditional Critical Race Theory term for this dominant ideology, to remove ableist language from my employment of theories of race (Annamma et al., 2017).
11 I capitalize the term "Students of Color" (and other "of Color" terms) in accordance with the writings of Latino Critical Race theorists (e.g., Lindsay Pérez Huber) who reject the standard grammatical norm and move towards the empowerment of these racialized groups.
12 Mujerista is a term used by Chicana/Latina feminists to refer "to a Latina-oriented 'womanist' sensibility or approach to power, knowledge, and relationships rooted in convictions for community uplift" (Villenas et al., 2006, p. 7).
13 The notion of "theoretical home" emerged from conversations with Zaynab Gates and friends/colleagues in the Department of Education Studies at UC San Diego that manifested in the publication of a special issue titled "Telling for Liberation: Using Critical Storytelling Methodology to Advance Racial and Social Justice" in UCLA's *InterActions* journal.

14 Platicando y Mapeando translates to talking and mapping.
15 Pláticas translates to relational conversations. It is a Chicana/Latina feminist methodology with a set of principles that honors lived experience, healing, reciprocity, vulnerability, and reflexivity.
16 (a) someone who makes/sells tacos, (b) butcher shops, (c) bakeries
17 This sentence is a tribute to the Indigenous academic and activist Lila Watson, who is often credited with the quote: "If you have come to help me, you are wasting your time. If you have come because your liberation is bound up with mine, then let us work together."

References

Annamma, S. A., Jackson, D. D., & Morrison, D. (2017). Conceptualizing color-evasiveness: Using dis/ability critical race theory to expand a color-blind racial ideology in education and society. *Race Ethnicity and Education, 20*(2), 147–162.
Bell, D. (1987). *And we will not be saved: The elusive quest for racial justice.* New York: Basic Books.
Bonilla-Silva, E. (2006). *Racism without racists: Color-blind racism and the persistence of racial inequality in the United States.* Lanham, MD: Rowman & Littlefield Publishers.
Crenshaw, K. (1991). Women of color at the center: Selections from the third national conference on women of color and the law: Mapping the margins: Intersectionality, identity politics, and violence against women of color. *Stanford Law Review, 43*(6), 1241–1299.
de la Torre, A., & Pesquera, B. (Eds.). (1993). *Building with our hands: New directions in Chicana studies.* Berkeley: University of California Press.
Delaney, D. (2002). The space that race makes. *The Professional Geographer, 54*(1), 6–14.
Delgado, R. (1989). Storytelling for oppositionists and others: A plea for narrative. *Michigan Law Review, 87*(8), 2411–2441.
Delgado, R. (1993). On telling stories in school: A reply to Farber and Sherry. *Vanderbilt Law Review, 46*, 665.
Delgado, R. (1995). *The Rodrigo chronicles: Conversations about America and race.* New York and London: NYU Press.
Delgado, R., & Stefancic, J. (2017). *Critical race theory: An introduction* (Vol. 20). New York: NYU press.
Delgado Bernal, D. (1998). Using a Chicana feminist epistemology in educational research. *Harvard Educational Review, 68*(4), 555–583.
Delgado Bernal, D., & Villalpando, O. (2002). An apartheid of knowledge in academia: The struggle over the" legitimate" knowledge of faculty of color. *Equity & Excellence in Education, 35*(2), 169–180.
Fierros, C. O., & Delgado Bernal, D. (2016). Vamos a platicar: The contours of pláticas as Chicana/Latina feminist methodology. *Chicana/Latina Studies, 15*(2), 98–121.
Haney López, I. F. (1997). Race, ethnicity, erasure: The salience of race to LatCrit theory. *California Law Review, 85*, 1143.
Lee, M. Y. H. (2015, July 8). Donald Trump's false comments connecting Mexican immigrants and crime. *The Washington Post.* Retrieved from https://

www.washingtonpost.com/news/fact-checker/wp/2015/07/08/donald-trumps-false-comments-connecting-mexican-immigrants-and-crime/

Lin, R. II, Gutierrez, M., & Chabria, A. (2020, July 28). Coronavirus ravages California's central valley, following a cruel and familiar path. *Los Angeles Times.* Retrieved from https://www.latimes.com/california/story/2020-07-28/coronavirus-ravages-californias-central-valley-following-a-cruel-and-familiar-path

Moraga, C., & Anzaldúa, G. (1981). *This bridge called my back: Writings by radical women of color.* Persephone Press.

National Farm Worker Ministry. (2022, September). *Low wages.* https://nfwm.org/farm-workers/farm-worker-issues/low-wages/#piece

National Integrated Drought Information System (NIDIS). (n.d.). *Historical data and conditions.* U.S. National Oceanic and Atmospheric Administration. Retrieved from https://www.drought.gov/historical-information?state=california&county Fips=06107&dataset=0&selectedDateUSDM=20110503

Pavlovskaya, M. (2009). Non-quantitative GIS. *Qualitative GIS: A mixed methods approach,* 13–37.

Pelaez López, A. (2018, September). The X in Latinx is a wound, not a trend. ColorBloq. Retrieved from https://www.colorbloq.org/article/the-x-in-latinx-is-a-wound-not-a-trend

Pérez Huber, L. (2016). Make America great again: Donald Trump, racist nativism and the virulent adherence to white supremacy amid US demographic change. *Charleston Law Review, 10,* 215.

Pérez Huber, L., Lopez, C. B., Malagon, M. C., Vélez, V. N., & Solórzano, D. G. (2008). Getting beyond the 'symptom,' acknowledging the 'disease': Theorizing racist nativism. *Contemporary Justice Review, 11*(1), 39–51.

Puente, M. (2022a). *Ground-Truthing en el Valle de San Joaquín: A Mixed Methods Study on Rural Latinx Spatiality and College (In)Opportunity.* UC San Diego. ProQuest ID: Puente_ucsd_0033D_21548. Merritt ID: ark:/13030/m59q09j9. Retrieved from https://escholarship.org/uc/item/4qj050xm

Puente, M. (2022b). A critical race spatial analysis of rural Latinx students' college (In)opportunities and conscious choices during the COVID-19 pandemic. *Journal of Latinos and Education, 21*(3), 304–318. https://doi.org/10.1080/15348431.2022.2051040

Puente, M., & Vélez, V. N. (2023). Platicando y Mapeando: a Chicana/Latina feminist GIS methodology in educational research. *International Journal of Qualitative Studies in Education,* 1–16. https://doi.org/10.1080/09518398.2023.2181432

Puente, M. (2023a). "Essential workers" or sacirifical labor? Applying the concept of racial capitalism to Mexican immigrant farm workers' disposability during the COVID-19 pandemic. In M. J. Villaseñor, & H. Jiménez (Eds.), *Latinx Experiences: Interdisciplinary Perspectives* (pp. 83–90), SAGE Publications.

Puente, M. (2023b). Reframing education deserts as places of desire: A case study of rural Latinx students' college opportunities. In T. Hallmark, S. Ardoin, & D. R. Means (Eds.), *Race and Rurality: Considerations for Advancing Higher Education Equity* (pp. 82–98), Routledge.

Russell, M. M. (1992). Entering Great America: Reflections on race and the convergence of progressive legal theory and practice. *Hastings Law Journal*, *43*, 749.

Solórzano, D. G. (1997). Images and words that wound: Critical race theory, racial stereotyping, and teacher education. *Teacher Education Quarterly*, *24*(3), 5–19.

Solórzano, D. G. (1998). Critical race theory, race and gender microaggressions, and the experience of Chicana and Chicano scholars. *International Journal of Qualitative Studies in Education*, *11*(1), 121–136.

Solórzano, D. G. (2023). My journey to this place called the RAC: Reflections on a movement in critical race thought and critical race hope in higher education. *International Journal of Qualitative Studies in Education*, *36*(1), 87–98.

Solórzano, D. G., & Delgado Bernal, D. (2001). Examining transformational resistance through a critical race and LatCrit theory framework: Chicana and Chicano students in an urban context. *Urban Education*, *36*(3), 308–342.

Solórzano, D. G., & Yosso, T. J. (2001). Critical race and LatCrit theory and method: Counter-storytelling. *International Journal of Qualitative Studies in Education*, *14*(4), 471–495.

Tuck, E. (2009). Suspending damage: A letter to communities. *Harvard Educational Review*, *79*(3), 409–428.

Tuck, E., & McKenzie, M. (2015). Relational validity and the "where" of inquiry: Place and land in qualitative research. *Qualitative Inquiry*, *21*(7), 633–638.

Vélez, V. N. (2012). *Del coraje a la esperanza (from rage to hope): A case study of the development of Latina/o immigrant parents as agents of change.* Los Angeles: University of California.

Vélez, V. N., & Solórzano, D. G. (2017). Critical race spatial analysis: Conceptualizing GIS as a tool for critical race research in education. In D. Morrison, S. Annamma, & D. Jackson (Eds.), *Critical race spatial analysis: Mapping to understand and address educational inequity* (pp. 8–31), Sterling, VA: Stylus.

Vélez, V. N., Torres, D. P., & Jaramillo, D. L. (2021). Trenzudas, truchas, and traviesas: Mapping higher education through a Chicana feminist cartography. In Nichole, M. Garcia, Cristobal, Salinas Jr, & Jesus, Cisneros (Eds.) *Studying Latinx/a/o students in higher education* (pp. 106–120). Routledge.

Villenas, S., Godinez, F. E., Delgado Bernal, D., & Elenes, C. A. (2006). Chicanas/Latinas building bridges: An introduction. *Chicana/Latina Education in Everyday Life: Feminista Perspectives on Pedagogy and Epistemology*, 1–9.

Villenas, S., & Moreno, M. (2001). To valerse por si misma between race, capitalism, and patriarchy: Latina mother-daughter pedagogies in North Carolina. *International Journal of Qualitative Studies in Education*, *14*(5), 671–687.

Whisnand, C. (2021, July 2). *East Porterville facing similar drought crisis to 2015*. The Porterville Recorder. Retrieved from https://www.recorderonline.com/news/east-porterville-facing-similar-drought-crisis-to-2015/article_8ed3d27e-db51-11eb-9c7c-332f636a09d4.html

Williams, P. (1987). Spirit-murdering the messenger: The discourse of fingerpointing as the law's response to racism. *University of Miami Law Review*, *42*, 127.

PART II

Racialization is an ongoing (settler) process

Leah D. Doane

In this section, "Racialization is an ongoing (settler) process", we read about the realities of racism and racialization as they unfold over time, from fleeting conversations to manifestations in neighborhoods and social structures. Importantly, this section invites readers to reflect on how the reinventing of racialization across time and place is a demonstration of ongoing settler colonialism and anti-Blackness. Authors recount stories of their first or ongoing experiences of racism and racialization across childhood and into adulthood, including accounts of growing up as a child of Mexican immigrants in Southeast Los Angeles to experiences of Islamophobia and anti-Muslim racism in a post-September 11th historical context. Importantly, they use their own stories of growing up to illustrate how and why theories of Blackness, Indigeneity, and racialization provided the groundwork and motivation for their own theorizing, as well as their current research with youth and families. Authors Dinorah Sánchez Loza and Goleen Samari attend to how ongoing generational practices of racialization informed their scholarly decisions and engagement in research and discourse on youth civic engagement and the influence of Islamophobia in the United States on health inequities.

Sánchez Loza writes from her perspective as a student of media, a veteran teacher, and a critical scholar of social and cultural processes examining the development of youth civic engagement. Sánchez Loza speaks of uncovering settler tracks in civic education and our schools such that a new understanding of race and racialization can emerge beyond treating race as an additive variable. Samari is both a Middle Eastern and Islamic studies scholar and a public health epidemiologist and demographer promoting

DOI: 10.4324/9781003303800-6

health equity. Samari describes how both the racialization of Muslim individuals and the invisibility or lack of acknowledgment of Middle Eastern and North African descent as a "racial" group has altered the health and well-being of her cultural and religious community. What becomes clear across these two chapters is that engaging in theorizations of settler colonialism and racialization is important across disciplines.

Both authors describe their family, neighborhoods, and daily life as their first "theorists"—the people and places that taught them how to be social critics and questioners from the margins. Importantly, both authors discuss the importance of learning through scholarship about their own communities while also joining "with Black, Brown, and Asian peers from diverse geographic and economic backgrounds with whom I organized and with whom I conspired in seminars to center marginalized voices and alternative narratives" (Sánchez Loza, this volume). Both authors identify the resounding influence of how and why racialization processes and racism shape youth and communities. Importantly, they illustrate the numerous interacting ways that racialization and racism have been understood across disciplines but often have been described using different words, different conceptualizations, and potentially different implications.

Dinorah Sánchez Loza shares her experiences of racialization both personally and within her own scholarly journey in "Tracking Race: Uncovering Settler Tracks in Civic Education as a Way to Theorize the Political Project of Racialization". Sánchez Loza sets the stage by describing her earliest experiences of critical social theorists as a child of Mexican immigrants living in neighborhoods where racial order and politics for Black, Brown, and Asian communities were complicated and driven by differing colonial histories (Tuck & Yang, 2012). She carefully describes how the stories of her neighborhood, and her family's critically engaged interpretations of such stories, were the root of her first lessons and theorizing on the role of the state that were given names—social reproduction, Critical Race Theory, and settler colonialism—once she entered graduate school. Sánchez Loza's experiences, first as an educator in her home neighborhood, and then as a graduate student, led her to explore how school could nurture the political development of Black and Brown youth where she found that "racialization is not a social condition, but a political one and civics education ... is inevitably implicated in its reproduction" (Sánchez Loza, this volume).

Sánchez Loza describes her uncovering of settler colonial tracks (Veracini, 2010) in civic opportunity gaps. She brings to attention the notion that civic education in schools, indeed the lessons taught, is steeped in political subjectivities, racialization schemes, and evolutionary settler politics. Importantly, her work has shown that in order to change these gaps we must focus on white youth political ideologies and civic engagement as opposed to much of the previous work which has focused on minoritized youth and how to make civic education culturally relevant. Drawing on theorists Junn (2004) and Veracini (2010), Sánchez Loza highlights that by moving the spotlight onto civic education for predominantly white schools and white youth, her work shifts the focus away from Black, Brown, and other marginalized youth and narratives laced in settler ideologies that have been dictated by racialized colonial processes over time.

In parallel to the previous chapter, Goleen Samari begins her chapter, "Anti-Muslim Racism: The Double Burden of Racism and Invisibility", with a poignant retelling of her experiences with anti-Muslim racism as a youth being pulled over by a police officer in Texas immediately following September 11, 2001. Samari shines a light on the intersection of belonging to an invisible community according to colonial categorizations—the Middle East and North Africa (MENA)—and a religious group that has been actively subjected to hate crimes, discrimination, and violence. Samari, as an early-career scholar, began to theorize through her own experiences by drawing from the Public Health and Critical Race Praxis (PHCRP) (Ford, 2016), as well as theories of structural racism and health (Gee & Ford, 2011; Gee & Hicken, 2021; Gee et al., 2019). She details her trajectory to promote better health outcomes and social justice for Muslim and Middle Eastern Americans through her active engagement in "self-reflexive, race-conscious research" (Samari, this volume). Samari began her scholarly endeavors through lessons and learning about racialization as a tool to discuss Muslim experiences. Indeed, her personal experiences highlight harmful racialization processes whereby structural contexts and agents of power assign "racial meaning to cultural traits of groups, some of whom may be white ethnics, resulting in their rejection from a white identity, even if their skin tone is white" (Samari, this volume), leading to creations of the "other".

Samari grapples with her experiences of being an insider and an outsider as a Western Muslim who faced challenges from mainstream public health and demography scholars who pushed back on the notion that Middle Eastern immigrants or Muslim communities were not a group that should be examined in public health. Drawing on the PHCRP, Samari details her path as a public-facing scholar where she has systematically demonstrated experiences of what she calls the "double burden of the racialized experience of Muslims and Middle Easterners: straddling erasure and racism induced public visibility, harm, and in some cases, mortality" (Samari, this volume). Many, in both the academy and public spaces, sought to silence her narrative, and her safety, instantiations of how institutionalized settler racialization processes continue to persist in multilevel ways from daily conversations to broad state policies and characterizations of cultural and religious groups.

Sánchez Loza and Samari share their stories and theories of racialization and settler colonialism across time, place, and discipline. I hope these chapters can be read by both early career and established Black and Indigenous scholars and scholars of color who may also find that their stories have been woven into the fabric of their research and theorizing and find echoes of their stories here. I hope this work stimulates new or re-engagement with theory, research, methods, and practices to help uncover the colonial structures that shape the lives of youth and families. Engaging in thoughtful discourse, laughter, and learning with Sánchez Loza and Samari while they worked on these chapters has stimulated important self-reflexive questions for me, a white scholar who grew up benefiting from daily and historical engagement with the institutional and systemic processes of racism and racialization. Collectively, I hope we can listen, learn, and ensure that the stories and theories of racialized communities are meaningfully engaged, and not silenced, erased, or distorted.

References

Ford, C. L. (2016). Public health critical race praxis: An introduction, an intervention, and three points for consideration. *Winston Law Review*, 477.

Gee, G. C., & Ford, C. L. (2011). Structural racism and health inequities: Old issues, New Directions 1. *Du Bois Review: Social Science Research on Race*, 8(1), 115.

Gee, G. C., & Hicken, M. T. (2021). Structural racism: The rules and relations of inequity. *Ethnicity & Disease*, 31(Suppl), 293–300.

Gee, G. C., Hing, A., Mohammed, S., Tabor, D. C., & Williams, D. R. (2019). Racism and the life course: Taking time seriously. *American Journal of Public Health*, 109(S1), S43–S47.

Junn, J. (2004). Diversity, immigration, and the politics of civic education. *PS: Political Science and Politics*, 37(2), 253–255.

Tuck, E., & Yang, K. W. (2012). Decolonization is not a metaphor. *Decolonization: Indigeneity, Education & Society*, 1(1), 1–40.

Veracini, L. (2010). *Settler colonialism*. Palgrave Macmillan.

5

TRACKING RACE, TRACKING SETTLERNESS

Theorizing the political project of racialization and uncovering settler tracks in civic education

dinorah sánchez loza

Lynwood as theory: Community as a curriculum on race

I begin this chapter from Lynwood, California. Though I am not physically there, this is where I am writing from. This city, referred to as part of the "urban fringe" just outside of the city of Los Angeles, served as the prominent geographical setting for my formative years and, as such, as my introductory curriculum to theories of race and racialization. That is what I mean when I say I am writing *from* this place. I also write as the daughter of immigrants who, (dis)located from Jalisco, Mexico, attempted to make a life in southeast LA. Neither sought to voluntarily leave their home but felt forced to do so for survival. Extractive and neoliberal economic policies which continually made Mexico untenable for many came to a head for my parents in the 1970s as they formed part of one of the largest movements of Mexican migrants to the United States in history.

As my parents and so many other people's parents made southeast LA home, so too did white flight, organized state abandonment, the crack "epidemic," increased gang activity, and accompanying state violence in the forms of over-policing and immigration raids (Gilmore, 2008). My parents arrived about five years after the Watts Rebellion and decades later as a middle schooler, I would come to see these same neighborhoods in south-central and southeast LA smoldering—smoke clouds on the horizon, neighborhood drug store in flames, liquor store looted—when a "not guilty" verdict absolved white officers in the beating of Rodney King. Lynwood, California served as the epicenter of my understanding of a racial order where Black people, Brown people, and poor folks with whom I was

DOI: 10.4324/9781003303800-7

in the community, were at the bottom. They were beaten by cops regularly, *only this time they were recorded*, where folks grabbed TVs and sneakers and diapers *'cause why the fuck not? They shot Latasha Harlins saying she stole some juice*. Where the racial politics among Black, Brown, and Asian folks were often in solidarity, at times in contention, but always complicated and intertwined in ways indicative of our respective colonial histories (Tuck & Yang, 2012). In many ways, the structures of colonialism emerging from 1492 and catalyzed through contemporary racialization schemes converged in and through 90262 and the people who called it home.

While the academic theories that helped give language to our conditions were not yet familiar to me, the stories I grew up around—of cops knocking down our doors and ransacking our houses looking for loved ones because they missed check-ins with their probation officers; of hiding in refrigerators at the factory when la migra decided to show up at our jobs; of being denied welfare assistance because we made $501 dollars a month and the cut off was $500—and our analyses of them served as curriculum teaching me through personal, familial, and extended community experiences how the state was not an abstract concept, but a very real material force that structured our everyday lives. The form and function of the stories themselves offered critiques of a carceral state, of colonial borders, of an unethical political economic system. It is why Critical Social Theories—ideas that critiqued the exploitative nature of capitalism, colonialism, white supremacy, heteropatriarchy—were so legible to me when they came into my life later in scholarly work. With my father as a sort of anticolonial narrator pointing out the ways coloniality persevered in our lives, my mother as a decolonial practitioner demonstrating ways to be in relation with each other and the land, and with peers as interlocutors making sense of what was happening to us and around us, these community pedagogies and curricula sowed the seeds for understandings that refused to pathologize those oppressed, but instead situated the problem with oppressive systems.

I start here to cite the community itself as a theorist given that Lynwood, with how *I* experienced and read it, provided a critical foundation on which I have come to build my scholarly inquiry. Although I highlight specific thinkers throughout this chapter, it is not often the case that the theorists in our moms and dads, in our aunties, cousins, friends, and neighbors, or the theorist of place are acknowledged. It was upon these theorists and lenses that the later language provided by academic theories like social reproduction, Critical Race Theory, and settler colonialism adhered to. It is undeniable to my scholarly trajectory that this predominantly Black and Brown urban enclave in the metropolitan area also known as Nuestra Señora Reina de Los Angeles, a place I would later understand as Tongva land, is the palimpsest on and from which I write and theorize.

Race through contrast and putting theory into (teaching) practice

Also undeniable to how I would come to theorize race was the curriculum that occurred through my displacement from LA to an elite university in the Midwest where for the first time I lived and learned in a predominantly white and economically affluent space. Zora Neal Hurston wrote in 1928, "I feel most colored when I am thrown against a sharp white background" and being a first-generation student of color at Northwestern was just that. Reading those words helped me to articulate how race was felt and experienced, how my Brownness was sensed (Muñoz, 2020), due to the contrast of existing against the "sharp white background" that was campus, classes, and course content. Throughout those four years, however, I found refuge in sociology courses where I learned about Marxist analyses that helped me make sense of class exploitation and in African American Studies courses that introduced me to Collins' (1991) intersectionality and Du Bois' (1903) double-consciousness. I also read Gloria Anzaldúa (1987) and engaged with her ideas of the borderland in the first Latino Studies course ever offered at the institution. This curriculum was pivotal in helping me to understand what theory was, that Black and Brown people could occupy theorizing space (Anzaldúa, 1987), and that it could offer language and concepts to explain how we lived race, class, and gender, including what I and my peers were experiencing.

Importantly, I engaged with this curriculum while in community with Black, Brown, and Asian peers from diverse geographic and economic backgrounds with whom I organized alongside and with whom I conspired in seminars to center marginalized voices and alternative narratives. One does not do theory in isolation. Our teaching and learning outside of the formal curriculum consisted of attempting to make sense of oppression and holding ourselves accountable for putting theory into practice. As we read about class struggle and gender and racial oppression, organized against racist professors, advocated for a Latino Studies program, and witnessed the Zapatistas engage in revolutionary praxis in Chiapas, we were inspired by the idea that one should not only theorize about the world, but act upon it and change it. This culminated in my return to Lynwood to become a teacher in the schools I had once experienced as a student and link theory to practice.

Drawn to the profession for its political possibilities, I was interested in the political development of Black and Brown youth. I saw my role as an educator as one that would nurture student knowledge and agency toward liberation not only in content but also through relations of teaching and learning. Enrolled in the Teaching for Social Justice teacher preparation program through UCLA Center X, I was introduced to the thinking of Paolo Freire, Bowles & Gintis, Gloria Ladson Billings, and Angela Valenzuela among many other theorists of education who attempted to make sense of race, class, and politics in and through schooling. Through the study of ideas like conscientization, correspondence theory, and culturally relevant pedagogy occurring alongside my day-to-day classroom experiences, I better understood the political role of teaching and how social structures were (re)produced via school. Schools could be oppressive, but also possess a liberatory potential. Yet, while I attempted to foster liberatory and transformative processes in my classroom, Black and Brown students overwhelmingly were forced to endure carceral processes, curricular violence, and a myriad of policies from the federal to the local level failing them. I began to question school's role in democratic (mis)education and in reproducing racial and social inequality and after seven years as an educator in the urban community that raised me, I entered academia to explore how Black and Brown youth come to think and act politically.

Race-property-politics: Racialization via settler colonialism and its impact on civic education

As I started my systematic inquiry into the relationship between school and how youth come to think and act politically, I read critical social theory alongside civic education literature and arrived at the point I now occupy regarding theories of racialization: "racialization" is not a social condition, but a political one. Further, racialization schemes derive from and are in service to the oldest political project in the US: settler colonialism. As such, civic education, being an educative practice in and of politics, is inevitably implicated in its reproduction.

When I began reading the civic education literature and scholarship that focused on the political development of youth, I was heartened to find work that focused on ameliorating educational inequality and increasing "civic learning opportunities" for students of color. I read a scholarship alerting us to low rates of youth political participation, tracing these trends to diminished civic education in the school curriculum, and attributed this decrease in civic learning opportunities to an educational landscape hyperfocused on testing (Westheimer & Kahne, 2004). Importantly, this scholarship drew linkages between unequal schooling experiences, inequality that fell along race and class cleavages, and how these not only impact academic achievement but negatively impact civic knowledge and engagement as well. Termed "civic opportunity gaps", these studies expose the difference between under-resourced and higher-resourced schools in providing democratic and civic learning opportunities and show that more rigorous academic school cultures and exposure to democratic learning environments in higher-resourced schools result in higher rates of youth political participation overall (Kahne & Middaugh, 2008; Levine, 2009). These studies also highlight the implications of unequal democratic participation and focus on how schools could improve civic outcomes for all young people. By equalizing the schooling inputs, we could democratize the political output so to speak.

At the time, the research questions I developed reflected my engagement with these texts. For example, I conducted one study with Latinx youth that explored their conceptualizations of politics. I found that these Latinx adolescents regarded themselves as not very politically engaged yet relayed many salient moments and experiences where they were just that. I argued that schools failed to connect the political work and knowledge these youth possess and recommended that schools do more to make civic education relevant for them. At that time, I believed that I was engaging in racial analyses of civic education for Latinx youth by focusing on a racialized population. I explicitly named racism as the root cause of their/our unequal social conditions. However, it was not until I read Charles Mills' *The Racial Contract* and Sandy Grande's *Red Pedagogy: Native American Social and Political Thought* that I began to understand citizenship and democracy in the US as white supremacist and colonial constructs.

In *The Racial Contract* Mills (1997) clarifies that the social contract undergirding liberal democracy is a racial contract where white supremacy functions as the political system, as "a particular power structure of formal or informal rule, socioeconomic privilege, and norms for the differential distribution of material wealth and opportunities, benefits and burdens, rights and duties" (Mills, 1997, p. 3). This understanding helped me recognize the co-constitutive nature of race and politics. Sandy Grande's analysis in Red Pedagogy was also critical offering insights into democracy as an imposition wherein inclusion into citizenship, while often idealized, serves as assimilation resulting in the undoing of tribalism. She also explained how citizenship worked toward eradicating Indigenous sovereignty and noted the inherent violence in making land into property. If liberal democracy was inherently racist and colonial, what did it mean to improve civic education and socialize students into this political system?

Of course, my reading did not happen linearly or in isolation. At this time, I also engaged with scholarship that grappled with ideas of race and whiteness across various disciplines. For example, the work of W.E.B Du Bois, and specifically the following quote, encapsulated for me one fundamental aspect of race: the link between race, property, and power. He writes,

"But what on earth is whiteness that one should so desire it?" Then always, somehow, some way, silently but clearly, I am given to understand that whiteness is the ownership of the earth forever and ever, Amen! (Du Bois, 1920)

In this quote, I understood Du Bois as pointing to the relationship between whiteness and ownership and the implications thereof for demarcating the field of citizenship, rights, and politics. Other scholarship on race that traces the relationship between whiteness and property include but are not limited to: Harris' (1995) pivotal demonstration of "whiteness as property" and its codification in US law, Roediger's (1999) engagement with Du Bois' conceptualization of the "public and psychological wages of Whiteness" (Du Bois, 1935/1998) through historical analysis of the materialization of these wages among the white working class, and George Lipsitz's (2006) argument of the existence of a "possessive investment in whiteness" where public policy and private prejudice work together to create and maintain a racial hierarchy founded on white supremacy. Critical scholars of race make clear that whiteness is not "a real, authentic, biological or cultural identity, rather it is a phenotypically secured and culturally produced enactment of racial dominance" (Alexander, 2012, p. 9). That "culturally produced enactment of racial dominance" is what Leonardo (2002) reminds us of when writing that whiteness functions as a set of ideals and practices that produce and maintain white power. This, along with Ansley's (1989) definition of white supremacy as "a political, economic, and cultural system in which whites overwhelmingly control power and material resources, conscious and unconscious idea of white superiority and entitlement are widespread, and relations of white dominance and non-white subordination are daily reenacted across a broad array of institutions and social settings," (p. 1024) made clear for me the political intentions and manifestations of race.

Reading Moreton-Robinson's (2015) work added nuance to this race-politics-property dynamic through the field of Indigenous Studies and engagement with the idea of sovereignty as a "white possession." In "The white possessive: Property, power, and Indigenous sovereignty", Moreton-Robinson discusses the possessive logics of white sovereignty that motivates land appropriation and rationalizes a racial hierarchy where white people are deemed the sole possessors and arbiters of rights. This provided important insight into the relationship between whiteness and citizenship and between ownership and land. She writes,

> As a means of controlling differently racialized populations enclosed within it borders, white subjects are disciplined (though to different degrees) *as citizens* to invest in the nation as a white possession. As citizens of this white nation, they are contracted into, and imbued with, a sense of belonging and ownership […] (emphasis added, p. 122).

The relationship between whiteness and ownership in this way delineates a relationship between the desirability and function of white supremacy wherein this hierarchy ensures those positioned in power (whites) enjoy control over and possession of property. Ownership and belonging constitute the crux of citizenship within settler colonial states like the United States and are supported and maintained through their racialized and political-economic structures. Thus, the dynamic between race and property constitutes a political relationship and converges with Lockean conceptions, wherein the justification of liberal democracy materializes through regimes and structures of individual liberty centered around property rights (Macpherson, 1962). As Moreton-Robinson (2015) writes, "white possession is a discursive pre-disposition servicing the conditions, practices, implications, and racialized discourses that are embedded within and central to White first world patri-archal nation-states" (Moreton-Robinson, 2015, p. xxiv). In this way, settler colonialism and resultant racialization schemes are central to the nation-state and to conceptualizations of citizenship and politics.

These ideas the social contract as a racialized scheme, citizenship as assimilation, whiteness as property, and white citizens as the sole proprie-tors of sovereignty and arbiters of rights—worked in concert to challenge my own liberal and ultimately colonial conceptions of citizenship and my own liberal and ultimately colonial conceptions of citizenship and helped me arrive at an understanding of race as a political condition. Starting from the "alternative starting point" (Glenn, 2015) of settler colonialism and understanding it as a structure and not an event (Wolfe, 2006) PROVIDES an overarching framework that demonstrates how coloniality structures every aspect of life, including race, politics, and education. In conjunction with Critical Race Theory, important scholarship theorizing anti-Blackness, and ideas from decolonial thinkers from the Global South (Grosfoguel, 2007; Quijano, 2000), these theories helped me understand that US pol-itics and racialization are functionally one and the same.

As I delved deeper into Indigenous and Black political theory, as well as theory from Decolonial and Settler Colonial Studies, I began to question whether civic education truly served as a public good. The colonial and racial structures shaping the political landscape for youth of color made me question the aims and practices of civic education in schools and the political ideologies it promotes. These ideas, including white sovereignty, the Racial Contract, and citizenship as assimilation, applied to research on youth in schools propelled me to interrogate how civic education may work to socialize and nurture students into investing in settler politics and the racialization schemes they create.

Pivotal scholarship in social studies has shed light on this issue. For ex-ample, Urrieta (2004) and Ladson-Billings (2004) note the Whitestream normativity in social studies and citizenship education. Calderon (2009, 2014) writes about rejecting colonial blindness in education and delineates the settler grammars that appear in textbooks, while Sabzalian and Shear (2018; 2019) argue for the importance of foregrounding Indigenous sovereignty in civic education. Starting with settler colonialism in civic education makes visible the ongoing legacies of colonialism and allows for different framings of the problems at the center of civic education research and practice. For me, this led to a research focus on communities that benefit most from settler politics: white youth in predominantly white schools.

The Ohio curriculum: Shifting the gaze onto white youth and predominantly white schools

As I developed my research around urban schools and youth of color, thinking about how schools mediate the political education of Black and Brown students, I began to question the schooling of white youth. These wonderings became ever more urgent as Donald Trump descended on the political scene and brought acute focus onto the "disaffected white working class." People asked how "we" arrived at a Trump candidacy and subsequent presidency. I, however, having newly arrived in Columbus, Ohio, and living in a red state for the first time, questioned why there was so little research on the civic education of white youth and the politics learned in predominantly white schools, given his popularity. Given the propensity with which research in education focuses on urban schools and urban youth as problems, I made the epistemological commitment to shift my research gaze onto the problem of white supremacy and onto white youth as racialized subjects. I wondered what new insights on race and politics might arise when predominantly white schools are situated as in need of research and when the civic education occurring therein is interrogated.

Of the civic education scholarship that explicitly engages with race and social inequality, most focus on students of color and the importance of making critical civic education accessible and culturally relevant to them (see Banks, 1990; 2001; Ginwright & Cammarota, 2007; Rubin & Hayes, 2010; Cohen et al., 2018). Junn (2004), for example, points to the ways that mainstream civic education may not provide the same benefits to students of color as to white students. Whereas civic education programs may be key in developing strong democratic citizenship among all the nation's youth, Junn (2004) argues that the positive effects of these programs may be unequally distributed given how social inequality structures the daily lives of non-white students. Junn (2004) writes, "The American democratic creed, tidy as it may sound when one is advocating its support, does not apply equally, but instead depends on where one is situated in relation to other" (p. 254). Therefore learning about one's rights is helpful only if it can be expected that those rights will be equally applied and respected. Accounting for the ways that inequality structures the lives of marginalized students is imperative for understanding how politics is understood and experienced differentially. I argue it is also imperative to account for how inequality structures the lives of White students as the beneficiaries of these unequal social conditions and how schooling may play a part not only in reifying particular conceptualizations of government and politics that are oppressive, but in fostering student's investments in them.

To be clear, it is not the case that white youth are absent in education research. A substantive field of scholarship focused on white youth in the U.S. explores the relationship between schooling and the development of white adolescents' racialized identities (Perry, 2002; Bucholtz, 2010, Hagerman, 2020) and the class nuances of identity and privilege acquired and maintained through schooling (Demerath, 2009; Khan, 2012). Yet, while studies may disaggregate data to illustrate how race and class impact voting or engagement, few delve into the specificities of white youth political ideologies[1] and less has been written about how these are negotiated, affirmed, or challenged in schools (GenForward, 2020). Swallwell's (2013) study is a notable exception highlighting the tensions and limits of nurturing "activist allies" and social justice education among white students in elite schools. Of the scholarship focused specifically on the substance of white youth politics and their racialized/racist implications, most analyses focus on right-wing youth in Europe or, if focused on the US, tend to focus on white youth involved in white supremacist gangs (Miller-Idriss, 2009; Miller-Idriss, 2018; Doosje et al., 2012; Reid & Valasik, 2018). This has recently begun to change. Rogers' (2017) extensive national study of teachers' experiences in the Trump era exposes the increase in hostile school cultures and points to ways white youth's employment of right-wing and white nationalist rhetoric contributed to their rise.

Concerned with a political landscape teeming with white nationalism and immersed in the new experience of living and learning in Ohio, I conducted an ethnographic study of two predominantly white high schools—one suburban and one smalltown—to explore how race and politics were made manifest in everyday school life. Through observations and interviews with both students and teachers, I found settler and right-wing ideologies (re) produced through teachers' pedagogical choices, students' own knowledge co-construction in the classroom, and the overall culture of schools and communities that silenced any alternative politics. For example, the benefits of "owning" Puerto Rico as a colony and of native erasure, disregard for civil rights legislation and the Black Lives Matter movement, these ideas were normalized as logical in the classroom space with hardly any sincere engagement with opposing ideas. Marginalized students—marginalized with regard to race and political affiliations—shared in one-on-one interviews that they refused to share alternative views on politics, including ideas around racism, for fear of ostracization. "They would just annihilate you," one of the girls of color in the suburban school shared.

Conversely, white and politically conservative students confidently and loudly shared their ideas both in class and in interviews; ideas that included eugenics, sexism, racism, and Islamophobia. Right-wing politics operated as the default as did white, male, conservative students as presenters of these ideas. Noting the second-class citizenship experienced by Afro-Caribbean students in the UK, Gilborn (1992) argues that citizenship is not only understood, but experienced differently through a hidden curriculum in schools where belonging, access, and participation are not abstract concepts, but real and "the degree to which Black students enjoy these entitlements in school transmits clear messages about the kind of citizenship they can look forward to in society at large" (p. 59). In the predominantly white schools I studied, the degree to which white students enjoyed citizenship also served to transmit clear messages, not only to the kind of citizenship they would look forward to, but to the kind of citizenship they already enjoyed and would continue to: white patriarchal sovereignty (Moreton-Robinson, 2015). My observations of the citizenship education occuring in these schools made clear the link between race, power, and politics showing how public schools, in the formal content and in the pedagogies of everyday school life, contribute to the reification of and investments in whiteness and a settler state.

Uncovering settler tracks in civic education: Settlerness as a problem in education research

Veracini (2010) discusses the particularities of settler colonialism in places like the United States where "the very invisibility of settler colonialism is most entrenched. The more it goes without saying, the better it covers its tracks" (pp. 14–15). To many interested in the civic education of young people, it seems settler colonialism is a forgone conclusion that "goes without saying." As a result, it more successfully covers its tracks and dictates the terms of debate by relegating what is and is not to be debated. According to the Merriam-Webster (2023) definition, *to track* means to follow the tracks or traces of, to search for by following evidence until found, to observe or plot the moving path. My approach to research, including research on youth in schools, is to be a tracker; that is, to track settlerness by engaging in research that documents how settlerness moves, note its location at various points, locate its manifestations in the present day, and contribute toward its dismantling. By uncovering settler tracks,

I am focusing the "damage" away from Black, Indigenous, and other communities of color (Tuck, 2009) and onto the damage that settlerness imparts and onto those communities most benefiting from its continuation. Mainstream civic and political education are racial/settler projects and framing them as such would serve as a crucial intervention that calls into question the very goal and existence of civic education—a field of research and practice that is too often idealized and unquestioned as a public "good". Starting from settlerness in our research on schools and with the young people who learn in them, allows for an approach to race work that does not fall into the trap of treating race as solely an additive variable or a social condition detached from the political motivations that make and remake it. On the contrary, starting from settlerness necessitates a situating of current racial processes that both temporally and spatially draw attention to the "how" and "why" structures that reify white supremacy, anti-Blackness, and anti-indigeneity are lived in the present day. Starting from settlerness brings to light all that is at stake.

Moreover, tracking settlerness in research points to the need for scholars of civic and democratic education to grapple with the tensions in liberal civic ideals that prove time and time again to have a chokehold on the field. Ideals like "tolerance of others' ideas," "teaching both sides", "pedagogical neutrality" serve to embolden white supremacy and settler politics when, however well-intentioned, they are given equal time. These form part of young people's community curricula on race and serve to tone police and discredit claims of racial justice and decolonization. Starting from settlerness in education research necessitates that we grapple with oppression as a feature of this political system and not a bug. Therefore, moving against the tide in civic education and starting from settlerness and the racialization it promotes, creates a possibility, an imperative, for unsettling civic education. When the "damage" that white supremacy and settler colonialism inflicts on society is placed front and center, perhaps we conclude that there is no saving civic education and what we need instead is a move toward anticolonial citizenship education with the goal of producing "land-based solidarities and inclusive conceptions of citizenship and justice that account for the well-being of land and all it sustains" (Sabzalian, 2019, p. 334). Only in acknowledging the colonial nature of the state and subsequent and enduring violence of the racial structures to which it has given rise, can new curricula centered on anticolonial citizenship emerge.

I end this chapter writing from Columbus, Ohio: a place whose city name honors the progenitor of colonialism in the Americas on the one hand; and on the other, a state name reminding us of whose land we are on. Not too far away, a train derailed with catastrophic environmental damage. Not too far away, police killed a young Black girl outside of her home, a Black man in his bed, another in his car, yet another in a Walmart. Not too far away they voted to roll back reproductive rights and to put forth legislation banning the teaching of "divisive concepts" like racial equity and gender justice. Not too far away is the headquarters of a popular right-wing propaganda site where the Proud Boys protested drag story time. It is not yet known what young people will theorize about race through this curriculum, but I am hopeful they will build on the ideas shared in these volumes and that a decolonial future may be not too far away.

Note

1 For examples of studies that have aimed to map the contours of adolescent political thinking please see Torney-Purta, Lehmann, Oswald, & Schulz's (2001); Flanagan & Tucker, (1999); Jennings & Niemi (2015); McDevitt (2006); and Ekström (2016).

References

Alexander, R. (2012). *Education by dispossession: Schooling on the new suburban frontier.* [Doctoral Dissertation, UC Berkeley]. Retrieved from https://escholarship. org/uc/item/5q28d3pm

Ansley, F. L. (1989). Stirring the ashes: Race, class and the future of civil rights scholarship. *Cornell Law Review, 74,* 993–1077.

Anzaldúa, G. (1987). *Borderlands/la frontera.* Aunt Lute Books.

Banks, J. A. (1990). Citizenship education for a pluralistic democratic society. *The Social Studies, 81*(5), 210–214.

Banks, J. A. (2001). Citizenship education and diversity implications for teacher education. *Journal of Teacher Education, 52*(1), 5–16.

Bucholtz, M. (2010). *White kids: Language, race, and styles of youth identity.* Cambridge University Press.

Calderón, D. (2009). Making explicit the jurisprudential foundations of multiculturalism: The continuing challenges of colonial education in US schooling for Indigenous education. In A. Kempf (Ed.), *Breaching the colonial contract: Anticolonialism in the U.S. and Canada* (pp. 53–77). Springer.

Calderon, D. (2014). Uncovering settler grammars in curriculum. *Educational Studies, 50*(4), 313–338.

Cohen, C., Kahne, J., Marshall, J., Anderson, V., Brower, M., & Knight, D. (2018). *Let's go there: Race, ethnicity, and a lived civics approach to civic education.* Chicago, IL: GenForward at the University of Chicago.

Collins, P. H. (1991). *Black feminist thought: Knowledge, consciousness, and the politics of empowerment.* Routledge.

Demerath, P. (2009). *Producing success: The culture of personal advancement in an American high school.* University of Chicago Press.

Doosje, B., van den Bos, K., Loseman, A., Feddes, A. R., & Mann, L. (2012). "My in-group is superior!": Susceptibility for radical right-wing attitudes and behaviors in Dutch youth. *Negotiation and Conflict Management Research, 5*(3), 253–268.

DuBois, W. E. B. (1903/2016). *The souls of black folk.* Dover Publications.

DuBois, W. E. B. (1920). *Darkwater: Voices from within the veil.* Harcourt, Brace and Company.

Du Bois, W. E. B. (1935). Inter-Racial Implications of the Ethiopian Crisis: A Negro View. *Foreign Affairs Magazine, 14,* 82.

Ekström, M. (2016). Young people's everyday political talk: a social achievement of democratic engagement. *Journal of Youth Studies, 19*(1), 1–19.

Flanagan, C. A., & Tucker, C. J. (1999). Adolescents' explanationsfor political issues: Concordance with their views of self and society. *Developmental Psychology, 35*(5), 1198.

GenForward. (2020, February). *Politics and the 2020 election by race and ethnicity.* http://genforwardsurvey.com/assets/uploads/2020/03/2020-02-February-Slide-Deck- Politics-and-the-2020-Election-by-Race-and-Ethnicity-final-.pdf

Gilmore, R. W. (2008). Forgotten places and the seeds of grassroots planning. In R. H. Charles (Ed.), *Engaging contradictions: Theory, politics, and methods of activist scholarship* (pp. 31–61). University of California Press.

Gillborn, D. (1992). Citizenship, 'race,' and the hidden curriculum. *International Studies in Sociology of Education, 2*(1), 57–73.

Ginwright, S., & Cammarota, J. (2007). Youth activism in the urban community: Learning critical civic praxis within community organizations. *International Journal of Qualitative Studies in Education, 20*(6), 693–710. 10.1080/095183 90701630833

Glenn, E. N. (2015). Settler colonialism as structure: A framework for comparative studies of US race and gender formation. *Sociology of Race and Ethnicity, 1*(1), 52–72.

Grande, S. (2015). *Red pedagogy: Native American social and political thought.* Rowman & Littlefield.

Grosfoguel, R. (2007). The epistemic decolonial turn. *Cultural Studies, 21*(2–3), 211–223.

Hagerman, M. A. (2020). *White kids: Growing up with privilege in a racially divided America.* NYU Press.

Harris, C. (1995). Whiteness as property. In K. Crenshaw, N. Gotanda, G. Peller, & K. Thomas (Eds.), *Critical race theory: The key writings that formed the movement* (pp. 276–291). The New Press.

Hurston, Z. N. (1999). How it feels to be colored me. In E. P. Stoller & R. C. Gibson (Eds.), *Worlds of difference: Inequality in the aging experience* (pp. 95–97). Sage.

Jennings, M. K., & Niemi, R. G. (2015). *Political character of adolescence: The influence of families and schools.* Princeton University Press.

Junn, J. (2004). Diversity, immigration, and the politics of civic education. *PS: Political Science and Politics, 37*(2), 253–255.

Kahne, J., & Middaugh, E. (2008). High quality civic education: What is it and who gets it? *Social Education, 72*(1), 34.

Khan, S. R. (2012). *Privilege: The making of an adolescent elite at St. Paul's School.* Princeton University Press.

Ladson-Billings, G. (2004). Culture versus citizenship: The challenge of racialized citizenship in the United States. In J. A. Banks (Ed.), *Diversity and citizenship education: Global perspectives* (pp. 99–126). John Wiley and Sons.

Leonardo, Z. (2002). The souls of white folk: Critical pedagogy, whiteness studies and globalization discourse. *Race, Ethnicity and Education, 5*(1), 29–50.

Levine, P. (2009). The civic opportunity gap. *Educational Leadership, 66*(8), 20–25.

Lipsitz, G. (2006). *The possessive investment in whiteness: How white people profit from identity politics.* Temple University Press.

Macpherson, C. B. (1962). The political theory of possessive individualism: Hobbes to Locke.

McDevitt, M. (2006). The Partisan Child: Developmental Provocation as a Model of Political Socialization. *International Journal of Public Opinion Research, 18*(1), 67–88.

Merriam-Webster. (2003). Track. In Merriam-Webster.com dictionary. Retrieved July 20, 2023, from https://www.merriam-webster.com/dictionary/track

Miller-Idriss, C. (2009). *Blood and culture: Youth, right-wing extremism, and national belonging in contemporary Germany.* Duke University Press.

Miller-Idriss, C. (2018). *The extreme gone mainstream: Commercialization and far right youth culture in Germany.* Princeton University Press.

Mills, C. W. (1997). *The racial contract.* Cornell University Press.

Moreton-Robinson, A. (2015). *The white possessive: Property, power, and indigenous sovereignty.* University of Minnesota Press.

Muñoz, J. E. (2020). *The sense of brown.* Duke University Press.

Oakes, J. (2005). *Keeping track: How schools structure inequality.* Yale University.

Perry, P. (2002). *Shades of white: White kids and racial identities in high school.* Duke University Press.

Quijano, A. (2000). Coloniality of power, ethnocentrism, and Latin America. *Neplanta, 1*(3), 533–580.

Reid, S. E., & Valasik, M. (2018). Ctrl+ALT-RIGHT: Reinterpreting our knowledge of white supremacy groups through the lens of street gangs. *Journal of Youth Studies, 21*(10), 1305–1325. 10.1080/13676261.2018.1467003

Roediger, D. R. (1999). *The wages of whiteness: Race and the making of the American working class.* Verso.

Rogers, J., Franke, M. , Yun, J. E. E., Ishimoto, M. , Diera, C. , Geller, R. C. ..., & Brenes, T. 2017. Teaching and Learning in the Age of Trump: Increasing Stress and Hostility in America's High Schools. Report from UCLA's Institute for Democracy, Education, and Access.

Rubin, B. C., & Hayes, B. F. (2010). "No backpacks" versus "drugs and murder": The promise and complexity of youth civic action research. *Harvard Educational Review, 80*(3), 352–379.

Sabzalian, L. (2019). The tensions between Indigenous sovereignty and multicultural citizenship education: Toward an anticolonial approach to civic education. *Theory & Research in Social Education, 47*(3), 311–346. 10.1080/009331 04.2019.1639572

Sabzalian, L., & Shear, S. (2018). Confronting colonial blindness in civics education. Recognizing colonization, self-determination, and sovereignty as core knowledge for elementary social studies teacher education. In S. B. Shear, C. M. Tschida, & E. Bellows (Eds.), (Re)Imagining elementary social studies: A controversial issues reader (pp. 153–176). Information Age Publishing.

Swalwell, K. M. (2013). *Educating activist allies: Social justice pedagogy with the suburban and urban elite.* Routledge.

Tuck, E. (2009). Suspending damage: A letter to communities. *Harvard Educational Review, 79*(3), 409–428. 10.17763/haer.79.3.n0016675661t3n15

Tuck, E., & Yang, K. W. (2012). Decolonization is not a metaphor. *Decolonization: Indigeneity, Education & Society, 1*(1), 1–40.

Torney-Purta, J., Lehmann, R., Oswald, H., & Schulz, W. (2001). Citizenship and education in twenty-eight countries: Civic knowledge and engagement at age fourteen. IEA Secretariat, Herengracht 487, 1017 BT, Amsterdam, The Netherlands.

Urrieta, L. (2004). Dis-connections in "American" citizenship and the post/neo-colonial: People of Mexican descent and whitestream2 pedagogy and curriculum. *Theory & Research in Social Education, 32*(4), 433–458.

Veracini, L. (2010). *Settler colonialism.* Palgrave Macmillan.

Westheimer, J., & Kahne, J. (2004). What Kind of Citizen? The Politics of Educating for Democracy. *American Educational Research Journal, 41*(2), 237–269.

Wolfe, P. (2006). Settler colonialism and the elimination of the native. *Journal of Genocide Research, 8*(4), 387–409.

6
ANTI-MUSLIM RACISM

The double burden of racism and invisibility

Goleen Samari

Early life course

When I was 16 years old, a Texas police officer pulled me over and told me "It's people like you that are ruining this country. Go back to your country." People who speed, I thought? People who are late for figure skating practice? I wasn't sure what he meant. What country was I supposed to go to? I was born and raised in Austin, Texas. Then, it dawned on me. It was a month after 9/11, and he meant Muslims. This experience was foundational to my identity formation in adolescence and young adulthood.

Islamophobia and anti-Muslim racism are so widespread that Muslim youth's positive identity formation is directly tied to how much Islamophobia they have experienced (Bakali, 2016). In the 20 years that have followed the Sept. 11 attacks, countless Muslims and Middle Eastern Americans who are assumed to be Muslims have been repeatedly exposed to hate, discrimination, and violence in the United States and around the world. In recent years, hate speech and crimes against Muslim Americans tripled after the San Bernardino and Paris attacks. Muslim Americans of all ages have been subject to violence, harassed on college campuses, they have lost jobs, mosques have been vandalized, Muslim charities have had their assets frozen, and racial profiling has occurred at airports and on the streets. Religion is the greatest source of bias for hate crimes following race/ethnicity. Since Trump campaigned and took office, anti-Muslim violence exponentially increased and was significantly higher than in the post-9/11 era. The highest number of assaults against Muslims in the United States peaked in 2017, and has remained elevated since 2015 (Samari, 2016).

DOI: 10.4324/9781003303800-8

In the 20 years that have followed the September 11 attacks, Muslim and Middle Eastern Americans have also remained invisible in research and social and health programming. According to the US Census Bureau and the Office of Management and Budget, populations from the Middle East and North Africa (MENA) are categorized as white yet MENA Americans are not perceived, nor do they perceive themselves to be white on the basis of ancestry, names, and religion (Maghbouleh et al., 2022). Muslim identity is not captured because of the exclusion of religion as a measure in the US Census. Legally and empirically, MENA populations and Muslims are not counted and remain invisible. Lack of data on certain subpopulations ultimately contributes to unmet needs by rendering groups invisible when policies are made, resources are allocated, and programs are implemented. Based on my lived experience at the hands of the actors and structures in the system of racism, the social experience of Muslims and Middle Eastern Americans is very visible, and that of the brown "Other" or minoritized racial groups. Thus, Muslim and Middle Eastern Americans are subject to the double burden of racism and invisibility.

Theoretical life course

The theoretical lens that guides my research on Muslim and Middle Eastern American health equity includes the Public Health and Critical Race Praxis (PHCRP) (Ford, 2016; Ford & Airhihenbuwa, 2010a; 2010b) and structural racism and health (Gee & Ford, 2011; Gee & Hicken, 2021; Gee et al., 2019). PHCRP draws on the distinguishing characteristics of critical race theory: racialization, social location and "centering in the margins," and the desire to not only understand, but to eliminate inequities to create a framework to guide public health research and practice (Ford & Airhihenbuwa, 2018). By centering my own experiences in the margins and racialization, I could begin to understand Muslim and Middle Eastern American healthcare experiences and the social conditions that lead to health inequities. PHCRP also seeks to generate empirical evidence that communities can use as part of their ongoing health equity and social justice efforts. Thus, my systematic process to conduct self-reflexive, race-conscious research on Muslim and Middle Eastern Americans ultimately should lead to better health outcomes and social justice for these communities. PHCRP includes four main phases: contemporary patterns of racial relations, knowledge production, conceptualization and measurement, and action (Ford & Airhihenbuwa, 2010b).

PHCRP is built on the acknowledgment of structural racism. Structural racism focuses on the totality of the ways in which society privileges white communities at the expense of non-white racialized communities (Braveman et al., 2022; Gee & Hicken, 2021). While health disparities have been referenced for over forty years, structural racism was only explicitly acknowledged as a driver of health inequity in policy documents and in federal agencies in 2019 (Zambrana & Williams, 2022). Structural racism emphasizes the role of structures (laws, policies, institutional practices, and entrenched norms) that provide the scaffolding for the system of racism which includes political, legal, economic, health care, education, and criminal justice systems (Braveman et al., 2022). Structural forms of racism, forms such as media coverage or political campaigns that call for a "ban on Muslims," help normalize racist attitudes and create the structures that reinforce the system of racism (Braveman et al., 2022).

PHCRP tells us that understanding racial health inequities and dismantling systemic racism requires an understanding of racialization in society and in one's personal life—the very place where I felt compelled to start and center my academic exploration. The first phase of PHCRP includes a focus on contemporary patterns of racial relations and understanding key character-istics of societal racialization (Ford, 2016; Ford & Airhihenbuwa, 2010b). To take a race-conscious orientation is to bring awareness of the ways in which racialization (not race) functions in society and may be relevant to the questions at hand (Ford & Airhihenbuwa, 2018). The concept of racializa-tion is a useful theoretical tool that provides the needed language to discuss the Muslim experiences as racial and subject to racism (Garner & Selod, 2014; Selod & Embrick, 2013). Racialization essentially delineates a line around all the members of a group and ascribes characteristics, sometimes because of ideas of where the group comes from, what it believes in, or how it organizes itself socially and culturally (Garner & Selod, 2014; Hochman, 2019). This "group" may not traditionally view itself as a racial or ethnic group and racialization is not the same as racial group formation because racialization is assigned by others. Racialization is the process by which racialized groups rather than races are formed (Hochman, 2019).

Racialization assigns racial meaning to cultural traits of groups, some of whom may be white ethnics, resulting in their rejection of white identity, even if their skin tone is white. As such, groups such as Muslims, Jews, the Irish, and Eastern European migrants have been racialized in Europe and America (Meer, 2013). Racialization of religious minorities in the United States makes them subject to racism and xenophobia similar to other racial minority groups (Meer, 2013). Understanding how creating a racial cate-gory out of a religious one is different from what typically encompasses a racial or religious category. Simply, a racialized religious category is based on what people with a specific set of religious beliefs and cultural traits are perceived, by those belonging to other groups, to look like. While the racialized experience of Muslims is largely attributed to the post-9/11 era (Sheth, 2017), since the transatlantic slave trade, Muslims in the United

States were not considered to be "real Americans," and Muslim identity was used to deny citizenship, including for Christians perceived to be Muslims (Rana, 2007).

Importantly, the key agents of racialization are those who exercise power within the state, media, and other authorities (e.g., immigration and customs enforcement, teachers and principals in schools, or police officers who interact with Middle Eastern and Muslim youth) (Garner & Selod, 2014). I still feel the physical response I had to that interaction with the police officer. Through experiences like that, as a teenager in Texas, I learned that I was a brown person, that I was different from white people, that it was bad to be different from white people, and that my version of brown was racialized to be Muslim no matter what my religious affiliation, and simply, that othering is taught. Muslims are often represented as coming from non-white groups, so their religious identity is linked with racial identity. In reality, Muslim Americans include many nationalities and racial categories, including black and white, and anyone who appears Muslim-like, Sikhs and many non-Muslim Arab, Iranian, and Indian Americans. This is simply the racialization of religious identity. The conceptualization of religious minorities as the "Other" is because they are seen as a threat to the "white nation" (Werbner, 2013).

Even children's discourses of "otherness" construct these differences as problematic and racialize Muslim children as the "bad Other" (Welply, 2018). As anti-Muslim racism has increased in society, anti-Muslim hostility and bullying have also increased in schools with ripping off hijabs, name-calling of youth as terrorists, and increased racism, implicitly and explicitly (Tabahi & Khayr, 2021). Ethnographic work with children in France and the United Kingdom shows that even in children as young as 10 and 11 years, there is an ethnocentric understanding of the place of "otherness" in peer group relations and discrimination towards Muslim children at the intersection of race, religion, language, and national identity (Welply, 2018). Muslim children internalize these differences and react by trying to hide their identity, silently accommodating, or tacitly resisting and employing strategies like proving they are "good Muslims" or distancing themselves from their countries of origin (Welply, 2018). The racialization of religion shapes Muslim children's identity and the way that they take up social space early in the life course and for many of us, this has lifelong implications.

The evolution of the "good Muslim"

My way of countering my experiences of othering and racism as a young person in Texas was to dive deeper into learning about the region and religion from which my family originated. Perhaps, I am merely trying to prove that I am a "good Muslim" or a "good Middle Eastern American." By focusing on Middle Eastern Studies as an undergraduate and on Islamic Studies as a graduate student, I wanted to take control of my own identity formation and not let experiences of racism leave the final mark. In parallel, I pursued a graduate education in public health and demography. Foundational to Islamic Studies is the notion of insiders, appraisers, and analysts of Islam that come from Muslims themselves, and outsiders, non-Muslim reviewers of Islam referred to as Orientalists (Said, 1978). Insiders are viewed as less objective because of their ideological interests, and outsiders' lack of objectivity is due to their propaganda-oriented study rooted in colonial interests (Abdul-Rauf, 1985). Orientalists' traditional work lacks the voices of Muslims and Muslim scholars and minimizes their contributions (Abdul-Rauf, 1985). Therefore, as a Muslim Western student, I knew I would juggle the duality of being an insider and an outsider. I was not sure how the humanities focus on the Middle East and Islam would factor into my identity as a researcher, but I knew it was both important for the theoretical underpinning of my work and necessary for my personal identity.

PHCRP posits that for the second phase, knowledge production, it is important to understand disciplinary norms or other considerations that, if unaccounted for, may inadvertently bias understanding (Ford & Airhihenbuwa, 2010b). Therefore, while I may not have been aware of it at the time, my public health training taught me to understand Islamic Studies disciplinary norms and to center Islamic principles and Muslim communities in my scholarship and work. There are some important guiding principles of Islam that have to be considered for disparities in work, health, or otherwise, with Muslim populations. Namely, Islam is a complete social, political, economic, and foreign policy system. Islam does not seek in any way to investigate observable and causal forces – the only sources for inquiry have already been revealed through the *Hadith* and *Quran*. Islam relies on concepts like the *Umma* (community of believers) and *assabiya* (group feeling) to account for all areas of social interaction. Thus, Islam, while often thought of at the individual level, is actually multilevel and situated in population dynamics by design. The foundation of public health is leveraging socioecological, and thus, multilevel population dynamics, to promote the fundamental right to health.

While in pursuit of my dual graduate educational track, my efforts were met with significant resistance from my public health and demography colleagues and mentors. For years, I was told that focusing on the public health of Muslim communities in the Middle East or of Middle Eastern immigrants was not a valid research endeavor. As a graduate student, I was repeatedly told that public health is "focused on health outcomes and not specific populations" or that "the Middle East is only a political science endeavor and not a region of focus for population health" or questioned, "why should Muslim populations garner public health attention?" The population health field was not open to acknowledging the health needs of Middle Easterners and Muslims around the world. The erasure and invisibility of these communities were embedded in the institution of academia itself, echoing themes of societal discourse: racism and invisibility. I was up against a glaring research gap on Muslim and MENA population health and institutional barriers to recognizing Muslim and racialized Muslim communities as valid populations for public health and health equity research. In my doctoral program, I changed academic advisors multiple times until I found a mentor and now colleague, Anne R. Pebley, who shared my values of knowing communities from within, taking a race-conscious approach, and engaging in work that reflects the social and policy environment. Professor Pebley believed in my interests in social inequities and the health of Middle Eastern and Muslim communities because it spoke to my identity and communities and the social world around us.

The public health field has very few strategies for meaningfully dealing with populations that do not fall into neat racial and ethnic categories or who are inherently intersectional, like Muslim Americans. Muslim Americans operate at the intersection of traditional racial and ethnic classifications and religion, but also gender, age, and sexuality, like any population group. In a field dominated by quantitative methodologies, it is difficult to identify datasets that contain the necessary intersectional factors to study Muslim communities so not only socioeconomic factors and the relevant health-related data but also measures of race/ethnicity and religion that include Muslim identity. Public health primarily uses conventional research approaches, such as those that set randomized controlled trials as the gold standard, even though it is neither feasible nor appropriate to use them to answer many research questions. The widespread reliance on conventional approaches to empirical research likely constrains the possibility of innovative research to address health disparities for populations subject to structural racism.

I assert that the invisibility of Muslims and MENA populations in health research and programs is a reflection of structural racism and academia as a vehicle for institutional racism. Institutional racism includes academic institutions that generate scholarship and knowledge on the detrimental effects of racism (Arday & Mirza, 2018). Practices across institutions include racialized rules or a set of explicit and implicit rules around the norms, principles, and regulations that reinforce racial hierarchy (Braveman et al., 2022; Williams, 1985). Academia is not immune to its own set of racialized rules (Arday & Mirza, 2018), which in my experience, includes the exclusion of Muslims in certain spaces and relegation of the study of Muslims to a politicized identity and stereotypes of war and terror.

Despite these barriers, with the support of one academic mentor, I continued with the knowledge production phase of PHCRP and pursued my interest in Middle Eastern and Muslim population health. I was fortunate to be situated at an institution with some of the leading anti-racism and health scholars, like Chandra Ford (see Ford, 2016), so my health disparities training was embedded in foundational theoretical approaches like those that I have described, namely, the Public Health and Critical Race Praxis. Simultaneously, I drew upon my Islamic Studies training to ask questions that centered on Islamic thought or Muslim communities like "How do Muslims conceptualize health disparities among Muslim youth?" or "What has Islam historically said about contraceptive use?" or "How can the relationship between social inequality and health be applied to Muslims or populations from the Middle East?" These questions are situated in PHCRP and Islamic Studies by reflecting historically on whether racialization already has informed existing knowledge on Muslim and MENA population health and whether the research findings advance knowledge on Muslim and MENA population health in ways that promote racial equity.

Birth of scholarship on anti-Muslim racism and health

In the third phase of PHCRP, conceptualization and measurement pushes scholars to use qualitative and theoretical approaches to operationalize racism-related constructs, the hypothesized relationships between these constructs, and the social contexts in which the constructs and relationships exist (Ford & Airhihenbuwa, 2010b). In 2015, there were two incidents of hate involving youth that were particularly striking: the murder of three Muslim students at the University of North Carolina Chapel Hill and a young teenager being expelled from school in Dallas for an engineered clock that was assumed to be a bomb. I was struck by how many years had passed since 9/11 and yet how rampant and pervasive anti-Muslim racism remained. Based on my own experience navigating instances of racism and my understanding of the relationship between racism, health, and health disparities, these incidents had clear multilevel population health implications at individual, interpersonal, and social levels. As both a scholar of Public Health and Islamic Studies, as a Middle Eastern immigrant from a Muslim country, I felt an innate obligation to speak on these issues and a responsibility to these communities to bring their experiences to the forefront. Middle Easterners who perceive more racism are more likely to embrace a MENA identity, which suggests that racial hostility activates a stronger group identity (Maghbouleh et al., 2022). Perhaps, these incidents were a catalyst for my academic racial identity. I was one of the few, if not the only, researchers who had the theoretical and methodological training and personal expertise to explain Muslim health disparities and specifically, speak to Islamophobia as a public health issue.

In 2016, my first article on "Islamophobia and Public Health in the United States" was published by the American Journal of Public Health (AJPH) (Samari, 2016) which explains how the racialization of religious minorities closely follows the multilevel effects of racism and stigma on health. Islamophobia is the term used to capture anti-Muslim racism and discrimination towards Muslims. Islamophobia is a social stigma towards Islam and Muslims, dislike of Muslims as a political force, and a distinct construct referring to xenophobia and racism towards Muslims or those perceived to be Muslim (Samari, 2016). Racialization of religion provides a framework for understanding how groups are rejected from whiteness and how race and racism mutate and change depending on the social and historical context. The article is widely read and cited as a groundbreaking extension of the relationship between racism and health to the racialized Muslim experience.

A lesser-known fact is that AJPH originally rejected this theoretical piece. While the reasoning for the rejection was not provided by the editor, this setback was another reminder of the realities and depth of the institutional pushback for research that considers Muslim and Middle Eastern communities. Academic publishing was yet another institutional space that I had to navigate and convince to acknowledge the racialized experiences of Muslim communities. I urged the editor and the journal to reconsider because of the social realities of Muslims and those racialized to be Muslim. My previous experience navigating institutional barriers in graduate school around my pursuit of Muslim population health as a research field emboldened me to push back on the editor's decision and engage the journal in this dialogue. Fortunately, they listened, and the work was reviewed and ultimately accepted. When applying a critical race lens to my journey, it is important to recognize that the acceptance and ultimate publication of the piece was due to the increasing anti-Muslim rhetoric in 2015 and 2016, including the Trump campaign's promise to implement a Muslim ban once elected. The system of racism had not changed; instead, the additional cracks and fissures in the overworked system created a space for my work to slip through.

In conjunction with my article, I wrote an op-ed that appeared in the *Dallas Morning News* in order to garner greater public and policy attention to the detrimental effects of Islamophobia. The argument at the core of my Islamophobia and health research is fairly simple: racism affects people's health, Muslims are people too, thus, racism affects Muslim's health. As a result of that opinion piece, my family received countless death threats and hate mail, I was accused of being a terrorist by right-wing trolls, I had to attempt to scrub the internet of my identifying information, and the FBI had to get involved to ensure my family's safety. From 2015 to 2017, anti-Muslim racism and Islamophobia were so rampant that it was simply too controversial to acknowledge Muslims as people who experience racism. Moreover, my intersectional identity, as a Middle Eastern woman, asserting the rights of Muslim communities offered additional challenges. Similar to the police officer who pulled me over in high school, assumptions about and racialization of my identity likely fueled the backlash. I reached out to academic op-ed experts, organizations, and institutions to better understand how to handle the backlash, and unsurprisingly, white experts, most often male, had little guidance on the issue as they had never received any backlash. Again, I was facing structures and systems that were not built for me and for the study of Muslims and MENA groups. Ironically, the most racism and racialization I have ever been subject to was due to writing public-facing work about anti-Muslim racism.

Islamophobia and health: A racialized experience

The health consequences of anti-Muslim racism for youth and people of all ages cannot be disentangled from all the evidence linking racism and poor mental and physical health. The religious minority experience in the United States is a racialized experience subject to racism and additional forms of discrimination. Delineating the health effects of Islamophobia across the life course is challenging as it affects diverse groups of people (geographically, racially, and socially) (Gottschalk & Greenberg, 2008). For example, in the United Kingdom, Muslims are primarily immigrant South Asians (Weller, 2006). In the United States, nearly 30% of Muslims identify as Black, another 30% are Asian, primarily South Asian, and the largest racial group of Muslims are classified as white, many of whom are from the Middle East (Ewing, 2008; Lipka, 2015; The Pew Research Center, 2017). In the United States, stereotypical representations equate all Muslims with populations from the Middle East and South Asia. Islamophobia and anti-Muslim racism target both Muslims and those who are racialized and thus, racially perceived as Muslims (Arabs, Iranians, Middle Easterners, Indians, Sikhs, etc.). Following my work, other scholars have written about anti-Middle Eastern racism or anti-Arab racism and health to try to distinguish those types of racism as having unique implications for health, yet these forms of racism are possible because of the racialization of Muslims, regardless of the religious identity of the targeted racial group. Thus, the pathways and implications for health remain the same.

Structural racism, including anti-Muslim racism, can lead to differential health outcomes and differential access to fundamental determinants of health such as education and employment. Moreover, when individuals are targeted based on their identity, persistent exposure to racism has a pervasive, negative effect on health (Williams & Mohammed, 2009; 2013). Being a victim of Islamophobia can be traumatizing, with severe and lasting health impacts, particularly for children and adolescents (Welply, 2018). Members of stigmatized groups have greater stress, strained social relationships, and unequal access to resources or medical care (Hatzenbuehler et al., 2013). Social marginalization also increases the physiological response to stress (Harrell et al., 2003), which can have damaging effects for children and throughout the life course. Discrimination against Muslim Americans has been linked to paranoia, psychological distress, and reduced happiness as well as preterm birth, high cholesterol, obesity, and other health problems (Samari et al., 2018; Samari et al., 2020). Islamophobia also prevents Muslim Americans from seeking health care (Samari et al., 2020), resulting in more late-stage chronic disease diagnoses.

Anti-Muslim racism: A double burden across the life course

As a teenager still navigating my own racial/ethnic identity formation, a once-off interaction with law enforcement reinforced my "otherness." As a graduate student, my interest in my communities was dismissed and Muslims and Middle Easterners were simply erased from Public Health research and knowledge production. As an early career academic, my theories of the racialization of Muslims were rejected as irrelevant to my field. In the meantime, socially and publicly, anti-Muslim racism and the detrimental side effects of morbidity and mortality were rapidly rising. This is the double burden of the racialized experience of Muslims and Middle Easterners: straddling erasure and racism induced public visibility, harm, and in some cases, mortality. Myself and other Muslim and Middle Eastern children and adolescents carry this double burden early in life as we experience racism and navigate racist incidents and then have no outlet to air grievances or gain any benefits from a minoritized status.

My theory of racialization includes close attention to how racism is historically and socially evolving and how the institutional response to that social evolution needs to situate and elevate the needs of Muslim and racialized Muslim youth and communities in timely and accurate ways. My research serves as the conceptual foundation for the study of anti-Muslim racism in public health, and my theoretical contributions to the racialization of religious minorities and anti-Muslim racism and health are widely cited (Samari, 2016; Samari et al., 2018). I continue to face resistance in the pursuit of this research program both in the academy and in public spaces, reflecting a social reality that remains structurally racist and Islamophobic. However, in phase four of the Public Health and Critical Race Praxis, researchers are charged with sharing the knowledge from their research with those involved with ongoing efforts to change the social conditions and racialized power differentials contributing to health inequities. My research is actively striving towards phase four of PHCRP to bring Muslim and Middle Eastern communities out of the shadows and reduce the double burden of racialization carried across the life course to promote health equity. While I may be on a lifelong journey to prove that I am a "good Muslim" or a "good Middle Eastern American" because of othering and racialization in adolescence, my goal remains the same—to promote well-being from within and between, for my communities.

References

Abdul-Rauf, M. (1985). Outsiders' interpretations of Islam: A Muslim's point of view. *Approaches to Islam in Religious Studies*, 175–188.

Arday, J., & Mirza, H. S. (2018). *Dismantling race in higher education: Racism, whiteness and decolonising the academy*. Springer.

Bakali, N. (2016). *Islamophobia: Understanding anti-Muslim racism through the lived experiences of Muslim youth* (Vol. 5). Springer.

Braveman, P. A., Arkin, E., Proctor, D., Kauh, T., & Holm, N. (2022). Systemic and structural racism: Definitions, examples, health damages, and approaches to dismantling. *Health Affairs (Millwood)*, *41*(2), 171–178.

Ewing, K. P. (2008). *Being and belonging: Muslims in the United States since 9/11*. Russell Sage Foundation.

Ford, C. L. (2016). Public health critical race praxis: An introduction, an intervention, and three points for consideration. *Wisconsin Law Review*, 477–491.

Ford, C. L., & Airhihenbuwa, C. O. (2010a). Critical race theory, race equity, and public health: Toward antiracism praxis. *American Journal of Public Health*, *100*(S1), S30–S35.

Ford, C. L., & Airhihenbuwa, C. O. (2010b). The public health critical race methodology: Praxis for antiracism research. *Social Science & Medicine*, *71*(8), 1390–1398.

Ford, C. L., & Airhihenbuwa, C. O. (2018). Commentary: Just what is critical race theory and what's it doing in a progressive field like public health? *Ethnicity & Disease*, *28*(Suppl 1), 223.

Garner, S., & Selod, S. (2014). The racialization of Muslims: Empirical studies of Islamophobia. *Critical Sociology*, *41*(1), 9–19.

Gee, G. C., & Ford, C. L. (2011). Structural racism and health inequities: Old issues, new directions 1. *Du Bois Review: Social Science Research on Race*, *8*(1), 115.

Gee, G. C., & Hicken, M. T. (2021). Structural racism: The rules and relations of inequity. *Ethnicity & Disease*, *31*(Suppl), 293–300.

Gee, G. C., Hing, A., Mohammed, S., Tabor, D. C., & Williams, D. R. (2019). Racism and the life course: Taking time seriously. *American Journal of Public Health, 109*(S1), S43–S47.

Gottschalk, P., & Greenberg, G. (2008). *Islamophobia: Making Muslims the enemy.* Rowman & Littlefield.

Harrell, J. P., Hall, S., & Taliaferro, J. (2003). Physiological responses to racism and discrimination: An assessment of the evidence. *American Journal of Public Health, 93*(2), 243–248.

Hatzenbuehler, M. L., Phelan, J. C., & Link, B. G. (2013). Stigma as a fundamental cause of population health inequalities. *American Journal of Public Health, 103*(5), 813–821.

Hochman, A. (2019). Racialization: A defense of the concept. *Ethnic and Racial Studies, 42*(8), 1245–1262.

Lipka, M. (2015). *Muslims and Islam: Key findings in the U.S. and around the world.* Retrieved from http://www.pewresearch.org/fact-tank/2015/12/07/muslims-and-islam-key-findings-in-the-u-s-and-around-the-world/

Maghbouleh, N., Schachter, A., & Flores, R. D. (2022). Middle Eastern and North African Americans may not be perceived, nor perceive themselves, to be White. *Proceedings of the* National Academy *of* Sciences *of the* United States *of America, 119*(7), 1–9.

Meer, N. (2013). Racialization and religion: Race, culture and difference in the study of Antisemitism and Islamophobia. *Ethnic and Racial Studies, 36*(3), 385–398.

Rana, J. (2007). The Story of Islamophobia. *Souls, 9*(2), 148–161.

Said, E. W. (1978). *Orientalism* (Vol. 1994). Vintage Books: A Division of Random House.

Samari, G. (2016). Islamophobia and public health in the United States. *American Journal of Public Health, 106*(11), 1920–1925.

Samari, G., Alcalá, H. E., & Sharif, M. Z. (2018). Islamophobia, health, and public health: A systematic literature review. *American Journal of Public Health, 108*(6), e1–e9.

Samari, G., Catalano, R., Alcalá, H. E., & Gemmill, A. (2020). The Muslim ban and preterm birth: Analysis of U.S. vital statistics data from 2009 to 2018. *Social Science & Medicine, 265*, 113544.

Samari, G., Sharif, M. Z., & Alcalá, H. E. (2020). Racial and citizenship disparities in health care among Middle Eastern Americans. *Medical Care, 58*(11), 974–980. Retrieved from https://journals.lww.com/lww-medicalcare/Fulltext/2020/11000/Racial_and_Citizenship_Disparities_in_Health_Care.7.aspx

Selod, S., & Embrick, D. G. (2013). Racialization and Muslims: Situating the Muslim experience in race scholarship. *Sociology Compass, 7*(8), 644–655.

Sheth, F. (2017). The racialization of Muslims in the post-9/11 United States. In Zack, Naomi (Ed.) *The Oxford handbook of philosophy and race* (p. 342). Oxford University Press.

Tabahi, S., & Khayr, L. (2021). Anti-Muslim racism and U.S. schools: Recommendations for practice, policy, and advocacy. *Children & Schools, 43*(1), 3–8.

The Pew Research Center. (2017). *U.S. Muslims concerned about their place in society, but continue to believe in the American dream: Findings from Pew research center's*

2017 survey of U.S. Muslims. Retrieved from http://www.pewforum.org/2017/07/26/findings-from-pew-research-centers-2017-survey-of-us-muslims/

Weller, P. (2006). Addressing religious discrimination and Islamophobia: Muslims and liberal democracies. The case of the United Kingdom. *Journal of Islamic Studies, 17*(3), 295–325.

Welply, O. (2018). 'I'm not being offensive but …': Intersecting discourses of discrimination towards Muslim children in school. *Race Ethnicity and Education, 21*(3), 370–389.

Werbner, P. (2013). Folk devils and racist imaginaries in a global prism: Islamophobia and Anti-semitism in the twenty-first century. *Ethnic and Racial Studies, 36*(3), 450–467.

Williams, D. R., & Mohammed, S. A. (2009). Discrimination and racial disparities in health: Evidence and needed research. *Journal of Behavioral Medicine, 32*(1), 20–47.

Williams, D. R., & Mohammed, S. A. (2013). Racism and health I: Pathways and scientific evidence. *American* Behavioral *Scientist, 57*(8), 1152–1173.

Williams, J. (1985). Redefining institutional racism. *Ethnic and Racial Studies, 8*(3), 323–348.

Zambrana, R. E., & Williams, D. R. (2022). The intellectual roots of current knowledge on racism and health: Relevance to policy and the national equity discourse. *Health Affairs (Millwood), 41*(2), 163–170.

PART III

Refusing to speak against ourselves and our communities

Eve Tuck and K. Wayne Yang

As a whole, this volume has prompted all of us to deepen our theorizing of racism and racial stratification, to become more precise in our discussions of racism in our research, and to be more accountable to the experiences of research participants and collaborators. At the same time, we have tried to build collective knowledge about the kinds of discourses of Blackness, Indigeneity, and racialization that are needed in social science research to reduce inequalities in the lives of young people. Our call for participants in this initiative was deliberate in emphasizing a storytelling approach, and the authors that we have gathered in this section are wonderful examples of that storytelling approach.

This section tells the stories of how authors refuse the damage-centered logics and assumptions that undergird their disciplines. These are logics and assumptions that dehumanize authors, youth participants, and their communities. In their chapters, authors Copeland, Houston, and Chaney describe their break from disciplinary traditions of social science research that continue to produce harmful stories about Black youth and Black families, and actively *absent* what Black people already know. Okamoto tells the story of the emergence and unattainability of the term Asian American. Authors attend to how unaddressed racial hierarchies need to be questioned, and how they are often built into the very theories that we've been taught to engage as core theories in a discipline. Authors also reflect on the works of scholars and community collaborators that offered them a way to account for structures and logics of anti-Blackness and to honor the ways that Black communities know and live.

The title of this section is "Refusing to speak against ourselves in our communities." We are so fortunate to be the people who edited this section,

DOI: 10.4324/9781003303800-9

because this idea of refusing to speak against ourselves and against our communities has been a throughline in our individual and collaborative works, and in many of our collaborations with others (Simpson, 2014; Tuck & Yang, 2014). Refusal is a central imperative, a guiding framework, of all of our research and scholarly activities. The authors in this section refuse the damage-centered logics and assumptions that undergird their disciplines, and how these damage-centered logics dehumanize both them and their communities.

We write in an ongoing pandemic and have no reason to believe that readers will be outside of this pandemic timeline. Almost certainly coming out of COVID-19 will be pandemic research, some explicitly addressing racial inequalities; other research that will leave it unnamed, hidden behind words like "high risk populations." These, too, will require some communities to speak against themselves. These are (re)newed racializations, and if left unquestioned, will become the implicit theories of race for the next generation of scholars, and for the young people they study (with, *study with*, we hope). We predict funded research projects that overlook community refusals, and take for granted that Latinx, Filipinx, and other racialized communities have greater risk of infection. Studies may presume that they are vectors of transmission, and thus research subjects for behavioral interventions. This is racialization, where structural racism becomes a projection onto the bodies of people of color, and communities. COVID-19 also illustrates the racialization of Asians, wherein old tropes of "yellow peril" are playing out in fears of contagion from an Orientalized other, illustrated by medical mythologies of people eating diseased bats, of secret laboratories manufacturing the virus.

Incidents of anti-Asian violence during the pandemic certainly echo into histories of racism. But this is also an example of contemporary racialization, where anxieties about China as a global superpower (competitor and foreign enemy Other) are projected onto Asian American bodies and communities. Hidden in all these minoritized racializations, is the racialization of whiteness, where certain communities and people (and their bodies) are presumed to be deserving of immunity, while other communities' medical precarity, most notably Black and Indigenous communities, is presumed to be expected.

Victoria Copeland's chapter, "Abolitionist Praxis and Black Geographies in Social Work," is a chapter we are thrilled to be able to publish in this volume. From our perspectives as those working outside the field of Social Work, the field is undergoing a massive transformation, in no small part because of the contributions of Black scholars, Indigenous scholars, and scholars of color who are intervening in the field's history of collusion with violent nation-states that harm communities, lands, and waters. Copeland's chapter is one that we anticipate will be circulated among those who wish to address the geographies of domination that are enacted in social welfare research. We have already recommended it to so many people! In part, Copeland works to confound the dismissal of research that attempts to reduce the harm of the discipline of social work on communities as "advocacy," and instead argues that it is central to the practice and future of this field. She connects this dismissal to anti-Black theories of Blackness that shape the field and its purposes. Copeland turns to the 1968 position statement by the National Association of Black Social Workers–standards set apart from the overwhelmingly white and colonial underpinnings of the field–in order to think about research and theory that might ensure the "survival, well-being, and liberation" of Black communities (NABSW, n.d., as quoted in Copeland, this volume). The NABSW position statement asserted a code of ethics that insisted on the accountability of social workers to Black communities, to social change, and to improving the lives of Black individuals and families. Copeland engages the work of Katherine McKittrick in *Demonic Grounds* (2015) to argue against the "divide and conquer" approaches of the discipline, linking these approaches to white supremacy in the field. Pointing to the ways that the ethics of the broader field are ethnically not sustainable, Copeland calls for letting go of the historical attachments of the field to paternalistic, racist, and carceral logics and systems (Copeland, this volume). The chapter is a fully considered invitation to think with Copeland about work in social work and beyond, where we come from, what we come to know, and how we learn.

Derek Houston's "Racialization, Quantification, and Criticalism: Finding Space in the Break" is a witty and vulnerable exploration into the perils of quantitative methods and into the radical unknown of QuantCRit. We imagine that quantitative researchers, especially graduate students making the choice to use quantitative methods, will read this essay with a lot of attention and reflection. Written from the perspective of a self-professed, "lover of all that is numbers," this piece invites readers who might otherwise be defensive of quantitative methods to dwell "in the break" away from the accepted rigor and objectivity of their training. Houston grapples with many of the unspoken practices of quantitative research. He compels us to think about the use of repetition as pedagogy, such as teaching students to practice on large data sets which are themselves often not problematized. He uncovers the prevalence of implicit theories about racialization that often pass unnoticed in the very design of studies, carried out by assumptions that race is causal, as having explanatory value illuminated through the manipulation of numbers. Today, so much of research is assumed to be antiracist because it focuses on inequality. Houston, in the legacy of W.E.B. Dubois, troubles this idea. He points out the foundational role that eugenics played in the advent of social scientific methods, and thus how race is presumed to be an explanation of inequalities. "Quantification is subjective but is assumed … to be objective," is one of many quotable moments that readers will likely underline in this chapter. Another is, "QuantCRiT operates and is operationalized in the break, at a nexus of two seemingly epistemologically and ontologically opposed research traditions, (post) positivism and constructivism." Ultimately, Houston writes in a lyrical way that humanizes even while unsettling quantitative methods, and brings quantitative researchers into communion with their qualitative, critical, poetic selves.

In "Undisciplining school discipline research: Refusing the racial paternalism to punishment pipeline," Mahasan Chaney compellingly tells three interlocking stories to make apparent the need to rethink and reframe theories and research on Black youth as troublemakers, and instead learn from their critiques of schooling, whiteness, carcerality, and unfreedom, in institutions that are in trouble. Chaney employs fugitivity as a methodology, refusing to take Black "troublemakers" as the objects of study, but rather to learn from their flights from the institutions that create the category of troublemaker in their likenesses. Chaney tells three stories that "walk" a reader through the antiBlackness at the center of who gets framed as a troublemaker, learning first from Anne Feguson's classic study Bad Boys (2000), a story of a restorative justice program in schools (that reduced the number of suspensions, but not the antiBlackness that Black students were subjected to in school), and a story of Mattie Jackson, re-told from Saidiya Hartman's critical fabulation of Jackson in *Wayward Lives* (2019). Showing how these stories might be told together, Chaney argues that fugitive theory can be a way for Black scholars to take a "generative stance toward refusing the violent discourses and racialized paternalism," that typifies research on Black youth (Chaney, this volume). We know that readers will turn to this chapter when they are unsatisfied with theorizing race and racialization, racism, and anti-Blackness in ways currently available to them. Indeed, this chapter highlights the different kinds of courage needed in reading and making fugitive texts. For Chaney, a fugitive text is "instructive in illustrating how writing of wholeness and complexity, scholars of race and punishment may free ourselves from rigid confines which might force us into reproducing categories we are attempting to reveal, undermine, and flee from," (Chaney, this volume).

In "Engaging with race and racism in research," Dina Okamoto also brings readers along in a story of learning to reflect fully on the ways that race and racism are conceptualized as constructs, as processes, and as categories within our research with youth. Focusing on the category that gets called Asian American, Okamoto revisits her earlier book *Redefining Race,* to tell the story of the disagreements, convergences, and solidarity goals of the term. Certainly, finding a way to combat anti-Asian racism is at the heart of the rationale for a pan-ethnic term, that does both so much and still covers over so much, as Asian American. Okamoto calls for engaging in rich conceptualizations.

In encouraging a storytelling approach, we hope that this is an approach that will be both pedagogically and personally meaningful to readers. However, we don't want authors, or readers, to feel that you need to be at the end of your learning story in order to think with these ideas of refusing to speak against ourselves and our communities. In fact, many of us are just at the beginning of our story. We hope that volume, and this section in particular, will, in fact, become part of your story, and the story of the research practices that emerge.

References

Simpson, A. (2014). *Mohawk Interruptus: Political life across the borders of settler states.* Duke University Press.

Tuck, E., & Yang, K. W. (2014). Unbecoming claims: Pedagogies of refusal in qualitative research. *Qualitative Inquiry, 20*(6), 811–818.

7

ABOLITIONIST PRAXIS AND BLACK GEOGRAPHIES IN SOCIAL WORK

Victoria Copeland

Bari Bari, saan ka agung-unget pari, ta pumukankami iti pabakirda kadakami.

I begin this journey with you from my kitchen in DC. It's 11:30 p.m., my grandma is in the hospital with congestive heart failure, and I am thousands of miles away unable to sit and properly form the words needed for this chapter. The quote above is a chant, or prayer rather, that keeps replaying in my head. It's a rendition of one that my grandma has recited since I was a child, the one she learned from her mother-in-law. My grandma is from Pangasinan in the Philippines and my late grandpa is from Ilocos Sur. To them the Bari Bari is more than just a simple ritual or chant, it's what bolsters physical and spiritual well-being. The Bari Bari is recited when one is ill with anything—from a slight sniffle to full-blown tumors. It's also recited when we depart from our elders. Whenever I was sick or simply saying goodbye, I would kneel and place my head between my grandma's hands. As she rubbed my forehead, my chest, my stomach, and the tips of my shoulders she would recite something akin to "Bari Bari, ta pumu-kankami ... daddy (referring to my grandpa) please watch over your granddaughter, help her finish school and keep her safe and well". As ex-plained by my grandma, the Bari Bari is a way to acknowledge the presence of our ancestors whether they are currently present or will be visiting in the future. She says, "their spirit might be with us, and want to just talk to you, that's why you feel sick". Where my grandparents are from, they believe that ancestors' visits can cause physical illness. There is no mal intent to this illness, it is simply a consequence of the tensions within the dimensions. It's

DOI: 10.4324/9781003303800-10

your ancestors' way of telling you hello and that they are watching over you. By reciting the Bari Bari, we acknowledge our elders, pay them respect, and ask them for protection and safety.

Based on scant scholarship, I found that Western researchers classify the Bari Bari as "mythology". However, for many Indigenous Filipino people, it has been referred to as a sacred practice offered to us by our Ilocano ancestors. According to Filipino researchers, artists, and writers, the Bari Bari was once considered a chant that inhabitants of Ilocos would say before cutting down trees in the mountains. The translation of Bari Bari is "do not feel bad my friend for we cut as we are ordered" (Gaverza, 2017). The people of Ilocos would recite this to the Mangmangkik, the anitos (secondary gods or spirits) found in the environment so that they would not be offended (Baglieri, 2021). If the anitos were offended they could inflict illness on the human (Anderson, 2013). Although the tradition of the Bari Bari may have shifted in its purpose over generations, it is far from being a mythological practice. The ritual continues to remind us that we are all connected to the land, to the ones before us, and to each other. It reminds us that knowledge is created by sharing stories with each other and passing down lessons to generations that come after us.

I start with this reflection on the Bari Bari to not only honor my grandmother, but to ground this chapter in what it means to challenge the ways in which we come to know, where we know from, and how we continue to learn (McKittrick, 2021). Our stories are beyond what some might consider mythology, they are intertwined with our physical realities, our material conditions, and the ways we both view and exist in the world. Thus, the theory is not inextricably tied to Western science, nor does it exist solely in the imagination of our captors—the ones who try to entrap us and force us into categories of the unknown or the abnormal. Just as the Bari Bari blends the lines between our dimension, the afterlife, and the liminal space between—approaching research and theory with relationality in mind holds space for and encourages complexity. It establishes new ways of learning together through recollecting memories and sharing lessons. It reconceptualizes forms of care and protection that are rooted in the community and encourages presence and vulnerability. Theory and research start with who we are, and what we are aiming to offer the world and each other.

Social work and geographies of domination

As graduate students, we often seek answers to the questions: what is theory and how do we use it? In the field of social welfare, the answer is not easily understood nor is it frequently described. As a student, I have heard endless echoes from professors telling me that social welfare has had no unique theoretical grounding. I watched as they struggled to describe the theoretical foundations of their work, and saw the spark disappear from their eyes as they outlined the ways that their theories and research questions were often tied to the funding of a research project. As students, we learned about the ways social welfare was trying to coalesce into the social sciences, and how the field is still struggling to form its identity today. Many of my professors claimed that theories frequently used by social welfare researchers originated from the social sciences, and as such research design generally required a sense of rigor that is made synonymous with quantitative methods and positivist or objectivist paradigms. Attempting to fit my research ideas into this box of "science" was extremely difficult. From Katherine McKittrick's (2021) work, I learned that "sharing stories is creative rigorous radical theory. The act of sharing stories is the theory and the methodology" (p. 73). Yet, my research questions did not fit with the theories I was learning and were never a match for the methods that were offered in our classes. When I used my experience as a foundation for my research I was told "that's advocacy, not research" and to try again. I was questioned about the novelty of the research area I was pursuing and was asked to identify and defend a special "research gap" that I was attempting to fill. There were no justifications for my research that were adequate enough for several of my professors. I came to realize that "the gap" that the academy prioritizes was not the same "gap" that I believed to exist. The gap I know to exist is where the academy does not focus, it's where the academy is complicit in harms inflicted upon communities, and where it abandons individuals for the sake of novelty. It's where the academy has rendered something as either inconceivable or insignificant.

Constructing "the gap" through dominant social work ethics

The tensions that I felt with social welfare's mission to mirror social science "disciplines", signified a deeper disconnect between my work and the foundational positioning of social work as a profession. Social work's foundations can be exemplified through the profession's "Code of Ethics" or "COE" which was created by the National Association of Social Workers in 1960. The COE aimed to be "the standard bearer for defining the values and principles that guide social workers' conduct in all practice areas" (National Association of Social Workers [NASW], n.d.). The COE defines several ethical principles that social workers are expected to adhere to including service, social justice, the importance of human relationships, integrity, and competence (NASW, 2021). Similarly, it includes ethical standards that dictate social workers' "ethical responsibilities to clients" including the right to self-determination, informed consent, competence, cultural competence, privacy and confidentiality, access to records, and more (NASW, 2021). Many of the NASW principles parallel revered value systems within the United States such as the prioritization of individualism, independence, and the right to participate in society. Thus, as innocuous and well-intended as the COE seems, in practice, it often recertifies certain ideals about what we should consider "normal". Consequently, this results in a reification of gendered and racialized hierarchies, frequently marking whiteness as the standard, which renders other communities as abnormal or something to be fixed.

As a Black and Filipina student, the incongruence between the NASW COE, my lived experiences, and my work felt incorrigible. Even though the code may seem innocuous, I knew that the systems and practices that social workers frequently engage in contradict our written ethical codes by justifying the continued surveillance, policing, and criminalization of Black families. This made me consider more deeply the individualistic and deeply embedded racialized intentions and interpretations of the COE, and how it protects certain communities while rationalizing ethical loopholes that lead to violence on others. The profession's insistence on relying on the NASW COE has had long-lasting consequences and has contributed to upholding geographies of colonialism and white supremacy—a perpetuation of the afterlives of slavery (Hartman, 2007). These harmful geographies and their requisite theories of whiteness and white saviorism continue to be proliferated through social work research and subsequent practices of family separation, law enforcement partnerships, and eugenic healthcare systems. Social work is thus not atheoretical. Rather, social work continues to be deeply reliant on a normalized theoretical grounding, one constructed by those who have had the power to make critical decisions regarding Black lives.

Though social work's complex history and struggle with racism spans back to the profession's conception, the formation of the National Association of Black Social Workers, or "NABSW" remains one of the most significant time points in the history of the profession. The NABSW was created at a time in which social work professional organizations and conferences, including the NASW and National Conference on Social Welfare, were contributing to the continued violence and erasure of Black communities. In efforts to preserve and fight for Black life, the group of Black workers set out to create separate standards that would work to ensure the "survival, well-being, and liberation" of Black communities (NABSW, n.d.). In 1968 the NABSW wrote a position statement that highlighted their concerns regarding white social workers' ignorance of and contribution to the plight of Black communities. In their statement, the

NABSW referred to the National Conference as a "white institution" that did not reflect the "ethnic composition commensurate with its expressed concern" (NABSW, 1968). They not only called for the representation of Black people on the boards, but they also demanded that "people who speak, write, research, and evaluate the Black community be Black people who are experts in this area" (NABSW, 1968). Further, the NABSW retracted any support for social welfare systems and programs that were designed to maintain "the unequal participation of the Black community", as many of the professional social work organizations at the time contributed to the traumatic experiences of Black people both in practice as well as in their theorizations about Black communities (NABSW, 1968). These theories were far removed from the lived experiences of Black people and were often woefully incorrect.

The NABSW and their code of ethics set out to: prioritize actions that would improve the social conditions for Black communities over any personal interests, adopt the concept of a Black extended family, hold workers responsible for the quality and extent of service performed as it relates to the Black community, protect the Black community from unethical and hypocritical practices by any individual, and utilize workers' skills to be an "instrument" for social change with particular attention to the establishment of Black social institutions (National Association of Black Social Workers, 2021). In addition to these codes, the NABSW adheres to core principles and virtues. The *Nguzo Saba* principles that guide their work are unity, self-determination, collective work and responsibility, cooperative economics, purpose, creativity, and faith (NABSW, n.d.). Their Seven Cardinal Virtues of Ma'at are right, truth, justice, order, reciprocity, balance, and harmony (NABSW, n.d.). Through these principles, ethical codes, and commitments that are rooted in ancestral knowledge and tradition—the NABSW presents its theory of Blackness. This theory is rooted in aliveness, ancestry, care, and relationality.

Compared to the NASW code of ethics, the NABSW code of ethics speaks against dominant practices of whiteness and white supremacy inherent to social work, rejecting anti-Blackness and individualism, and instead centering on Black well-being. This direct contestation of the dominant and prevailing geographies in social work acts as a rupture in how social workers theorize and define their relation to Black communities. Through this centering of Black voices and Black life, the NABSW points to the barriers placed on Black people that stem from systems and society rather than adhering to the individualized and criminalized blame that is inherent to hegemonic social work discourse and practice. The NABSW Code demarginalizes Black communities, presenting them as significantly constitutive of our society and not marginal, not property, not commodity.

For me, the NABSW's differentiated code of ethics signified that there were alternate pathways to think through how theorizations of Blackness can disrupt hegemonic discourses in social work.

Oppositional geographies of the "unimaginable" gap—Black women's geographies as demonic grounds in social work

The conflicts between my experiences, my research interests and questions, my ethics, and the social work "discipline" perplexed me in a haunting way throughout the initial years of my education. I continue to struggle through the paradoxes between my training in social welfare and my experience as a Black and Filipina woman. These tensions have allowed me to reorient myself and dedicate energy to learning from the traditions and scholars of Asian American and African-American studies. These traditions helped me find a synergy between my experiences, my observations of the world, theory, and subsequently my research design. When I search for answers about theory, I continue to find myself meditating on and conversing with various offerings from Black scholars, some of whom identify as Black Feminists and others who do not. Particularly, I sit with Sylvia Wynter and Katherine McKittrick's offerings on the concepts of the human, Man, and the "demonic grounds" or geographies of Black women (McKittrick, 2006; 2015). McKittricks "Demonic Grounds" weaves together Wynter's demonic model and description of "the grounds" to highlight the ways that Black womanhood is both present and "outside the bounds of reason", calling us to question how we might understand race and humanness if "black women legitimately inhabited our world and made their needs known" (McKittrick, 2015, p. xxv). Demonic grounds are further described by McKittrick as a geography that is "genealogically wrapped in the historical spatial unrepresentability of black femininity" (McKittrick, 2015, p. xxv). McKittrick's offering of demonic grounds has allowed me to understand the importance of Black women's geographies as oppositional geographies and beyond, geographies that are threaded through and often created within violent systems of capture, confinement, and violence. As recounted by McKittrick, Black women's geographies are "central to how we know and understand space and place" (Spillers as cited in McKittrick, p. 62), and directly contest the normalized meaning of Man as Human that has been threaded throughout social work practice. Through this process of re-learning, I realized that theory was not to be confined to the white imagination, nor to the boundaries of academia. Theory is not *always* neat and methodical— it is fun, creative, depressing, enlightening, and complex. Theory is deeply personal, but also deeply interpersonal.

Family policing

This vision of theory deeply resonated with me. My experiences in this world have impacted my work and have been the reason I maintain a particular focus on carceral institutions like the "child welfare" system better known as the "family policing system"—a term used by my colleague Brianna Harvey and I. Aside from my own family's experiences with the family policing system, much of my work has been driven by previous experiences working alongside peers in my neighborhood who were involved in the family policing and juvenile injustice systems. Through this work, I was able to witness and experience the rampant discontent and disregard that the family policing and juvenile injustice systems had for Black children. I saw how caseworkers would construct narratives of criminality onto Black families to keep them separated, all under the guise of "child protection". I saw that Black family preservation was either an impossibility or an afterthought. Due to these experiences, I remained critical of social workers and wanted to understand their roles and their decision-making powers more clearly. I wanted to problematize the phrase "falling into the cracks" as I believed that children did not fall into the cracks, systems placed them there.

As I pursued my graduate degree to conduct research on the family policing and juvenile injustice systems, I recognized that these systems not only work in tandem they also utilize the same carceral logic. The family policing system in the United States is a network of agencies and organizations that investigates suspected child maltreatment cases and is deeply entangled with the criminal legal system and its foundational logics. The family policing system claims to "promote the well-being of children by ensuring safety, achieving permanency, and strengthening families" and largely completes its mission through the deputization of social workers (Child Welfare Information Gateway, 2020). Social workers within the system are tasked with investigating reports of child abuse and neglect, removing children when they are deemed unsafe, and deciding if parents are worthy enough to be reunified after separation (Child Welfare Information Gateway, 2020). A normative hegemonic social work view of the "child welfare" system holds that regardless of its efficiency, the system should continue to be responsible for "protecting" child well-being. Thus, the NASW COE and accompanying theories of social work rationalize the tactics of power that are used by the system's effort to "save children" from their "risky" Black parents. Dominant social work geographies and theorizations about Black families as "high risk" have been exacerbated through social work programs that funnel students into the family policing system, and have expanded into community-based and mental health organizations in which social workers are employed to be the eyes and ears of child protective services. This has led to the continuation of a cycle of terror, one that has been endured by Black families for generations.

Contrary to the dominant social work view then, a Black epistemology rooted in Black geography brings forth an understanding of the ways that state violence and genocidal aims to eradicate Black life have continued through dominant social work geographies. From these Black places and spaces of knowing it is made clear that Black suffering is not simply a "byproduct" or "outcome" of the system, but a fundamental requirement for the family policing system to exist. The family policing system is fueled by the continuous capture and tracking of poor Black communities, often because Black families and Black places are often seen as uninhabitable, insufficient, or nonexistent. These are demonic grounds. Black women's geographies shows that the system is incapable of being a "protective" system because it relies on criminalization, assumptions, and punishment practices that are antithetical to the well-being of Black communities and their liberation as outlined by the NABSW. It calls into question the system's claim of "protection" and unsettles the normalization of its role in society.

The family policing system has gone unquestioned because of its seemingly benevolent mission and societal responsibility to keep children out of "harms" way. Social workers have continuously failed to grapple with who is being deemed a threat by the system, and why. These geographies of domination, upheld by social works ethical conundrums, render Black women both unimaginable and unrepresentable (McKittrick, 2006, p. 128). And yet, as McKittrick states in Demonic Grounds, Black women still find ways to create pathways to fugitivity, liberation, and resistance. Black women's stories and their accompanying theorizations allow us to truly interrogate the system, making central the ways it attributes "risk" and "threat of harm" to Black women in attempts to control their past, present, and future. Through my dissertation, I was able to chart these pathways—these oppositional geographies, alongside Black mothers.

DCF: Divide and conquering families—theorizing within a matrix of domination

I spent a considerable amount of time thinking about what the dominant geographies of social work were attempting to hide, and who they were leaving out in the process. Through my own organizing efforts, I recognized that many community partners I worked with were deeply impacted by the family policing system and were simultaneously creating pathways to thrive despite the system's ceaseless attempts to confine them. Because of this the Stop LAPD Spying Coalition, Los Angeles Community Action Networks—Downtown Women's Action Coalition, and I decided to partner together to chart the oppositional geography of mothers in Skid Row who experienced surveillance through the family policing system.

Skid Row is a community in Los Angeles that consists of predominantly residents of color who have been impacted by unrelenting structural racism and organized abandonment, leaving many people extremely low-income or experiencing homelessness (Los Angeles Community Action Network, 2021). Skid Row is a community of people who have endured egregious state surveillance and violence but have stood up for the rights of all residents despite it all. It is a community that attempts to thrive despite the ramifications of racial capitalism and anti-Blackness. It is demonic ground.

In Skid Row we sat together to plan and host "community sessions" directly within the community and with mothers in Skid Row who had their children taken away from the Department of Children and Family Services "DCFS" in Los Angeles. Through our community sessions, mothers were able to share their stories in a way that made sense for them, ways that included laughter and tears. To many mothers, and to myself it was a form of liberation and healing. I would meet with mothers every week throughout the summer to discuss, cry, and imagine together. Through dialogue, we were able to contribute to a shared consciousness, discussing how Black mothers conceptualize "protection", what it meant to counter and resist surveillance, and how we could move forward together towards a better world. Each week the mothers would use language that contested social works' claims of protection. All of their stories confirmed that the social work dominant code of ethics was not only contradictory to "child welfare" practices but was actively harmful to their experiences as mothers. Thus, from these community sessions and the stories shared, mothers constructed their own theories around racialization and social work through the family policing system or DCFS. Mothers called it "DCF" or "Dividing and Conquering Families".

DCF was a way for mothers to theorize the ways that social work has incited violence in their communities. DCF was a theorization and story about how social workers in the family policing system violently treated mothers and their children as commodifiable objects, putting price tags on children through adoption and erasing Black mothers through control and punishment. For Black mothers and Latine mothers in Skid Row, DCF(S) was about conquest and capture—it was about the power to keep poor Black and Latine families "subordinated" through the "dismembering of families" generationally. Mothers used their theorizations about DCF and dismemberment to think through ways that they have collectively survived and subverted the system. Through their counternarratives, they charted their oppositional geographies in Skid Row by highlighting the importance of strong, trusting, and mutually accountable relationships. They told stories about how their neighbors looked after them when they were younger, so their parents could rest or work. They shared details that flipped the narratives about living in tents, describing the immaculate decorations that remained inside peoples' homes and the beautiful kitchens that families created in their tents. Mothers demanded reparations in the form of housing deeds and talked about creating self-sustaining villages. They talked about cultivating crops on their own land, hosting single mothers' marches, and writing a book with their stories in it— stories as liberation and stories as healing. One mother said that by sharing stories she could unravel the knot inside of her stomach that was created by years of trauma within the system. She shared:

> When something is happening to you, you feel like you're the only person that it is happening to, and it's a big load there. But when you hear somebody share, you give another person an opportunity to kind of release the fear, and the hurt, and the pain that you carry within yourself because it's knotted up there. It's only happening to you. And that's what I like about certain situations when people can come in groups like this and talk about it.

They discussed this all while acknowledging and working through the ongoing state violence that attempted to enclose them.

Oppositional geography as a possibility

The NABSW Code highlights the same foundational concerns that mothers outlined through their theorization of DCF. They both make central the importance of improving the material conditions for Black communities that have been ravaged by those in power. Both mothers and the NABSW call out the unethical and hypocritical practices of most social workers and the lack of attention paid to establishing and building up Black social institutions. Further, they both define the "protection" of Black families' by using completely different language and framing than social work dominant geographies, geographies that are rooted in whiteness. Rather than claiming that Black children *need to be protected from their parents*, the NABSW and mothers in Skid Row believe that Black communities need to be *protected from harmful systems and practices*. This is one of the most important distinctions made clear through these converging yet oppositional geographies.

If I adhered to the theories and methods that I was taught within my formal social work education, I would not have been afforded the opportunity to sit with and learn from mothers in Skid Row. I would not have been able to resonate and build with a community to push forward against discourses of individualized blame and criminalization. This was research, and this was advocacy. It was theory, and it was action. Part of the violence we endure is the attempts by people and systems in power to confine us within these dichotomous categorizations. Thus, part of our liberatory task is to learn and re-learn how to move dynamically through theory and action— through experience and knowledge creation. Inherent to this liberatory task is creating space for and prioritizing storytelling and story-making. Being in dialogue with one another requires us to slow down and be intentional, and for those in the academy, it requires us to abandon much of what we know. According to McKittrick, storytelling signifies more than a simple exchange of words or materials between two people—sharing "signals collaboration and collaborative ways to act and engender struggle" (2021, p. 7). Sharing stories "is creative rigorous radical theory" (McKittrick, 2021, p. 73). Through storytelling, we reaffirm Black life in a world that almost always necessitates the perpetuation of the Black death. The "terrain of struggle" occurs through the sharing of ideas, which enables us to collaboratively create and envision a different future together (McKittrick, 2021, p. 25).

Grounding myself in a Black woman's geography has shifted my research in unimaginable ways. It has allowed me to be accountable for my part in dismantling systems of violence that are predicated on the commodification, exploitation, and harm of Black families. It has reminded me that with care and dialogue, we can grow a consciousness within the community and in our research. Moving forward requires us to acknowledge a different way, another way that many of us, like me, a Black and Filipina student, find fundamental to the way we question the world around us. Liberatory pathways through the rupture and beyond the white gaze have emerged through the collective work I have engaged in with Stop LAPD Spying Coalition (SLSC) and LACAN-Downtown Women's Action Coalition where we organized against state violence and surveillance (Browne, 2015). Our research addressed how biocentric Western frameworks perpetuate ideologies of Black insufficiency and death (McKittrick, 2021; Gilmore & Kumanyika, 2020) but can also be counteracted through community and through storytelling. Through this work, we created spaces to reflect on the paradoxes and challenges inherent to imagining a counter-hegemonic anti-carceral future. Through continued conversations we discuss the role social workers play—if any, in carrying this out. McKittrick leaves us with an offering:

Wynter taught me that radical theory-making takes place outside existing systems of knowledge that this place, outside (demonic grounds) is inhabited by those who are brilliantly and intimately aware of and connected to existing systems of knowledge (as self-replicating), and that this awareness provides theoretical insights and projections of humanity that imagine a totally new way of being that observes how our present mode of being functions unjustly and cannot sustain itself ethically. (McKittrick, 2021, p. 24)

The normalized ways of approaching and practicing social work *cannot sustain themselves ethically.* We do not have to be complicit in continuing unethical habits. The contrast between the NABSW and NASW code of ethics indicates a struggle to grapple with problems that have no easy answer—if any answer at all. The calls for anti-racist social work practice, research, and pedagogy have been reverberating throughout the academy, many of which lack a direct reflection of the internal social work ethics and values that perpetuate and uphold systematically violent and racist infrastructures. Due to the historical attachments of the field of social work to paternalistic, racist, and carceral logics and systems, there is a need to reflect internally on how the field of social work approaches care, help, and "protection" under this dominant geography (Jacobs et al., 2020; Law, 2020; Sacks & Chow, 2018). These values run through our practices, policies, and our research.

We need to dramatically shift our overarching attachments to the Western episteme and dominant geographies by relinquishing claims to power. In other words, we have to more closely consider how we come to know, what we know, and where we know from (McKittrick, 2021). We must prioritize Indigenous thinkers, Black thinkers, and scholarship that do not rely on hegemonic ideologies of domination. Additionally, if we are seeking a world that drastically operates differently, we must acknowledge that our involvement may not be desired by those whom social work assumes need our help. Instead of saying that we are "working ourselves out of a job" social workers must reorient themselves to think about why we believe the jobs we have *are necessary* for the progress that community members are seeking. Often they are not. Part of our commitment to address the inherent contradictions and power hierarchies invoked by social work and the academy requires us to work through these complexities and to build trusting and dynamic relationships. This can allow for spaces of new theory-creation and new relationalities.

Through Black geographies, we can continue to see that relationality is how we begin to move away from repurposing the harms that are inflicted upon us. Relationality is part of a "liberatory tasks" that requires us "not to measure and assess the unfree—and seek consolation in naming violence—but to posit that many divergent and different and relational voices of unfreedom are analytical and intellectual sites that can tell us something new about our academic concerns and our anticolonial futures" (McKittrick, 2021, p. 50). When we read across text and consider the plethora of creations by Black people that encompass art, imagery, thoughts, and actions, we move towards a different way of relating to one another—one that is not predicated on violence and exploitation. McKittrick (2021) advises us that we are responsible for working out how our different perspectives and contributions relate to one another and open unique ways of talking about liberation, Blackness, and knowledge. These stories, these fictive creations allow us to "practice radical interdisciplinarity without fraying its connection to black life, honor a black sense of place and where we know from" (McKittrick, 2021, p. 121).

My approaches to theory come from the creators before me who believed in the undisciplined, from the mothers who come from the unimaginable. They believed that we must contest structured and constrained processes of creating and sharing knowledge. We are never alone in our experiences. Black Studies leave us with a genealogy of knowledge that allows both fugitivity and care to become reality. Black communities enable beauty, love, nourishment, possibility, and care. As seen in my recollection of the Bari Bari, we are connected to one another through stories, history, and memory—through prayers at night and laughs with friends at the park. We are connected through collective knowledge, and through our will to chart different pathways towards liberation.

References

Anderson, B. (2013). *The age of globalization: Anarchists and the anticolonial imagination*. Verso Books.

Baglieri, K. (2021). *In order to escort her* [Master's thesis, City University of New York]. CUNY Academic Works. Retrieved from https://academicworks.cuny.edu/cgi/viewcontent.cgi?article=1765&context=hc_sas_etds

Browne, S. (2015). *Dark matters: On the surveillance of blackness*. Duke University Press.

Child Welfare Information Gateway. (2020). *How the child welfare system works. U.S. Department of Health and Human Services.* Administration for Children and Families, Children's Bureau. https://www.childwelfare.gov/pubs/factsheets/cpswork/

Gaverza, K. (2017, May 28). *Mangmangkik: Tree Spirits in Ilocos Norte.* Aswang Project. https://www.aswangproject.com/mangmangkik-spirits-trees/

Gilmore, R. W., & Kumanyika, C. (2020). Ruth Wilson Gilmore makes the case for abolition. Intercepted Podcast by JeremyScahill.

Hartman, S. (2007). *Lose your mother: A journey along the Atlantic slave route.* Farrar, Straus, and Giroux.

Jacobs, L. A., Kim, M. E., Whitfield, D. L., Gartner, R. E., Panichelli, M., Kattari, S. K., Downey, M. M., McQueen, S. S., & Mountz, S. E. (2020). Defund the police: Moving towards an anti-carceral social work. *Journal of Progressive Human Services. 32*(1), 37–62

Law, V. (2020). *Prison by any other name: The harmful consequences of popular reforms.* The New Press.

Los Angeles Community Action Network. (2021). *The impact of structural racism: On women in skid row.* https://cangress.org/publications/

McKittrick, K. (2006). *Demonic grounds: Black women and the cartographies of struggle.* University of Minnesota Press.

McKittrick, K. (Ed.). (2015). *Sylvia Wynter: On being human as Praxis.* Duke University Press.

McKittrick, K. (2021). *Dear science and other stories.* Duke University Press.

National Association of Black Social Workers [NABSW]. (1968). *Our Roots: Position Statement of the National Association of Black Social Workers.* Retrieved from https://cdn.ymaws.com/www.nabsw.org/resource/resmgr/position_statements_papers/nabsw_30_years_of_unity_-_ou.pdf

National Association of Black Social Workers [NABSW]. (n.d.). *Our mission statement.* NABSW. https://www.nabsw.org/page/MissionStatement

National Association of Social Workers [NASW]. (n.d.). *History of the NASW Code of ethics.* NASW. https://www.socialworkers.org/About/Ethics/Code-of-Ethics/History#:~:text=NASW's%20Delegate%20Assembly%20approved%20the,conduct%20in%20all%20practice%20areas

National Association of Social Workers [NASW]. 2021. *The code of ethics.* NASW. https://www.socialworkers.org/About/Ethics/Code-of-Ethics/History#:~:text=NASW's%20Delegate%20Assembly%20approved%20the,conduct%20in%20all%20practice%20areas

Sacks, T. K., & Chow, J. C. (2018). A social work perspective on police violence: Evidence and interventions. *Journal of Ethnic & Cultural Diversity in Social Work, 27*(3), 10.1080/15313204.2018.1476197

8

RACIALIZATION, QUANTIFICATION, AND CRITICALISM

Finding space in the break

Derek A. Houston

Southern Illinois University Edwardsville exists in and serves a region that includes the lands of the Kiikaapoi (treaty in Edwardsville, 1819); The Illinois Confederacy, including the Peoria, Kaskaskia, Michigamea, Cahokia, and Tamaroa (treaty in Edwardsville, 1818); Dhegiha Sioux peoples; and others. I acknowledge and affirm their contemporary and ancestral ties to the land and their contributions to this place. I acknowledge my connection to place and honor the land as a relative.

I am a Black man, a father and partner, the son of two working-class Black parents, brother of two Black siblings, the biological progeny of mixed-race relations, and a fourth-generation college graduate. I am allowed to engage in this work because of the foundations built by my Black grandparents, and continued by my parents, aunts, uncles, and community from which I come. I am responsible to this community and those like it. I stand on the shoulders of giants, with the responsibility to lift as I climb.

Refusing, rethinking, and reimagining are liberatory acts. For me, as a scholar who works in methods of quantification, refusing is the process of not accepting the normativity of a convention; rethinking is critiquing and questioning the understanding of the convention; and reimagining is moving beyond the critique of the convention toward the speculative space of what could be. To refuse, rethink, and reimagine is a continuous process. I choose to refuse the normative conventions of quantification, I actively engage in rethinking my understanding of current and past conventions, and I am reimagining what quantitative conventions could be.

I always thought myself good with numbers and at a certain point in graduate school, I had to make a choice about the methods I would use in

DOI: 10.4324/9781003303800-11

pursuit of my PhD. So, I chose the path that made the most sense to my sensibilities, quantitative methods. Hell, I even obtained a Master's in Statistics in addition to the PhD. So, my joy for numbers and quantification is and should be readily apparent. I spent my time learning about the "how to" and the mechanics of statistics, both correlational and causal inferences. I engaged with theories of measurement and grappled with the mechanics of survey design. Yet, what was limited across the multitude of quantitative-based courses was a lack of a critique of the social construction of meaning around race, sex, and/or class, which also meant limitations of these methods to address racism and racialization, sexism, and discrimination against poor people. Outside of the assumptions of quantification or measurement, the assumptions about the social construction of race were rarely, if ever, discussed or challenged. Some mentors engaged in critical ways through their scholarship. Yet conversations specifically about quantification and racialization were non-existent. In this chapter, I engage conceptually with Zuberi's (2001) critique of how race is used in social science search, Moten's (2003) theorization of repetition and how repetition is found in the pedagogical practices of quantification, and Dixon-Román's (2017) argument that quantification in the social science is a subjective rather than objective exercise. Furthermore, I offer two examples at the nexus of quantification and criticalism, first a discussion of Du Bois' quantitative "art" and second a summary of a quantitative empirical article grounded in criticalism. The critique in this chapter is offered in the spirit of hard love and the need for continuous study to move the work of quantification beyond static engagements of race and racialization.

How quantification gets race and racialization wrong

Quantification is subjective but is assumed, by most, to be objective. Researchers choose how and what to assign to that which is quantified, how and what to assign to that which is used to measure, and how and what to then analyze the measures of quantification. The processes of scientific quantification, a subjective task, have been and are still used in the quantification of human experiences. The foundational principles of quantification within social science research are grounded in the dehumanizing and racializing practices of eugenics (Zuberi, 2001). The assumed and unchecked objectivity of quantification within social science research allows for the continued possibilities of dehumanization.

Zuberi (2001) provides a history of quantification within the social sciences. He discusses how quantification, specifically demography, was used to understand population characteristics along the lines of race and class. This history charts the path of how the scientific method (experimentation, control, treatment, and measurable outcomes) came to prominence in the social sciences. Most specifically, Zuberi (2001) argues that the scientific method applied to social sciences provided an avenue for the justification of racial stratification, e.g., racialization. Zuberi (2001) highlights the development of IQ tests as ways to measure intelligence and the use of IQ tests to differentiate between individuals, specifically the racialization within the United States. Inherent in the scientific method is the desire to assign causation, A causes B, or X causes Y, to a human condition or set of conditions in order to understand the machinations of the social order. Under the scientific method and without critical examination, human characteristics (race, class, gender, income, living conditions) were linked to cognitive measures of intelligence and non-cognitive outcomes of poverty.

An essential argument of Zuberi (2001) is the need for better causal theorizations. He critiques how the scientific method has been used to assign causality to non-manipulable human characteristics. Specifically, his critique centers around the use of race as a cause of the differences in IQ scores or other academic measures between Black and white students/ people. Zuberi (2001) notes:

Because most social science research studies causal effects for the purpose of making inferences about the effects of manipulation to which groups of individuals in a population have been or might be exposed, causes are only things that can, in theory, be manipulated or altered" (p. 127) … It must make sense in the context under examination that for any individual the causal variable might have been different from the value actually taken. Thus, race is not a causal variable but rather an intrinsic property of the individual … Race and gender as unalterable characteristics of individuals are not causal variables in inferential statistical analysis (p. 129).

Here, Zuberi (2001) summarizes the purpose of causal quantitative inquiry, the mechanism of manipulation or change by which cause can be estimated, and how the concept of race is not subject to manipulation, rendering the use of race as a causal mechanism problematic.

The foundation of the scientific method, which leads to understanding a causal mechanism/factor, requires manipulation. As in, the factors in the experiment must be able to take on a different form or be manipulated in some way. Although racialization has a political and social history of manipulation, the immediate social contexts by which individuals exist do not allow for their race to be manipulated in the way of the scientific method. Zuberi (2001) argues the same for sex. Whereas other factors of the human condition can be manipulated (income, school attended, etc.), a person's race cannot be changed. As such, Zuberi (2001) notes that the language of causation (impact, effect) is used inappropriately when addressing differences in outcomes by race. Because race is a non-manipulable human characteristic, race can't cause anything.

It is wrong to say that race (the social/political classification assigned to an individual) causes differences in educational outcomes. How we talk about the use of non-manipulable variables (race/sex) in quantification is extremely pressing. The language of association (relationships) centers on the human condition, whereas the language of causation assigns blame to that which is unable to change. Zuberi (2001) adds the following:

> "Along these lines we could attempt to engage in social statistics in a way that keeps the human being and human effort evident. This effort requires that we avoid studying society while rejecting the humanity of the population under consideration. In order for modern social statistics to make efforts to pursue this direction of research, we much change some of our ideas about the study of racial statistics" (p. 106).

Given the rooted history of social science quantification in the dehumanizing pseudoscience of eugenics, continuing to assign cause to race reinforces a still present racial stratification (racialization). It also allows researchers to avoid discussing the structural conditions that are manipulable and likely have causal implications for raced folks, including white folks. In the training grounds of higher education, choosing not to directly refuse, rethink, and/or reimagine how race or other non-manipulable characteristics are discussed in quantitative methods courses is a form of pedagogical repetition, a space where normative conventions are unchallenged and passed from one generation of scholars to the next.

Repetition and quantification

Moten (2003) asks us to

> "think the relation of convention [of quantitative methods training] to repetition, think the way convention's dependence upon repetition is the condition of its (in)security. So that if we imagine a space between repetition then we imagine something impossible to locate. The moment between moments presents massive ontological problems ..." (p. 69).

I want to sit with Moten (2003) to think about the break. The moment between moments, the space between repetitions, the break, offers the possibility of what could be, that which challenges and disrupts the norms of convention. In this case, thinking and operating in the break interrupts convention, such that what is does not necessarily have to be, what has not can be, and what remains unimagined is no longer a dream. For the convention of quantitative methods training, if what is taught continues to be taught, it could be assumed to be right and the conventional norm, creating a pedagogical power paradigm that is unlikely to be challenged. In short, repetition happens without disruption and maintains convention.

Convention, in this case, is the general form of quantitative methods training typically found in the graduate classrooms of the academy. Quantification and quantitative methods in the social sciences are, at their foundation, grounded in (post)-positivism, as previously discussed. Unchallenged assumptions about race and racialization presented within these conventions are allowed to repeat semester to semester, year to year, and from generation to generation. The repetition of not challenging the assumptions of race and racialization, among other things, within quantitative methods training can lead to acritical examinations of outcomes that point an individual's or group's race as a cause of disparities and not the social and structural conditions of racialization and racism.

I surmise that these conventions likely have been maintained because the core pedagogy, or processes of teaching and learning quantitative methods, is repetition. Repetition is found in the types of assignments used to reinforce learning and mastery, in the textbooks used from course to course across the academy, and in the passing along of pedagogical methods and tools (read sharing slides) from instructor to student. A disruption of that repetition is hard, particularly when the how-to-disrupt is found in critical places unlikely to be occupied by quantitative scholars. There is a security in acritical quantitative methods training that reinforces the assumptions of objectivity and avoids the messiness of the subjective. Maybe repetition helps to squash the imagination of burgeoning quantitative researchers. Maybe the structures and the systems that control who is heard and what is read restrict the scholarly bounds by which future quantitative scholars abide. Maybe seeing, in general, acritical repetitions (repetitions that lack a critique of power) of quantitative scholarship reinforces the norm and provides the condition of security needed to maintain convention.

My guess is that this still happens. My sense is that in a statistics course, race or sex are regularly described in a regression model and these categories are used without theorization or conceptualization. It is regular practice when an instructor fails to conceptualize what they mean by race or sex or if the instructor assumes a shared knowledge of what is meant by race or sex, a point of unchecked repetition. Zuberi (2001) describes race and other readily unchangeable human characteristics (e.g., sex) as non-manipulable. In statistics, it is a desire to assign causality to a phenomenon based on the estimation of a model. To assign cause, as Zuberi (2001) argues, is to assume that there are at least two conditions of the experienced phenomenon, both equally likely for the participants in the data. This phenomenon would be considered manipulable because of the likelihood of participants in the data experiencing one of the two conditions. Relating back to the instructor, I want to address passive assumptions around the use of race or other non-manipulable human characteristics in the teaching of statistics as one example of a form of repetition.

It would not surprise me if a regression textbook on your bookshelf included a statistical model that uses race and/or sex along with other factors like prior math test scores to predict future math scores without conceptualizing race and/or sex. It would also not surprise me if there was a similar model discussed during a lecture on regression without a discussion about the assumptions of race or sex. While not intentional, the impact of an act is always more important than the intent. By not addressing the assumptions of racialization in this case or theoretically grounding the use of race in the model, the instruction of statistics passively reinforces at least two assumptions. The first is that differences in future math scores are caused by some inherent differences in race and/or sex, reinforcing stereotypes associated with non-white, non-male-identified people. The second assumption is that non-manipulable human characteristics (e.g., race, sex) are treated as manipulable when discussing the predicted model, likely leading to causality being assigned. To understand the long-range implications of not questioning how non-manipulable human characteristics are discussed in statistics, perform a Google Scholar search for the phrases "effect of race" and "education." Over 14,000 documents include the term "effect of race." Race, when measured, is not manipulable because it does not meet the conditions described above. It is not equally likely that participants experience two or racialized categories. As such, the term "effect of race" is wrong and reinforces the first assumption above. I could call out scholars but because this is so commonly taught, I'd rather call in folks to understand what the possibilities could be if we adjusted how we talk about race and other non-manipulable human characteristics when explaining statistical models. Engaging with this seemingly mundane change in how we teach quantification adjusts the focus from race as cause to focusing on racialization and racism and the social and structural contexts resulting from them.

As a pedagogical practice, to engage in the process of learning quantitative methods without examining the assumptions upon which methods are built is repetition. The break between those repetitions is space to ask about the why of quantification in addition to how the space is made to acknowledge the multiple whys. If introductory statistics courses are taught how our instructors were taught, using the same or similar texts, it is likely that the students who become instructors will follow the same path. Repetition manifests itself in the unchanging approaches to uncritical approaches to the passing along of quantitative methods. Repetition exists in the unsaid and the assumed. Zuberi penned his work in 2001. The foundational work of my quantitative training began a decade later. The discussion of manipulability and causality, let alone theory, was scant, providing room for unchecked repetition by way of silence.

Quantification and new materialism

Given the historical foundations of quantification within social science research on race, it was critical to think about subjectivity and objectivity within quantification. In doing so, I chose to enter the break, an unknown space between the repetitious conventions of objectivity within quantification. In one instance, Moten (2003) described the break as a space that is "the site of … ensemble: the improvisation of singularity and totality and through their opposition" (p. 10). Singularity, in this case, could be the repetitions of singular conventions that permeate quantification while totality could be the unknown possibilities at the nexus of criticalism and quantification, the break. Moten (2003), in the same discussion, posits that "Lingering in that space is not but is of deconstruction, the oscillation between ghostly poles" (p. 89). To be in the break, outside of the bounds of convention, the spaces between repetitions, is to begin to (re)imagine, (re)consider, and/or (re)construct what was to what could be. Maybe the break is somewhere in the axiological yearnings of my existence, the valuing of humanity and, in particular, Black humanity. Maybe my desire to think thoughtfully about the humanity within the data I was using gave me pause; that data quantifies the human experiences of someone's child/ren, somebody's baby, somebody. My role, given my methodological training, love for all things quantification, and love for Black people, was to engage in the rehumanizing of data which has been whittled down to a set of numbers. This process of rehumanizing was unknown to me but it was necessary because of the power (un)consciously bestowed upon quantification in the social sciences to shape the lives of people usually found at the margins.

And, yet, quantification and criticalism have historically spent time in the diametrically opposed epistemological and ontological research traditions of positivism and constructivism. Dixon-Román (2017) offers a foundation by which to move into the break, the unknown at the nexus of quantification and criticalism. Dixon-Román (2017) deeply engaged with the epistemological and ontological assumptions of quantification, specifically disrupting the quant/qual binary, and provides an intellectual foundation from which to build from:

"There continues to be an abyss between the work of cultural studies and critical inquiry and the dominant uses of quantitative studies on social reproduction … Scholarship in cultural studies and critical inquiry has maintained a hermeneutics of suspicion toward the critical possibilities of quantitative methods at the cost of not accounting for what is inherently, in part, a question of quantification: the materialist analysis of power relations … The dominant orientation toward quantitative social science research on social reproduction has eschewed critical theories, maintained a positivist posture toward the data, and assumed privileged access to the "truths" of natural phenomena via the logics of mathematics" (p. xvii).

Dixon-Román (2017) offers a nuanced critique of the epistemological assumptions of both positivism and constructivism, identifying what he refers to as the problem of comparison. A problem where each epistemic tradition engages in comparative analyses to identify differences between groups. His critique is not limited to acritical positions, as he engages the work of CRT and Black Feminisms, purporting that these traditions offer limited analyses beyond difference.

Dixon-Román (2017) posits that a new-materialist approach to the study of differential outcomes allows for criticalism to co-exist with quantification. Central to his argument is the relational entanglements of nature and culture, which can be associated with the epistemic traditions of positivism and constructivism. In discussing how to think about these entanglements, Dixon-Román (2017) argues that one is not separate from the other, suggesting that "cultural processes are not predated by nature but rather are nature" and noting that "the challenge both ontologically and epistemologically is how we understand and produce knowledge of the category of the human in the world" (p. 23). Unlike the critiques offered above regarding a focus on difference, new materialism, notes Dixon-Román (2017), is less interested in the concept of difference, as focusing on difference can create an assumption that there is a singular cause for said difference. Instead, a new materialist approach addresses empirical research through a multitude of inter- and intra-related social conditions, complicating the idea of causality and predictability which underscore the traditions of quantification. His argument employs the use of conditional and contextual interpretations of statistical estimates. Dixon-Román (2017) argues that

"some methods and text are more amenable and advantageous to the study of particular phenomena but the diffractive reading of the data from each method through the other methods can allow that which would have been missed otherwise to emerge and complicate/enrich the social understanding of any particular phenomena" (p. 71).

Dixon-Román's argument makes room for criticalism and quantification because the ontological assumptions are such that the human condition under study is explained by both.

As discussed above, the process of quantification is a subjective task, where the what, why, and how of measurement are decided subjectively. Dixon-Román (2017) notes that "measuring apparatuses are boundary-making practices that produce separations within phenomena that designate determinate boundaries of what matters and is excluded, of what's possible and impossible, and of what's intelligible and unintelligible" (p. 61). The process of measurement has subjective consequences, where those conse-quences equate to a choice. Said subjectivity may or may not be informed by theory and/or prior literature but what is included, and subsequently excluded, is chosen by the researcher. To think about the inter- and intra-relatedness of what, why, and how positions the researcher to acknowledge relationships beyond those captured in the singular statistical model.

Dixon-Román complicates what some would call the quant/qual binary. He builds from the work of Zuberi (2001) and Zuberi and Bonilla-Silva (2008), along with others, to clearly articulate how choice, subjectivity, are foundational in quantification, measurement, and statistics. Dixon-Román would probably argue that the quant/qual binary should have never existed in social science research. Although this is the case, traditional epistemo-logical boundaries are not quickly eroded. As such, for burgeoning meth-odologists, graduate students, and quants thinking about criticalism, the quant/qual binary still exists in the normative bounds of the academy and, unfortunately, society. A value has been placed on that which is assumed to be objective, quantification, and quantitative methods. That value elicits power and defines power relations. In the academy, it helps define what is and what is not considered good research, listened-to and trusted research, and funded research. Because value is placed on quantification, "produced knowledge from social statistics becomes part of the enumeration of power" (Dixon-Román, 2017, p. 54). Where future researchers have to find their place is at the nexus of quantification and criticalism. That space of lightly treaded adventure that asks that the researcher to think beyond that which has been taught in quantitative research courses, to imagine the need to theorize about the social contexts of social science, and to not rely com-pletely on the value of a single story, regardless of how robust the estimates. It is in the best interests of the community you are working for and/or with to theorize beyond just allowing the numbers to speak.

Quantitative + criticalism

Here, I attend to critical race theory (CRT) and, more specifically, QuantCRiT (Garcia et al., 2018) as they have helped shape the doing of my research practice and, more importantly, the thinking around my research practice. CRT is grounded in critical legal studies and is generally thought about as moving beyond the color-blind assumptions of neutrality in law. Similarly, quantitative + criticalism (Quant CriT), grounded in the tenets of CRT, is thought about as moving beyond the color-blind assumptions of neutrality in quantification (Gillborn et al., 2018). Building off the work of Zuberi (2001), Sólorzano et al. (2005), and Zuberi and Bonilla-Silva (2008), QuantCrit is a way that criticalism is operationalized/engaged quantitatively. I say it is a way, one of many ways, in which this happens. Criticalism is not relegated to one liberatory theoretical framing, as there is not a single theoretical framework used in the pursuit of liberation. My engagement beyond the walls of traditional academic arenas led me to Robinson (2000), hooks (2015), Kelley (2002; 2018), Moten (2003), Harney and Moten (2013), Collins (2019), Crenshaw (1989), and Smith (2012) on Indigenous Research Methodologies, and Taylor (2017) on the Combahee River Collective. Most importantly in my development, it led me back to Du Bois, who I had read acritically in undergrad. QuantCRiT operates and is operationalized in the break, at a nexus of two seemingly epistemologically and ontologically opposed research traditions, (post) positivism and constructivism. I offer a discussion of Du Bois' quantification along with two examples, one from him and the other from me, of how criticalism has been operationalized quantitatively.

The art of social quantification

Du Bois, likely most known for his work *The Souls of Black Folks* published in 1903, has finally started receiving his flowers as a key founder of American sociology. His groundbreaking work explored the lives of Black Americans in Philadelphia and shaped how quantification is used to study, understand, and try to better the human condition (see Du Bois, 2014). Du Bois humanized the dehumanized, quantifiably, methodically, and methodologically. His use of demography, along with surveys that collected quantitative and qualitative data, helped shape the story of Black American life that embraced modernity. In working through the broad-reaching impacts of Du Bois' work, I began to see how his humanizing process of quantification, that which I seemed to take for granted, provided a foundation for critical quantitative inquiry. Du Bois' meticulous efforts to use data and a "scientific" process, a measured and repeatable process to collect and make sense of data, was used to humanize the lives of Black Americans. It amplified "the how" quantitative social science researchers should think about, and "the who" they are working with, and for what purposes quantitative social science researchers are doing the work. In his case, Du Bois was working with Black Americans to humanize them and their conditions and engage in truth-telling about the impacts of social and societal contexts, pushing back on the narratives purported by sociology based on assumptions or conjecture and not on rigorous methods and evidence.

Du Bois' work is also foundational to the work of CRT scholars. As such, I want to situate Du Bois and Du Bois' critical quantification. Specifically, I want to think about Du Bois' oft-referenced concept of double consciousness and, as Charles R. Lawrence, III (1991) posits, the duality of perspective while exploring the contributions of Du Bois to critical quantification. Du Bois' understanding of duality could be thought of as an understanding of the multidimensionality of perspective and purpose. The idea of double consciousness suggests that Black folks are gifted with perspective beyond perspective, multiple ways of seeing beyond that which is readily apparent, and multiple ways of understanding the why beyond that which is immediately described. This duality of perspective, argues Lawrence III (1991), is seen in a duality of empathy, story, and purpose. A duality of empathy provides room to critique but love, achieve, and not leave behind. That of the story to explain but also reimagine, to tell but also re-tell. And a duality of purpose allows for an understanding of doing that appeases but liberates, calms but empowers, subdues but uplifts. It is not lost on Du Bois that duality is an engagement with power, who has it, and what can be done to subvert it. Furthermore, the duality of perspective means an understanding of the need to be quantitatively and methodologically sound while also pursuing work that humanizes folks, particularly Black folks, and changing the narratives of dehumanization.

The duality of perspective is evident in the data visualizations produced by Du Bois' and his team of sociologists from the Atlanta school for the 1900 Paris World Fair. Seen in the carefully crafted volume edited by Battle-Baptiste and Rusert (2018), they note that "the cross-fertilization of visual art and social science here marks an important transitional moment in the history of the disciplines while offering alternative visions of how social scientific data might be made more accessible (p. 13). Du Bois' unique use of the visual arts to display statistical patterns found in the lives of Black Americans provides a foray into what is critical quantification. In addition to appeasing white Americans, the stories told through the ingeniously crafted colorful charts and graphs provide counter-narratives that offer a unique interpretation of numerical data that already existed in demography tables. Du Bois's work showcased the numerical data to tell a story, the Black American story, a different Black American story, instead of allowing the already-existing data to "speak for itself."

Numerical data does not speak for itself. Social science numerical data, that which has been quantified to represent aspects of the social conditions and human experiences of human beings, cannot and does not speak for itself. The context by which numerical data happens along with the assumptions about the collection, measurement, and analysis of numerical data shapes that which is understood about the numerical data. Du Bois' efforts to change how numerical data is understood, viewed, and absorbed, were arguably his way of speaking for the numerical data. Not about but for the numerical data, knowing that the numerical data represented human beings, the Black Americans assumed to be lesser than humans, for who he was speaking and telling their (counter)stories. In his work *The Philadelphia Negro: A Social Study*, originally published in 1899, Du Bois offers visual evidence (plate 59) of the relationship between the lived social conditions of Black Americans and their mortality rate (Du Bois, 2018). Interestingly, Du Bois, over 120 years ago, offered an example of that which foreshadows the direction of critical quantification today. On plate 14, Du Bois documents the literacy rates of Black Americans for each decade beginning in 1860, highlighting the growing trend in literacy (Du Bois, 2018). Importantly, he offers an example of critical quantitative speculation. The data presented for the 1900s includes a question mark, a mark of unknown (Du Bois, 2018). Du Bois, here, foreshadows the possibilities of Black Americans based on recognizable patterns in already measured numerical data.

A first foray into the break

A personal example of the operationalization of criticalism is a recent co-authored manuscript that explored education and special education degree production. Through the almost six-year development of this manuscript, I learned that sometimes your work is just not ready. The evolution of this project is evidence of my growth and continued evolution as a critical scholar. In 2015, my advisor suggested to a colleague studying special education that he should approach me to help him with an aspect of his research. The idea would be to understand which institutions were awarding education and special education degrees, with attention placed on to Black students. Simple enough, I said. The numerical data existed (IPEDS) and the project sounded interesting. In retrospect, I approached the project both a-theoretically and acritically. I thought the data was going to speak for itself. We were to show trends in the number and percentage distribution of education and special education degrees awarded by racialized categories, along with who "produced" the most degrees for each racialized group. And, well, that's what we did, even presenting the work at a conference the following year in 2016.

Fast forward to 2020 and, after multiple attempts, the manuscript had yet to find a home. I am about three years into this journey at the nexus of quantification and criticalism. I had not truly re-read the work that was produced in 2016 and I thought it best to do so with a different perspective, a different me. As a quantitative study, my work led the direction of the paper, and it was my a-theoretical and a-conceptual that limited the manuscript. I am of the orientation that any form of quantification that engages race, racialization, or racism must be approached critically. So, that's what we did. Outside of updating the analysis to include newer waves of IPEDS data, the data essentially did not change. What did change was the overall conceptualization of the study. We thought about the why of our purpose and how this work would be seen. We wrestled with the ideas of how this numerical data should be contextualized and how the systems that produced the numerical data were complicit in the disparities found within. We grounded the work through a QuantCRiT framework (Garcia et al., 2018) while also exploring facets of Ray's (2019) work on racialized organizations. The manuscript addressed outcomes specifically for each racialized group, looking at trends over 25 years of the number of degrees awarded for each racialized group, and statistically relating the number of degrees awarded for each group to institutional factors (e.g., Carnegie classification, enrollment by race). Most importantly, the conceptualization, implementation, and discussion of the study were centered on critical frameworks. Through the lenses of critical theorists, we spoke for the data, those humans represented by the data, instead of assuming the data would speak for itself.

The results of the study are important (see Cormier et al., 2021). The journey to the final draft of the manuscript is equally, if not more, important for me. This manuscript was the first, my first, foray into the application of and engagement with criticalism within the empirical realm of quantification. Borrowing the words of a student from a critical quantitative course, this work is hard. But hard is never an excuse when that which is at stake (liberation and freedom) is so grand.

Being in the unknown

The push and pull of quantification grounded in criticalism is an unknown. The quantification of social science data and the use of quantitative methods are subjective tasks. Thus, objective "truth" and objective "reality" are subjective and contextual. I have and continue to struggle with the reality of the messiness within quantification and, therefore, the reality of heterogeneity in outcomes. As in, there is a struggle to think about the multiple quantifiable and contextual truths. Lawrence III (1991), in critiquing universalism within the law, notes that "universal accounts are particularly pernicious when the assertion of universality is left unstated" (p. 2252). The harmful impacts of assumed universal truths have helped create anti-liberating systems and structures, many of which are supported by acritical quantification. Embracing subjectivity within quantification is an act of fugitivity and liberation and, in doing so, creates space for counter-narratives/stories that can humanize. Lawrence III (1991) offers that "when we use language to refer to ourselves, we do more than offer another possible description of the world around us; we define ourselves and our relationship to the world" (p. 2265). Furthermore, if we choose not to engage quantification critically, we continue the normative processes of universalism and exclusion.

A few years ago, I started to think about the space between the repetitions of what I had known to be quantification. I read and continue to read, and I continue to explore the space in the break, the space of possibilities in the break of quantification and criticalism. That break is burgeoning and unknown and unrehearsed, one that exists. It will exist, whether allowed to or not, when and where space and place are made for it, fugitively (Harney & Moten, 2013).

Fugitivity, planning, and study, Black study, are aspects of the Black radical tradition (Harney & Moten, 2013). Fugitivity, often considered in the escape from, can also be thought of as a journey towards. In this case, fugitivity is the refusal of and disengagement from what is the norm, specifically, the normative conventions of quantification, and a journey towards the unknown possibilities of quantification and criticalism. Planning, an act of collective engagement, is a process of fugitivity, one that is outside the normative bounds of the dominant order, one that is self-sufficient and "reproduces in its experiment not just what it needs, life, but what it wants, life in difference" (Harney & Moten, 2013). And study, deep study, Black study, ground the processes of planning and fugitivity in a critique of what is known or said or has been done such that the futures, the possibilities, are guided by a collective critique of the past. Scholars are engaging in acts of fugitivity. These same scholars are planning and studying the movement toward a future, a set of possibilities that do not currently exist. Scholars like Shanyce Campbell, Heather McCambly, and Sarah Peko-Spicer, organizers of the #Quant4What critical quantitative convening are finding space in the break, the space between the repetitions of the norms of quantification. They embody the call of La paperson (2017) and become cyborgs, extracting and repurposing institutional resources for fugitive acts and collective purposes.

The joy, the beauty, of liberating and collective work is that I am not alone, my journey is not the only one. Critical quantification is an act of fugitivity, one that requires a love of humanity, a deep study of criticalism and quantification, and a willingness to struggle with the complexities of the break (see Kelley, 2018). The break, the unknown possibilities at the nexus of quantification and criticalism, will exist, whether allowed to or not, when and where space and place are made for it, fugitively (Harney & Moten, 2013).

References

Battle-Baptiste, W., & Rusert, B. (Eds.). (2018). *WEB Du Bois's data portraits: Visualizing Black America*. Chronicle Books.

Collins, P. H. (2019). *Intersectionality as critical social theory*. Duke University Press.

Cormier, C. J., Houston, D. A., & Scott, L. A. (2021). When salt ain't enough: A critical quantitative analysis of special education and education degree production. *Teachers College Record, 123*(10), 3–30.

Crenshaw, K. W. (1989). Demarginalizing the intersection of race and sex: A Black feminist critique of antidiscrimination doctrine, feminist theory and antiracist politics. *University of Chicago Legal Forum, 1989*, 139.

Dixon-Román, E. J. (2017). *Inheriting possibility: Social reproduction and quantification in education*. University of Minnesota Press.

Du Bois, W. E. B. (2014). *The souls of black folk*. Dover Publications. (Original work published 1903)

Du Bois, W. E. B. (2018). *The Philadelphia Negro: A social study*. Oxford University Press (Original work published 1899).

Garcia, N. M., López, N., & Velez, V. N. (2018). QuantCrit: Rectifying quantitative methods through critical race theory. *Race Ethnicity and Education, 21*(2), 149–157.

Gillborn, D., Warmington, P., & Demack, S. (2018). QuantCrit: Education, policy, 'Big Data' and principles for a critical race theory of statistics. *Race Ethnicity and Education, 21*(2), 158–179.

Harney, S., & Moten, F. (2013). *The undercommons: Fugitive planning and black study*. Minor Compositions.

hooks, b. (2015). *Feminist theory: From margin to center*. Routledge.

Kelley, R. D. (2002). *Freedom dreams: The black radical imagination*. Beacon Press.

Kelley, R. D. (2018). Black study, black struggle. *Ufahamu: A Journal of African Studies, 40*(2), 153–168.

La paperson. (2017). *A third university is possible*. University of Minnesota Press.

Lawrence III, C. R. (1991). The word and the river: Pedagogy as scholarship as struggle. *Southern California Law Review, 65*, 2231.

Moten, F. (2003). *In the break: The aesthetics of the Black radical tradition*. University of Minnesota Press.

Ray, V. (2019). A theory of racialized organizations. *American Sociological Review, 84*(1), 26–53.

Robinson, C. J. (2000). *Black Marxism: The making of the black radical tradition*. UNC Press.

Smith. L. T. (2012). *Decolonizing methodologies: Research and Indigenous peoples 2nd Edition*. Zed Books.

Sólorzano, D. G., Villalpando, O., & Oseguera, L. (2005). Educational inequities and Latina/o undergraduate students in the United States: A critical race analysis of their educational progress. *Journal of Hispanic Higher Education, 4*(3), 272–294.

Taylor, K. Y. (Ed.). (2017). *How we get free: Black feminism and the Combahee River Collective*. Haymarket Books.

Zuberi, T. (2001). *Thicker than blood: How racial statistics lie*. Minneapolis, MN: University of Minnesota Press.

Zuberi, T., & Bonilla-Silva, E. (2008). *White logic, White methods: Racism and methodology*. Lanham, MD: Rowman & Littlefield Publishers.

9

UNDISCIPLINING SCHOOL DISCIPLINE RESEARCH

Refusing the racial paternalism to punishment pipeline

Mahasan Offutt-Chaney

In the 1968 poem, *Nikki Rosa*, poet and writer Nikki Giovanni shares her memories of growing up in a Black community, weaving observations of challenges with familial understanding, happy times, and birthdays. She writes, " I really hoped no white person ever has cause to write about me … they'll probably talk about my hard childhood and never understand that all the while I was quite happy" (Giovanni, 2009, p. 53). Here, she acknowledged that, yes, she was poor, though poverty wasn't the whole of her reality. The poem is more of a lament that Black children are too often confined to simplistic narratives of poverty and hardship. "Childhood remembrances," she begins "are always a drag if you're Black" (Giovanni, 2009, p. 53).

Research and teaching about racial inequality is riddled with the same lament. Like many scholars who study racial inequality in education, I have had to confront a central tension in my research and teaching; wanting to ensure Black children have the right to engaging, challenging, fun, and enriching educational experiences without relying on unending stories of Black failure as a means toward advancing educational opportunity. That is, by engaging with and speaking to existing research, we tend to rely on familiar education refrains about the persistent achievement gap, dropout rates, and learning loss in urban communities, narratives that not only pathologize students and families but ultimately provide the rationale for their punishment (Mervosh & Wu, 2022). Research and policies designed to treat the "at-risk," the school dropout, and to prevent crime, teenage pregnancy, or any number of outcomes deemed troubling, not only foreclose the possibility that children may

DOI: 10.4324/9781003303800-12

have happy and beautiful lives, despite their proximity to poverty. However, these narratives tend to locate the problems of education inequality and therefore structure reforms aimed at fixing the actions and behaviors of Black students (Dumas, 2016). Framing Black education through narratives of hardships and in presuming student wrongdoing or their *potential* for wrongdoing contributes to continuous surveillance and punishment. I want to offer fugitivity, refusals, and an embrace of the wayward as a means of escaping the dualistic reinforcement of paternalism and punishment—so that researchers might reimagine new ways to *write with and instead of against ourselves.*

In this chapter, I want to walk through three stories that demonstrate the anti-Black dualism between race-based pathology and punishment. I want to offer that fugitive research as a practice of subversion and refusals may provide education researchers with an alternative path of escaping the damage imagery that pervades education research and policy-making (Givens, 2021; Scott, 1997; Sojoyner, 2017; Tuck, 2009). When considering school discipline research, damage imagery defines children as pitiable and *potentially* criminal and always on the *brink* of being labeled as "bad and therefore punishable" (Ferguson, 2000). The first is a story of school discipline and the institutional practices and cultural assumptions that make Black children punishable and therefore subject to punishment. The second story reflects upon my time working to reform racially disproportionate discipline practices. It demonstrates how anti-Black depictions or damaged imagery persists through reform which purportedly tries to improve discipline.

The last story explores fugitivity as a method to "read against," existing research, archival absences, and disciplinary norms, that again name Black youth as either *potentially a problem*, or a problem in need of correction. Saidiya Hartman's (2019) fugitive history of the wayward, reveals, "the paradox of cramped creation, the entanglement of escape and confinement, flight and captivity" (Hartman, 2019, p. 227). In the tradition of decolonial scholar Sylvia Wynter, fugitivity as research praxis "demands a delinking of oneself from the knowledge systems we take for granted (and can profit from) and practicing epistemic disobedience" (Mignolo, 2015, p. 107; Wynter, 2003). In doing so, scholars might produce research that offers more complex representations of youth—that free youth and ourselves from "the cramped creation" as always on the brink of "troublemaking" (Mignolo, 2015, p. 6). Fugitivity calls attention to the structures that youth and educators subvert (Givens, 2021). While leaving space to consider the possibility—of Black youth's beautiful lives and to consider the possibility that "all the while we were quite happy" (Giovanni, 2009, p. 53).

A story of school punishment: How anti-Blackness makes troublemakers

Anne Ferguson's (2000) now classic study of school punishment, *Bad Boys: The Making of Black Masculinity* opens with a quote from an African American staff member, who, pointing at a ten-year-old, a student the school has deemed a "troublemaker," asserts that the child had "a jail-cell with his name on it" (Ferguson, 2000, p. 1). Ferguson's (2000) work has become a foundational text in the social reproduction function of school punishment. Ferguson (2000) theorizes, "Just as children were tracked into futures as doctors, scientists, engineers, word processors, and as fast-food workers, there were also tracks for some children predominantly male that led to prison" (p. 2). By theorizing race and masculinity, Ferguson (2000) details how practices of school punishment socialized Black boys into "trouble-makers". Ferguson's research story follows twenty boys through hallways, classrooms, neighborhoods, and exclusionary spaces like the "punishing room" and "jailhouse" at Rosa Parks, an intermediary school. The "pun-ishing room" or the Student Specialists' Office is the "first tier of the disci-plinary apparatus" (Ferguson, 2000, p. 26). Ferguson (2000) writes that it is the place where stories are told, truth is determined, and judgment is passed" (p. 34). The "jailhouse", a hidden room on campus, is where detention is held, and where students serve in-house suspension (Ferguson, 2000, p. 26). As I discuss herein, I have personal experience working in one of these "punishment rooms'" or school "jailhouses" through a program seeking to restore school discipline practices. But first, I want to focus on Ferguson's (2000) writing on her own story; how she came to question her initial way of distinguishing the "bad boys" from other students, and in doing so, she came to understand the ways schools created the "troublemakers", the students with their name written on jail cells (p. 1).

Ferguson (2000) writes that, at the outset of her study, she was deter-mined to learn about the differences between what the school identified as schoolboys who do well in school, and others who were deemed trouble-makers (i.e., children who got into trouble, had been suspended, and received class referrals). Upon reflecting on her initial findings, she decided to approach the project very differently: Ferguson (2000) turned her focus away from the Black "schoolboys" and "troublemakers", and instead began to look into the ways race and gender operate in the schools that help create these categories in the first place. Ferguson (2000) writes that she "grad-ually realized that to see Schoolboys and Troublemakers as fundamentally different was to make a grave mistake. As African American males, schoolboys were always on the *brink* of being redefined into the trouble-maker category by the school." (p. 10). Ferguson (2000) teases out the ways punishment operates and is revealed by institutional practices that perpetuate beliefs about all low-income Black children as already or yet to become troublemakers. That is, schools and adult staff made assumptions about Black masculinity—assumptions that were ensnared with racist beliefs about the children's propensity to delinquency and criminality as "at-risk", "troublemakers", and "unsalvageable" (Ferguson, 2000). Schools produced social identities and therefore *made* troublemakers. Once labeled, children were at risk of becoming more visible within the classroom, and more likely to be singled out and punished (Ferguson, 2000, p. 92). Ferguson's (2000) study demonstrates how dualistic framings of children as either "schoolboys" or "troublemakers" ultimately reinforce the idea that all Black children are punishable.

My own story of participating in discipline reform demonstrates that while schools respond to race-based discipline disproportionality with reforms like restorative justice and positive behavior interventions and supports, they often still engage in labeling practices, leaving them unproblematized. These approaches don't address Ferguson's (2000) central finding that institutional practices, racist assumptions, and labeling practices name children as a problem and represent them as endangered, "at risk", or criminal. Reforms still name and sort children.

A story of reform: And the persistence of paternalistic damage imagery

Since first encountering Ferguson's (2000) *Bad Boys* as an undergraduate student, I have found myself returning to Ferguson's observations that school practices are ensnared with racist beliefs about children's propensity to criminality. As I moved in and out of various roles, from student to practitioner to researcher, I have grown increasingly interested in how assumptions of Black students as damaged, "at risk," or "uneducable" are used to not only rationalize punishment practices, but these same beliefs inform both research and reforms attempting to redress them. Even reforms that aim to be in service of Black youth produce policies that further discipline and punish Black children—they are marked by "belatedness and insufficiency" (Best & Hartman, 2005, p. 2). In this section, I demonstrate this point through my experience as a restorative justice coordinator seeking to shift discipline practices at the high school that I also attended as a young person.

For two years, I served as a restorative justice coordinator at my alma mater Berkeley High School. Not unlike the school in Ferguson's study, Berkeley High has been infamous for its stark racial disparities between white and Black students (Noguera, 2003). Amongst them, Black students at Berkeley High were over-represented along various indicators of school discipline, particularly on campus suspension and school suspensions. The program I coordinated, Youth Court, was meant to intervene in the school disciplinary process by offering an alternative to school suspension. In lieu of suspension, students would receive alternative consequences which might include some combination of tutoring, counseling, community service, letters of apology, anger management, and a "jury duty" on a future disciplinary trial.

This process depended on students taking responsibility for their actions so they could "restore the harm" caused by their transgressions. By my second year coordinating the program, it became apparent that far from intervening in what critics refer to as a "school to prison pipeline", the restorative justice program that I coordinated, our "youth court," reproduced carceral practices in the school. The structure of our restorative justice program reminded me of Ferguson's (2000) description of the punishing room:

> The Punishing Room is the first tier of the disciplinary apparatus of the school. Like the courtroom, it is the place where stories are told, truth is determined, and judgment is passed (p. 55).

Modeled after a court system, our restorative justice program required that students who transgressed school rules play defendant to avoid suspension. Students who got into trouble would plead their case to a peer advocate, together they would assign consequences and later in the week they would appear before a judge, or a jury of their peers and receive consequences. While the program may have intervened in-school suspensions, restorative justice did not disrupt the school practices identified in Ferguson's (2000) text which made Black children punishable. While restorative justice could repair individual moments of "harm," those caused by cheating, fighting, or hallway pranks, to name a few of the incidents that came across my desk, the program left untouched the practices that made Black students more likely to be punished in the first place. There was no such program that could restore the harm caused by the anti-Black punishment practices that led to Black children being over-represented in both suspension and our restorative justice program.

The phenomenon identified by Ferguson (2000)—that schools make bad boys—seeps into the reforms that attempt to mitigate the harms of that making. Both punishment and reforms like the program I coordinated rely on assumptions of Black wrongdoing. Our Restorative justice program, like the broader punitive practices it might redress, relied on a discourse of individual behavior and personal choice— liberal logic that left untouched the institutional culture, practices, and racist beliefs that made "troublemakers". For instance, one of my students told me that he had been suspended every year since kindergarten! His experience aligned with the broader literature on race-based discrepancies in school discipline practices. Not only are Black students more likely to be referred to the office for offenses that were more subjective and less serious (Skiba et al., 2002). But racial stereotypes also impact how teachers interpret "wrong doing" as a pattern across time (Okonofua & Eberhardt, 2015).

Even programs like restorative justice that served to correct the problems identified by Ferguson (2000) had so greatly missed the mark. "Bad boys" were given an alternative to suspension, but they were still seen as the sole source of the punishment problem. Our program left teachers and staff's ideas and practices unchallenged, which makes routine punishment plausible. These arguably beneficial programs, as Michael Dumas (2016) argues, undermine fundamental change in practices like school punishment, by locating problems to Black boys rather than the social and economic order (Dumas, 2016, p. 97). Students may not have been suspended, but instead, Black children may have just been disproportionately funneled into restorative justice programs, disproportionately taking responsibility for "restoring" their actions and the problems of discipline within the school.

School discipline reforms may rely on—instead of challenge—what Daryl Scott (1997) calls racial damage imagery. Scott (1997) argues that racial damage imagery, which depicts Black personalities as psychologically damaged, has threaded through liberal and conservative social science thought. On the one hand, conservatives use claims of Black pathology, sexuality, and violence to rationalize segregation, justify exclusionary policies, and justify cuts to social programs. On the other, liberals evoke racial damage imagery, often to evoke white sympathy toward Blacks and justify policies of inclusion and rehabilitation. Beliefs about black children as criminal or *potentially* criminal similarly fit within this damaged imagery frame. Not only have notions about racial violence propelled the development of the carceral state (Hinton, 2016; Murakawa, 2014), but policymakers similarly rely on these ideas to justify the expansion of punitive practices including zero tolerance policies, or deploy them to help justify discipline reforms. The effect, Scott (1997) argues, is that liberal damage imagery makes Black rights contingent on white sympathy. Black children are framed "as damaged objects of pity," rather than citizens "whose rights had been violated" (Scott, 1997). This tendency, as Eve Tuck (2009) argues, is based on a faulty theory of change, and "establishes harm or injury in order to achieve reparation" (Tuck, 2009, p. 413). The theory of change in programs like restorative justice is that school suspension policies harm Black children—and leave them subject to more punitive exposure to incarceration. Yet research on school discipline reforms confirms the experience I had coordinating restorative justice programs, that is, even reforms put in place to eliminate detentions and limit school suspension may still reenact the logics of Black punishment and disposability (Shange, 2019). These reforms tend to mask the gendered and anti-Black stereotypes that persist through new discipline programs (Smith-Purviance, 2021).

Damage imagery demonstrates how anti-Blackness is reproduced through *punitive* practices of school discipline and *paternalistic* strategies of school discipline reform. At play is a dualism that maps children as both pitiable and punishable- as "at risk" and endangered or "criminal." Programs like restorative justice that target the "at risk," those on the *brink* of becoming, or those who have already been labeled "bad," may replace the problems of suspension, but it may leave unchanged the broader institutional patterns and practices that individualized wrongdoing. That is bad boys, and not the schools, were responsible for restoring harm. Restorative justice, as redress, is insufficient and "seems always to arrive too late" (Best & Hartman, 2005, p. 4). *Fugitivity as refusal.* Because of this, I left this job.

A fugitive story of the wayward and undisciplining research on youth

Histories and theories of anti-Blackness refusal and fugitivity provide the language to think across the brink—that is to trouble—Black troublemaking. They do this in part by framing paternalism and punishment as part and parcel of the same racial project, while also refusing methods that would have us categorize these treatments as different. Saunders, as quoted in Sharpe (2016) posits,

> Producing legible work in the academy often means that Black academics must adhere to research methods that are drafted into the service of a larger destructive force … we must become undisciplined" (Sharpe, 2016, p. 13).

For historians, undisciplining has meant attending to archival absences and using narrative to make more whole those relegated to silence in the historical record (Trouillot, 1995). For ethnographers like Anne Ferguson, fugitive methods took form as she theorized institutions instead of theorizing youth behavior. As Tuck and Yang argue (2014) prominent forms of refusal in designing studies "resist the urge to study people (and their "social problems") and to study instead institutions and power" (p. 815). By embracing fugitivity as a method, as a theoretical framework, and in a narrative, educational researchers can challenge the discourse of reports, research, and reveal the fuller lives of youth typically forced into anti-Black representations that dominate education policy and education research.

In *Wayward Lives, Beautiful Experiments*, Saidiya Hartman (2019) draws on her method of critical fabulation to write what she sees as a "fugitive text" of 20th-century wayward Black women—demonstrating research refusals, the limit of reform, and the recreation of new vocabularies. Hartman's critical fabulation extrapolates stories from archives in order to recreate narratives of the historical figures typically excluded from or pushed to the background of the historical record (Hartman, 1997). Hartman demonstrates how the archival record—made up of surveys, monographs of sociologists, trial transcripts, the accounts of social workers, and parole officers, interviews with psychiatrists and psychologists, and prison case files—reduce 20th black women to pathological descriptions of black women as always "potentially" deviant and criminal, in short—as a problem. These records limit *who we can know* as historical actors (are Black girls' records kept in the archive?) and *how we might know* them (through the paternalistic gaze of researchers, social workers, and the state). Hartman's (2019) fugitive text recreates the radical imagination of Black women in 20th-century cities like New York City and Philadelphia (p. 7), and in doing so, enables new possibilities and new vocabularies than what might otherwise be possible.

Hartman's (2019) depiction of Mattie Jackson, a fifteen-year-old newly arrived in the docks of New York City from Hampton Virginia is an instructive example of the ways fugitivity as a counter-narrative untangles the intertwined descriptions of wayward women as potentially delinquent and therefore criminalizable. At the beginning of the chapter, Mattie has just arrived in New York City: "New York was her first adventure" (Hartman, 2019, p. 17). By the end of the chapter, readers encounter the words Mattie wrote to her mother from behind the walls of the New York State Reformatory for Women. Mattie's traverses from New York migrant, "her head was full of dreams", to being imprisoned in a reformatory (Hartman, 2019, p. 4). Black life on the *brink*—a space created by social scientists, and reformers, and reinforced through the state and police. Laws like New York's Wayward Minor's Act criminalized sexual delinquency and subjected girls to probation or reformatory institutions to protect them from "future criminality" (Hartman, 2019, pp. 14–15). Others like New York State's Tenement House Act (1901) did little to improve the housing of the Black poor. Its benefits and protection were overshadowed "by the abuse and harassment that accompanied the police presence inside private homes," and consolidated Blackness and criminality, by placing Black domestic life under surveillance (Hartman, 2019, p. x). Mattie and the other cast of girls and women featured in Hartman's (2019) account straddle "the fault lines of immorality" and this proximity marks them as pitiable and potentially salvageable (Hartman, 2019, p. x). Paternalistic policies like New York State's Wayward Girls Acts rationalized sentencing a first offender to a three-year sentence. Punishment here is weaponized and indeed rationalized as a means to protect what's left of Mattie's morality and as a preventative measure for her becoming more like her mother. This scene reveals how girls like Mattie straddle "the fault lines"' between paternalized and pitied to punished.

Mattie's story, and Hartman's (2019) telling of it is an instructive tool in the ways it reveals the messiness of a fugitive approach to research and writing. Fugitivity as a counter-narrative allows for wholeness, and complexity that social scientists want to clean up through pre-defined and enduring categories. Throughout the chapter, we follow Mattie through scenes that because of their messiness and complexity, are at times difficult to read. Mattie worked as a domestic because factories, shops, or offices "would not hire colored girls." She visited parties with her older lover and lived out of wedlock with others—just as her mother had done. She openly disregarded the property of others—an offense that though being her first (or perhaps more accurately, her last given her previously perceived moral failings) helped rationalize her incarceration. Hartman (2019) writes away from paternalism, or deficit, and instead attends to "beautiful experiments" of women deemed wayward. Hartman (2019) tells her story by imagining how Mattie may have described herself on her terms thereby freeing her from the paternalistic judgment of the archival records that would otherwise be left to speak for her.

Toward new stories of refusals

Childhood remembrances, researching, and teaching of black education may not always have "to be a drag" (Giovanni, 1970, p. 29). For educators and researchers interested in confronting anti-Blackness and punishment in education, fugitivity provides a portal into exploring the wholeness of Black life, it allows for complex personhood (Gordon, 2008). We can refuse subjecting children and their families to either side of a punitive brink, as those subjected to categories of despised or pitied. Instead, fugitivity provides a lens to see how Black students are confined by the logics that thread through school practices, research, and policies and reveals the "constant straining against said confinement" (Givens, 2021).

In this chapter, I have walked through various stories of research, reform, and historical refusals as a way to counter dominant stories of failure or Black potential. Fugitive accounts provide a counter-narrative to imagine beyond the limits of the archival sources or other dominant research frames that might otherwise determine how Black children are defined and understood. In his account of the Black education heritage and tradition of Black education, Jarvis Givens (2021) refers to fugitive pedagogy "as the plot at the heart of the matter—the story and the scheme" (p. 16). A fugitive theory tells a fuller story by considering Wayward/troublemaker define themselves outside of the problematics of pitiable/punishable. Ferguson (2000) for instance considers how troublemakers' "subverse," and offers a "reverse discourse" and a *counter-narrative* to the school project (pp. 4–5). The students she follows "disidentify" and engage in "not learning" as a *desirable* alternative to the school's characterization of them as criminal or endangered (Ferguson, 2000). They exercise and define their life on the brink through an alternative dualism of *desire and refusal.* Hartman, considers the radical imagination of "ordinary colored girls" (Hartman, 2019, p. xiv).

> *Mattie's "desires mattered to no one but herself. If she didn't decide how she wanted to live, then the world would dictate, and it would always consign her to the bottom. Refusing this, Mattie carried on as if she were free, and in the eyes of the world that was no different from acting wild* (Hartman, 2019, p. 68).

Through fugitivity we attend to the radical imagination and wayward practices of youth, thereby describing the world through the eyes of young people instead of from the perspective of researchers or reformers who label the imaginings punishable. Joining with Black youth's practices of refusal may allow researchers to consider how youth strain against the confines of research description, educators' beliefs, and police enforcement.

Theories of anti-Blackness and fugitivity are instructive for policymakers, reformers, and researchers of education policy. Fugitivity asks to be attentive to the continuities and the persistence of punishment—to refuse rather than accept or even assume linear notions of progress (Dumas & Ross, 2016). Ferguson's (2000) telling of the good boys vs the troublemakers; Scott's (1997) description of the pitied and those held in contempt; Hartman's (2019) history of the wayward, all signify how labeling practices and racist dualities continued through and constitute various "scenes" of subjection (Hartman, 1997). What fugitivity does is shift how we ask questions about those on the brink—or perhaps more accurately those *brinked* by school rules, and liberal reforms aimed at reforming the "at risk." The stories of fugitivity and the lessons we might glean from them encourage us to shift the direction of our research. As we imagine new ways to address school discipline, or even opportunity policies in education more broadly, we must refuse "repackaged analytical and practical paradigms labeled as solutions" (Sojoyner, 2017, p. 533).

Lastly, attending to fugitive theory also allows Black researchers to take a generative stance toward refusing the violent discourses and racialized paternalism that persists through studies, reports, and research on Black youth (Tuck & Yang, 2014). A fugitive text is instructive in illustrating how in writing of wholeness and complexity, scholars of race and punishment may free ourselves from rigid confines that might force us into reproducing harmful categories we are attempting to reveal, undermine, and flee from. More specifically, this research offers insights into how Black scholars of education, Black students of Black educational "failure," might reveal and counter pathological narratives that are still dominant within liberal approaches to education and reform. Approaching a fugitive praxis in education research, means embracing wholeness, supplanting outcomes with "desire," and freeing ourselves from the confines of writing against ourselves. Fugitivity requires that we counter our own fields and our own training—that we fill in "archival absences" by seeking out and offering counternarratives to those preserved in existing bodies of research and knowing. It means that sometimes we leave space for "agentic absence," some students may not want to be studied, followed, or found (Shange, 2019, p. 120). In the absence we might make space for asking new questions that consider for instance all the ways black children may be "quite happy" (Giovanni, 2009, p. 53). Doing so may allow us to see ourselves alongside our students—in all the ways they may be beautifully wayward—as part of a longer, and broader subversive tradition (Givens, 2021).

References

Best, S., & Hartman, S. (2005). Fugitive justice. *Representations*, *92*(1), 1–15.
Dumas, M. J. (2016). Neoliberal education reform and the foreclosure of brown futures. *Urban Education*, *51*(7), 765–791.
Dumas, M. J., & Ross, K. M. (2016). Black lives matter in public schools: Interrogating the root causes of state violence. *Theory into Practice*, *55*(1), 13–20.
Ferguson, A. A. (2000). *Bad boys: Public schools in the making of black masculinity (Law, Meaning, and Violence)*. University of Michigan Press.
Giovanni, N. (1970). *Black Feeling, Black Talk/Black Judgement*. 1968. Reprint, New York: Morrow Quill Paperback.
Giovanni, Nikki (2009). *The collected poetry of Nikki Giovanni: 1968–1998*. Harper Collins, 2009.
Givens, J. R. (2021). *Fugitive pedagogy: Carter G. Woodson and the art of black teaching*. Harvard University Press.
Gordon, E. T. (2008). "Why we must ask of love what we really want": Learning to hear Black girl fugitivity. *Educational Foundations*, *22*(1–2), 35–56.
Hartman, S. (1997). *Scenes of subjection: Terror, slavery, and self-making in nineteenth-century America*. Oxford University Press.
Hartman, S. (2019). *Wayward lives, beautiful experiments: Intimate histories of riotous black girls, troublesome women, and queer radicals*. W. W. Norton & Company.
Hinton, E. (2016). *From the war on poverty to the war on crime. The making of mass incarceration in America*. Harvard University Press.

Mervosh, S., & Wu, J. (2022, January 28). *Learning loss in America: Disparities grow as schools race to reopen.* The New York Times. https://www.nytimes.com/2022/01/28/us/learning-loss-reopening-schools.html

Mignolo, W. (2015). Chapter 4. Sylvia Wynter: What does it mean to be human? In K. McKittrick (Ed.), *Sylvia Wynter: On being human as praxis* (pp. 106–123). Duke University Press. 10.1515/9780822375852-005

Murakawa, N. (2014). *The first civil right: How liberals built prison America.* Oxford University Press.

Noguera, P. (2003). *City schools and the American dream: Reclaiming the promise of public education.* Teachers College Press.

Okonofua, J. A., & Eberhardt, J. L. (2015). Two strikes: Race and the disciplining of young students. *Psychological Science, 26*(5), 617–624.

Scott, D. M. (1997). *Contempt and pity: Social policy and the image of the damaged Black Psyche, 1880-1996.* The University of North Carolina Press.

Skiba, R. J., Michael, R. S., Nardo, A. C., & Peterson, R. L. (2002). The color of discipline: Sources of racial and gender disproportionality in school punishment. *The Urban Review, 34*(4), 317–342.

Shange, S. (2019). *Progressive dystopia: Abolition, anti-blackness + schooling in San Francisco.* Duke University Press.

Sharpe, C. (2016). *In the wake: On blackness and being.* Duke University Press.

Smith-Purviance, S. (2021). The politics of black women's grief. *Feminist Studies, 47*(1), 175–200.

Sojoyner, D. M. (2017). Another life is possible: Black fugitivity and enclosed places. *Cultural Anthropology, 32*(4), 514–536.

Trouillot, M.-R. (1995). *Silencing the past: Power and the production of history.* Beacon Press.

Tuck, E. (2009). Suspending damage: A letter to communities. *Harvard Educational Review, 79*(3), 409–428.

Tuck, E., & Yang, K. W. (2014). Unbecoming claims: Pedagogies of refusal in qualitative research. *Qualitative Inquiry, 20*(6), 811–818.

Wynter, S. (2003). Unsettling the coloniality of being/power/truth/freedom: Towards the human, after man, its overrepresentation—An argument. *CR: The New Centennial Review, 3*(3), 257–337.

10
ENGAGING WITH RACE AND RACISM IN RESEARCH

Developing a racial analysis

Dina G. Okamoto

Given the renewed attention to racial inequality, scholars are thinking about ways to more deeply engage with race and racism in their own research. Despite the fact that race is a social construct with no biological basis, it remains one of the most powerful and persistent group boundaries in American life today. It can produce significant material and social impacts, and create stark disadvantages over generations. Yet race and racial boundaries can also generate communities with shared experiences and identities, which has implications for people's social experiences, perceptions, and behaviors.

What does it mean to develop a racial analysis? By definition, a racial analysis has race and racism as its central objects of examination. Race and racism can be investigated and analyzed in myriad ways, and one approach is to investigate how they are embedded within policies and practices. Scholars of economic inequality and education, for example, have focused on discriminatory governmental policies that have contributed to racial segregation, which in turn has shaped racial differences in homeownership, wealth, and access to differently-resourced schools (Krysan & Crowder, 2017; Massey & Denton, 1993; Oliver & Shapiro, 2013). Race can also be understood and studied as a schema or ideology that infuses interactions within institutions, which can maintain, exacerbate, or reproduce inequalities. Scholars who study workplaces, schools, and the criminal justice system, for example, have documented the ways in which racial schemas shape hiring and promotion decisions, as well as perceptions of who is valued and deserving, and who is considered delinquent or criminal (Lewis & Diamond, 2015; Miller & Stuart, 2017; Okonofua & Eberhardt, 2015;

DOI: 10.4324/9781003303800-13

Pager, 2003). Additionally, race can be examined as an expressive identity and a central part of one's social experience. Scholars have found that a strong and positive racial identity can be protective for minority youth and raise self-esteem (Rivas-Drake et al., 2014). Such research agendas put race at the center.

Scholars who do not primarily engage with race and racism in their research need not entirely shift their research agendas, but should seriously consider how to engage with race in their work moving forward and to learn from and collaborate with scholars who have such expertise. To engage with race more fully in our own research, we first need to reflect upon how we conceptualize, address, and locate race as a social construct, process, or category within that research.

Using race as an organizing tool or control variable

For many researchers, race is not the central object of analysis. Instead, race is an organizing tool, and a social construct and category used as shorthand to describe groups and populations. It is a useful way to enumerate individuals and groups and to describe variation in our samples. For example, scholars may analyze interview data and describe the racial composition of the study context, whether it be a neighborhood, school, or county, as well as its interviewees. Researchers often analyze large samples of survey data and use race to measure disparities in poverty, incarceration, and dropout rates. In general, race is a useful and important classification tool to describe and potentially interrogate differences.

Analytically, scholars who use quantitative methods often use race as a variable to be controlled in statistical models. We do this because race and racial differences may be related to a particular outcome we are interested in explaining, such as well-being, college completion, or civic engagement. If we hold race constant in our models, we can understand how other key variables work to produce an outcome.

What sometimes gets lost is the fact that racial differences exist at the baseline. We often do not stop to think about how race may be an important driving force for these differences. Considering race as a central driver or fundamental social force can lead us to a racial analysis—an analysis that centers on race and uses racial explanations to understand differences in group outcomes and experiences.

No matter how we use race in our research—as an organizing tool, as a way to describe our samples or variations in outcomes, or as a control variable—we need to be mindful of the implications. Racial categories are not natural or fixed entities. They are socially constructed and can be quite limiting because they often mask diversity and heterogeneity within such categories, which can lead to erroneous understandings of social processes and outcomes. Thus, we need to think about the samples we collect (who is included and who is not), how we use racial categories to generalize about populations, and what it means to see variation in outcomes by race.

Shifting toward a racial analysis

My own experience of shifting toward a racial analysis in my research developed in graduate school. I came to graduate school to do research in the areas of gender and small group processes. I had excellent training in social psychology, which was focused on group dynamics such as cooperation and trust, and individual processes related to social identity, self-concept, and social perceptions. The mainstream approaches in the field were focused on social psychological processes that were generalizable across populations, not concepts and theories related to specific groups characterized by gender, race, or class. Much of the research that I was exposed to was based on experiments conducted in lab settings, where conditions could be manipulated to test and advance general theories about status, cooperation, and identity. However, race and ethnicity were nowhere to be found in these studies or the central readings in social psychology.

I took a graduate course on race, which introduced me to Omi and Winant's (2014) *Racial Formation*. It pushed me to think beyond paradigms of ethnicity and class and to think about what it means for race to be a fundamental process and axis of stratification. I was inspired by scholars such as W. E. B. DuBois whose groundbreaking work on the Black community in Philadelphia has informed my scholarship on how space and stratification work. Race and ethnicity scholars such as Herbert Blumer, Eduardo Bonilla-Silva, Elaine Kim, Stephen Cornell, Mary Waters, and Larry Bobo moved me to think beyond the individual and to examine the structures and processes through which racial inequality is reproduced. These scholars highlighted the fundamental nature of the racial hierarchy in the United States, and how it remains durable and operates to reproduce inequalities despite the progressive shift in racial attitudes. They also emphasized that racism is alive and well, but simply in different forms. I learned about colonialism and white supremacy—about the ways in which power, politics, and consciousness intertwine from thinkers and scholars such as Franz Fanon, Malcolm X, Stokely Carmichael, and Robert Blauner. I wondered how this work interfaced, if at all, with my training in social psychology.

After years of conducting research on gender and small group processes, I began to gravitate toward theories and ideas related to race and ethnicity.

Studies of race at the time focused on documenting experiences and patterns of racial inequality, and generating new concepts, frameworks, and explanations (see Bonilla-Silva, 1997; Feagin, 1991; Williams et al., 1997). These studies also primarily focused on the Black-white divide. I wanted to think about Asian Americans, a group that few people studied at the time. And rather than focus on disparities, I wanted to study agency and social change.

I became interested in broader questions about collective identity and the data collection strategies of social movements scholars. The collective action problem that I studied in social psychology—the age-old problem of how to explain collective action given that the risks can be high, interests can be cross-cutting, and people can simply free-ride on others' efforts—was on my mind. So I began to gather data on Asian American protests and organizations across the United States and over time, to gain insights into how Asians and Asian Americans created new narratives and organized themselves through the decades, along ethnic and pan-ethnic lines. I eventually developed a project on race and collective action, and those general social psychological concepts and processes provided the foundation for my research.

Unpacking racial categories

Racial categories are not inherent or natural, even though they can sometimes take on a life of their own. I came to understand the importance of unpacking racial categories as I began to develop my research on Asian Americans. Scholars have documented and analyzed the process of racialization as it applied to Asian Americans (see Kim, 1999), and how the racial category of Asian can flatten differences and reproduce racial stereotypes such as the "model minority" (Kim, 1999, p. 107). I wanted to move beyond a focus on how Asians are racially classified to interrogate the Asian American category itself.

In my book, *Redefining Race*, I examine the emergence and construction of the Asian American category and identity. Before 1968, there was no "Asian American" category or consciousness that linked Asians from different national origins. In fact, immigrants in the United States from China, Japan, Korea, India, the Philippines, and other parts of Asia did not readily form alliances or cooperate, nor did they see themselves as part of the same racial category (Okamoto, 2014). Instead, they built separate ethnic communities, depended on their own systems of social and economic support, and at times, intentionally distinguished themselves from one another. The category and identity of "Asian American" emerged in the late 1960s, well before the US Census Bureau and other federal agencies adopted it as an official racial category in 1980. Asian activists built a political movement based on the shared experiences and struggles of all Asian ethnic groups in the United States, and developing the new pan-ethnic label and identity was a key part of that movement (Okamoto, 2014). Alongside their national origin, linguistic, cultural, and religious differences, they constructed a narrative about the shared racialized histories of Asian ethnic groups—as cheap laborers and unassimilable foreigners without access to US citizenship, land ownership, civil rights, and at times, even entry into the United States (Okamoto, 2014).

This new pan-ethnic label used to organize for equal rights and build coalitions for social change was in many ways quite fragile. Organizing as "Asian Americans" was not a natural process because of the cross-cutting differences and histories of conflict among the different Asian ethnic groups; it was a social achievement. In my work, I detailed the histories and social processes that led to such an achievement (Okamoto, 2003; 2014), as well as the early and contemporary narratives of Asian Americans—in their own public writings and commentary. The early narratives, which took place in the decade of the 1970s, addressed how Asian Americans struggled to find their place in American society, and how they viewed their own communities, especially in relation to established racial minorities such as Black and Native/Indigenous Americans (Mora & Okamoto 2020a, 2020b). I also studied how contemporary activists and leaders navigated the use of the term "Asian American" to advocate for the broader community, as it could detract from the significant disparities within and between various groups comprising Asian Americans.

Instead of taking racial categories for granted or considering them natural, my work looks beneath the surface to understand the structures and processes that encouraged Asian Americans to develop and utilize this pan-ethnic label to protest anti-Asian racism and other forms of inequality. In this case, race and racial categories became my objects of analysis.

Developing a racial analysis

So how do we move toward a racial analysis in our own research? We need to dig deeper into racial constructs and think about what the implications are when and how we use those constructs. We need to further unpack the racial categories of Black, White, Asian, Latinx, and Native/Indigenous to understand the populations that comprise them. Using racial categories without scrutiny can mask the socially constructed nature of race and reify race as natural and biological. It can also gloss over the heterogeneity within such categories, producing inaccurate representations and understandings of a population. These inaccurate understandings, in turn, can lead to misinformation among policymakers, institutional stakeholders, and the larger public. At the same time, we need to recognize that racial categories remain durable because of the shared histories and contemporary experiences of race, and that for some individuals and groups, these categories have meaning, contribute to identities, and shape behaviors.

As scholars, we need to **develop a racial analysis or explanation for the patterns and disparities that we see.** If we find stark racial disparities in rates of incarceration, educational attainment, or civic engagement, for example, we may look toward the ways in which racial inequalities are embedded within institutions and systems. We cannot understand these thorny contemporary issues without comprehending the broader history of racialization in the United States, and its ties to the history of citizenship, exclusion, and institutional discrimination. Racism is not simply comprised of overt acts and implicit bias in everyday interactions, but is often built into institutions, policies, and the structures of our society. Race and racial hierarchies also shape informal norms and practices regarding who is deserving (and who is not), which can in turn influence policy outcomes. It even follows that race-neutral policies and practices can have implications for racial inequality and operate in non-neutral ways. As an example, historical tax (Brown, 1998; 2018; 2022) and land use laws (Rothwell & Massey, 2009; Trounstine, 2020), as well as contemporary felony disenfranchisement and drug sentencing laws (Manza & Uggen, 2008) are all race-neutral in that they do not explicitly mention race, but they do have racially disparate impacts. These laws have systematically disadvantaged racial minorities and advantaged Whites in terms of wealth accumulation, employment, housing, and voting rights. In the arena of education, school organizational rules related to school discipline, track placements, and parental interventions are ostensibly race-neutral, but in practice, they lead to racial differences (Lewis & Diamond, 2015; Morris, 2005). All of these social facts often go unrecognized because of the lack of racial analysis in research.

Where do we go from here?

Here are some questions we can ask ourselves as we develop our research. I initially posed these questions for others, but below I attempt to answer them as well, as a way to start a discussion about how we can move toward a racial analysis in our work.

What are the larger implications of using established racial categories in a study?

Researchers use established racial categories on a regular basis to describe populations and samples, and to discuss the experiences of different groups. Racial categories are important because they are recognizable and a collective public understands, more or less, which groups we are talking about when we say "Black" or "Latinx." But that said, using established racial categories can potentially prime racial stereotypes and race-based belief systems, and even more dangerously, reinforce the idea that race is biologically determined (see Morning, 2011). Without recognizing these potential implications, researchers can contribute to reproducing inequalities and power structures.

I use and refer to established racial categories in my work. When I discuss Asian Americans, for example, I emphasize that not all people who are categorized as Asian share the same ethnic background, social status, language of origin, economic position, citizenship status, political ideology, or everyday experience. All people who are categorized as Asian may not even identify as Asian American. But I continue to use racial categories in my research because they are meaningful; they shape the way that individuals and groups are treated, and how individuals may come to see themselves. My work on Asian Americans demonstrates how race shaped the lives of Asian Americans, and how activists and community members were able to organize as a pan-ethnic group and create a platform for social change efforts. Some argue that using a racial category as the basis for a social movement is problematic, but activists and leaders came to redefine the meaning of the racial label in the 1960s and are continuing to do so today, creating their own collective histories, cultures, and identities, and organizing together to address racial inequalities.

How might we understand the variation within established racial categories?

As researchers, one way to understand the variation within established categories would be to gather larger samples of data so that national origin, language, and social class, as well as citizenship and legal status differences are captured. Case studies can provide new insights into the experiences of different ethnic, national origin, or language groups within established categories and can also help to demonstrate that established racial categories are socially constructed, and that while subgroups may share a racialized position and some experiences, they do not comprise a static grouping and have multiple needs.

In my own research, I have conducted interviews and gathered archival and documentary data to further understand how, for example, different Asian-origin groups view one another and perceive barriers to pan-ethnic organizing; what the distinctive needs and challenges are for the different generations and national origin groups; and how the issues that Asian-origin groups organized around changed over time. By unpacking and highlighting the diversity and social dynamics within the Asian American population, we have a more complex understanding of the variation within an established racial category.

How can we construct more complex measures of race?

Race is a difficult concept to capture. The most common measure is self-identified race, where people are provided with racial categories to choose from on a survey. This measure is an important way to classify groups so that we can understand how social, economic, and political outcomes vary by race. Unfortunately, it does not capture the *multiple dimensions of race* (Roth, 2016), which also include how a person subjectively identifies their race (racial identity), how an individual believes others perceive them racially (perceived race), and aspects of one's racial appearance. These dimensions may not all necessarily align, but they are important to measure because they each matter for understanding different types of social outcomes. As an example, racial identity can shape perceptions of discrimination, feelings of belonging, and self-esteem (Gong et al., 2017; Hughes et al., 2015). Perceived race can help us to further understand the multi-racial population, which does not fit neatly into one racial category nor have a uniform racial appearance (see Heilman, 2022). Skin tone and other measures of racial appearance have been useful for predicting socio-economic outcomes such as educational attainment, employment, earnings, and occupational status, regardless of self-identified race (Abascal & Garcia, 2022; Flores & Telles, 2012; Frank et al., 2010; Keith and Herring, 1991; Monk, 2014; 2019).

As scholars, we can continue to develop more complex measures of race by understanding the daily experiences of various groups and populations. We can also continue to conduct research on race in a comparative way, examining experiences within and across groups, as well as within and outside of the United States, to provide some leverage on the new dimensions of race and new ways that race is experienced.

How can we address the complexity of race in our research designs?

As researchers, we can address the complexity of race by understanding race as multidimensional and socially constructed, and as racial hierarchies reinforced through interactions, policies, and practices. We can also use mixed-methods research designs. Such designs can capture the ways in which racial disparities may appear in survey or experimental data, and then qualitative data can help to understand the processes that drive such disparities. Studies could also start with qualitative data based on interviews, observations, and case studies, which can help to theorize about the complexity of race, by examining the experiences of different racialized groups. The insights unearthed from qualitative research can be used to develop new concepts, theorize about processes, and identify mechanisms, which could be tested with quantitative data. But mixed-methods designs are not a panacea. I encourage scholars to read widely in their fields so that quantitative research can engage with and effectively build upon the work of scholars who leverage qualitative data; and research generated from interviews, archival data, and observations can be informed by quantitative analyses, all with the goal of pushing forward a more complex understanding of race.

As we move toward a racial analysis, we also can consider how race intersects with other dimensions of difference or stratification, such as language, citizenship, immigrant status, and legal status, as well as gender, class, and sexual orientation. While some of these dimensions correlate, they do not always move together in the same direction. Scholars who use qualitative methods are often able to capture the dynamics of race and their intersections, as observations and interviews can highlight meaning-making and unfolding processes. For scholars who use quantitative methods, it can be more challenging to address the fact that race is dynamic rather than fixed, but one approach is to take into account the ways that race may have different effects on a particular set of outcomes, depending on context. Another approach is to examine how the effects of race change over time. Either way, drawing upon qualitative work to understand the mechanisms and processes that may underlie these effects would help us to more fully understand how race and other dimensions of difference are operating to produce or diminish inequalities.

How can we take into account the ways in which race is manifested in institutions and policies?

Research that focuses on individuals operating within institutions, whether they be schools, labor markets, or healthcare systems can benefit from a deeper understanding of the ways in which such institutions potentially operate with a racialized lens or according to rules and regulations that support the dominant group (see Ray, 2019). In more specific terms, researchers can examine how historical practices, laws, and institutions have shaped contemporary outcomes. As an example, scholars have used quantitative data to examine how slavery has shaped contemporary patterns of poverty rates, school enrollment, and legal executions (Baker, 2022; Reece & O'Connell, 2016; Vandiver et al., 2005). Other studies examine the long-term effects of historical racial violence on homeownership rates (Albright et al., 2021), and how past governmental policies continue to shape contemporary health outcomes (Graetz & Esposito, 2022; Lynch et al., 2021;

Nardone et al., 2020). In this way, we need to continue to think about how race is manifested in historical institutions and practices, which have down-stream effects on contemporary groups and communities. At the same time, we also can continue to think about and study how contemporary organizations and practices—those that claim to be race-neutral or even attempt to address inequalities (e.g., diversity initiatives)—can further racial inequality if they are not interrogated.

What are the implications of not addressing racialized structures and institutions?

By not taking racialized structures and institutions into account, we risk overlooking processes and conditions that may address the outcomes that we find in our data, whether we are interested in differences in access to health care, labor market earnings, neighborhoods, or contact with the criminal justice system. By overlooking racialized structures and institutions, we risk targeting our policies in ways that do not address the deeper structures at work that generate inequality. That said, it is important to note that not all researchers are studying differential outcomes by race and racial inequality per se, but such studies could still benefit from understanding the background within which interactions are occurring or certain groups have privilege over others. Not all studies need to engage with race per se, but it is useful to think about how one's account or explanation may be informed by the history of immigration and race since the two are intertwined in many societies. For my own work, addressing the history of racist exclusionary policies directed at Asian-origin immigrants provided a context to understand why on the one hand, Asians built separate ethnic communities and did not organize across ethnic lines during the early immigration era, and on the other hand, how Asians could draw upon that past history to build a new collective identity based on shared experiences.

Conclusion

The current moment calls upon us to reorient our approaches to research. If we continue to look beyond race, we will overlook the fundamental ways that race and racial hierarchies are power structures that produce unequal outcomes and shape current and future experiences and trajectories. We need to move toward examining the ways in which systems and practices sustain durable racial inequalities, so that our research can more effectively inform policymakers about pathways for change. We need to develop a racial analysis that begins to center on race and racism and learn from scholars whose research agendas have been dedicated to the study of race, racism, and racial inequalities.

References

Abascal, M., & Garcia, D. (2022). Pathways to skin color stratification: The role of inherited (dis) advantage and skin color discrimination in labor markets. *Sociological Science, 9,* 346–373.

Albright, A., Cook, J. A., Feigenbaum, J. J., Kincaide, L., Long, J., & Nunn, N. (2021). *After the burning: The economic effects of the 1921 Tulsa race massacre (No. w28985).* National Bureau of Economic Research.

Baker, R. S. (2022). The historical racial regime and racial inequality in poverty in the American South. *American Journal of Sociology, 127*(6), 1721–1781.

Bonilla-Silva, E. (1997). Rethinking racism: Toward a structural interpretation. *American Sociological Review, 62*(3), 465–480.

Brown, D. A. (1998). Racial equality in the twenty-first century: What's tax policy got to do with it. *The University of Arkansas at Little Rock Law Review, 21,* 759.

Brown, D. A. (2018). Homeownership in black and white: The role of tax policy in increasing housing inequity. *University of Memphis Law Review, 49,* 205–245.

Brown, D. A. (2022). *The whiteness of wealth: How the tax system impoverishes Black Americans--and how we can fix it.* Crown.

Feagin, J. R. (1991). The continuing significance of race: Antiblack discrimination in public places. *American Sociological Review, 56*(1), 101–116.

Flores, R., & Telles, E. (2012). Social stratification in Mexico: Disentangling color, ethnicity, and class. *American Sociological Review, 77*(3), 486–494.

Frank, R., Akresh, I. R., & Lu, B. (2010). Latino immigrants and the US racial order: How and where do they fit in? *American Sociological Review, 75*(3), 378–401.

Gong, F., Xu, J., & Takeuchi, D. T. (2017). Racial and ethnic differences in perceptions of everyday discrimination. *Sociology of Race and Ethnicity, 3*(4), 506–521.

Graetz, N., & Esposito, M. (2022). Historical redlining and contemporary racial disparities in neighborhood life expectancy. *Social Forces,* soac 114.

Hughes, M., Kiecolt, K. J., Keith, V. M., & Demo, D. H. (2015). Racial identity and well-being among African Americans. *Social Psychology Quarterly, 78*(1), 25–48.

Heilman, M. (2022). The racial elevator speech: How multiracial individuals respond to racial identity inquiries. *Sociology of Race and Ethnicity, 8*(3), 370–385.

Keith, V. M., & Herring, C. (1991). Skin tone and stratification in the Black community. *American Journal of Sociology, 97*(3), 760–778.

Kim, C. J. (1999). The racial triangulation of Asian Americans. *Politics & Society, 27*(1), 105–138.

Krysan, M., & Crowder, K. (2017). *Cycle of segregation: Social processes and residential stratification.* Russell Sage Foundation.

Lewis, A. E., & Diamond, J. B. (2015). *Despite the best intentions: How racial inequality thrives in good schools.* Oxford University Press.

Lynch, E. E., Malcoe, L. H., Laurent, S. E., Richardson, J., Mitchell, B. C., & Meier, H. C. S. (2021). The legacy of structural racism: Associations between historic redlining, current mortgage lending, and health. *SSM-population health*, 14, 100793.

Manza, J., & Uggen, C. (2008). *Locked out: Felon disenfranchisement and American democracy.* Oxford University Press.

Massey, D. S., & Denton, N. A. (1993). *American apartheid: Segregation and the making of the underclass.* Harvard University Press.

Miller, R. J., & Stuart, F. (2017). Carceral citizenship: Race, rights and responsibility in the age of mass supervision. *Theoretical Criminology, 21*(4), 532–548.

Monk, E. P. (2014). Skin tone stratification among Black Americans, 2001–2003. *Social Forces, 92*(4), 1313–1337.

Monk, E. P. (2019). The color of punishment: African Americans, skin tone, and the criminal justice system. *Ethnic and Racial Studies, 42*(10), 1593–1612.

Morris, E. W. (2005). "Tuck in that shirt!" Race, class, gender, and discipline in an urban school. *Sociological Perspectives, 48*(1), 25–48.

Mora, G. C., & Okamoto, D. G. (2020a). Boundary articulation and emergent identities: Asian and Hispanic panethnicity in comparison, 1970–1980. *Social Problems, 67*(1), 56–76.

Mora, G. C., & Okamoto, D. G. (2020b). Postcolonialism, racial political fields, and panethnicity: A comparison of early 'Asian American' and 'Hispanic' movements. *Sociology of Race and Ethnicity, 6*(4), 450–467.

Morning, A. (2011). *The nature of race: How scientists think and teach about human difference.* University of California Press.

Nardone, A. L., Casey, J. A., Rudolph, K. E., Karasek, D., Mujahid, M., & Morello-Frosch, R. (2020). Associations between historical redlining and birth outcomes from 2006 through 2015 in California. *PLoS One, 15*(8), e0237241.

Okamoto, D. G. (2014). *Redefining race: Asian American panethnicity and shifting ethnic boundaries.* Russell Sage Foundation.

Okamoto, D. G. (2003). Toward a theory of panethnicity: Explaining Asian American collective action. *American Sociological Review, 68*(6), 811–842.

Okonofua, J. A., & Eberhardt, J. L. (2015). Two strikes: Race and the disciplining of young students. *Psychological Science, 26*(5), 617–624.

Oliver, M., & Shapiro, T. (2013). *Black wealth/white wealth: A new perspective on racial inequality.* Routledge.

Omi, M., & Winant, H. (2014). *Racial formation in the United States.* Routledge.

Pager, D. (2003). The mark of a criminal record. *American Journal of Sociology, 108*(5), 937–975.

Ray, V. (2019). A theory of racialized organizations. *American Sociological Review, 84*(1), 26–53.

Reece, R. L., & O'Connell, H. A. (2016). How the legacy of slavery and racial composition shape public school enrollment in the American South. *Sociology of Race and Ethnicity, 2*(1), 42–57.

Rivas-Drake, D., Seaton, E. K., Markstrom, C., Quintana, S., Syed, M., Lee, R. M., Schwartz, S. J., et al. (2014). Ethnic and racial identity in adolescence: Implications for psychosocial, academic, and health outcomes. *Child Development, 85*(1), 40–57.

Roth, W. D. (2016). The multiple dimensions of race. *Ethnic and Racial Studies, 39*(8), 1310–1338.

Rothwell, J., & Massey, D. S. (2009). The effect of density zoning on racial segregation in US urban areas. *Urban Affairs Review, 44*(6), 779–806.

Trounstine, J. (2020). The geography of inequality: How land use regulation produces segregation. *American Political Science Review, 114*(2), 443–455.

Vandiver, M. (2005). *Lethal punishment: Lynchings and legal executions in the South*. Rutgers University Press.

Williams, D. R., Yu, Y., Jackson, J. S., & Anderson, N. B. (1997). Racial differences in physical and mental health: Socio-economic status, stress and discrimination. *Journal of Health Psychology, 2*(3), 335–351.

PART IV

Our stories are the heart of theory

Joanna L. Williams

This section, "Our stories are the heart of theory," invites readers to consider storytelling as a way of making theory in the world. Storytelling is, of course, central to the larger volume. Authors reflect upon and tell stories of how they grow in their learning and understanding of Blackness, Indigeneity, and racialization and explain how such learning informs their current work and research with young people. Given the importance of storytelling to the full volume, this final section of the book is especially meaningful. The authors, Dani Ahuicapahtzin Cornejo, Antar Tichavakunda, and Stephanie Toliver, center the stories that animate their own theorizing. By sharing the stories that inform their own social science research, they also make room for more capacious understandings of not only what counts as a theory, but also who can make a theory.

Cornejo explores the possibilities that emerge from reclaiming and rebuilding holistic, Indigenous knowledge systems shattered by colonial violence and encourages us to "build mosaics with the pieces and repurpose those mosaical teachings in service of our communities in the present" (Cornejo, this volume). Tichavakunda reflects on what it looks and feels like to call oneself a "theorist" and shares how academic spaces can work to sever us from our stories and render them meaningless. Finally, Toliver uses speculative storytelling to bring us on her journey of becoming a "story listener" who, with strong guidance from her own story listeners, breaks the hold of the antiBlack stories that dominated her education and learns to listen to the stories of ancestors, elders, Afrofuturist scholars, and youth.

These chapters do a great deal of work, and readers are invited to see multiple possibilities within each of them. On one level, they are personal

DOI: 10.4324/9781003303800-14

narratives in which authors dare to be vulnerable. They push back on the inclination to write defensively, a reflex we often learn in the process of academic socialization, and instead lay bare their challenges and vulnerabilities. In writing from the heart, the authors give readers "permission to connect their head knowledge to their heart knowledge and speak more powerfully from that place" (Williams, Cornejo, Tichavakunda, & Toliver, 2023). Such vulnerability is not without risk, however, as the stories may be misinterpreted and misused (Tuck & Ree, 2013). Historically, stories perpetuated by those in power get retold as theory, and dominant theories get (mis)taken for reality (Archibald et al., 2019; Tuck & Ree, 2013). Thus, the authors' stories also function to challenge dominant theories of racialization and Indigeneity and push back against "the violence of colonial storytelling" (Archibald, et al., 2019). In keeping with methodological traditions of Indigenous storywork (Archibald, 2008; Cornejo, this volume) and counter-storytelling (Solórzano & Yosso, 2002), the authors challenge master narratives of biological determinism and racial deficiency.

In "Our stories are the heart of theory: Walking the mosaic path and exorcising the ghosts of missionaries past," Cornejo builds on Jo-Ann Archibald's (2008) "storywork" tradition, which centers Indigenous storytelling and story-listening as essential practices for theory-making and learning. Archibald notes that despite the assault on "storied memories of Indigenous people ... Indigenous Elders and storytellers kept embers of original Indigenous stories alive in their hearts, minds, bodies, and spirits, waiting for the time to spark the return of these storied memories" (Archibald, 2018, pp. 238–239). Cornejo reflects this in his discussion of the "mosaic path" as one that offers opportunities for (re)creation and renewal. He writes, "by seeking out, gathering, honoring, repurposing, and applying the fragments of our Indigenous traditions in service to our communities and ourselves in the present, we can not only survive and navigate the western world but begin/continue forging Indigenized de-colonial and emancipatory educational spaces" (Cornejo, this volume). Walking the mosaic path requires wrestling with ghosts, and Cornejo shows us how exorcising ghosts from the archival record of a Christian missionary can open space for the archived knowledge and traditions captured in the hearts, bodies, minds, and oral traditions of Ópatan people. Cornejo reminds us that "Our stories are grounded in struggle and context. They are the ground from which we emerge and the ground whose nutrients feed the substance of our beings."

Cornejo lays the groundwork for storytelling as a way of making theory, and Tichavakunda pushes us further by asking questions about which stories are deemed worthy of informing and becoming theory in, "Your theories are too small: Beyond stories of the hunt." As Tichavakunda (this volume) writes,

"Stories shape our social realities, how we view ourselves and others, how we understand history and what histories we tell, and what we imagine is possible for society." He recounts how his stories of being a Black educator in Washington, DC public schools were discounted in graduate courses about race and education. Importantly, this led to the realization that "the problem was that my graduate program's approach to theorizing and teaching theory was too small." This assertion opens us to "bigger ideas for theory and for [ourselves] as thinkers." The inextricable link between story and theory motivates Tichavakunda to question the stories that have taken hold and dominate theories of racialization. He works through his relation to the proverb of the hunter and lion, which, on its surface, reminds us of the one-sided nature of dominant stories (i.e., those told by the hunter). This work pushes Tichavakunda towards scholars like Nascimiento (in Smith et al., 2021), Tuck (2009), and Quashie (2012) who reveal how damage-, oppression-, or resistance-centered narratives of Black and Indigenous peoples mask the complexity of human experience. Tichavakunda writes, "Through resistance, and resistance centered frameworks, we understand the lion's story only in relation to the hunt," and notes our failure to ask, "What life did the lion have outside of the hunt?" He implores us to embrace the connection between theory and story without neglecting the importance of stories that may lay outside of our traditional analytic gaze.

Finally, Toliver transports us with her speculative storytelling to the worlds she inhabits in, "An Afrofuturist dreams of Black liberations: Disentangling Blackness from fatalism". She traverses the education system in her incarnation as a Black child/not child, a "monster" in the eyes of peers and teachers. She reveals the pain of existing as a contortionist, "I must disfigure myself, my blackness, let it become mangled in the gears of whiteness because this monster must endure" (Toliver, this volume). While the violent tools of antiBlackness render Toliver broken and disfigured, we are privy to the cries of her story-listener, who implores her to (re)connect to the wisdom of ancestors, family members, and scholars shared through an intergenerational feedback loop. "The story listener whispers, for the connection has been made once again. 'Follow the thread of story. Find your map to the future. Forget monstrosity and remember your humanity. Forge a path that leads to the (re)searching of Black past, present, and future'" (Toliver, this volume). On this new path, Toliver, as story listener, reconnects herself to Black people "across space and time" by engaging with Afrofuturist scholars like Ytasha Womack (2013), Alondra Nelson (2000), and Isiah Lavender (2019). From Toliver's chapter, we understand that theory-building begins with story-listening, and that story-listeners must "think about the numerous connectors that bind Black futures to Black pasts and Black presents." For, as Toliver has learned from these teachers, "dreaming of a world in which Black people are valued for who they are, not for who they can contort themselves to be, is a concept as old as Blackness itself" (Toliver, this volume).

Cornejo (this volume) writes, "when we remember that our stories are the heart of theory our knowledge has no ledges." We, as story listeners, have work to do, and each author offers a glimpse into how this work might manifest. Collectively, the chapters in this section push us to think more expansively about story and theory. The authors share the missteps, misinterpretations, and mistellings that informed restricted and deficit-centered theories of race, racialization, and Indigeneity. They remind us to attend to forgotten pasts and take care in their retelling, and to imagine possible futures as a way of re-envisioning, repairing, and reclaiming knowledge and theory.

References

Archibald, J. (2008). *Indigenous storywork: Educating the heart, mind, body, and spirit.* UBC Press.

Archibald, J. (2018). Indigenous storytelling. In P. Tortell, M. Turin, & M. Young, (Eds.), *Memory* (pp. 233–241). Peter Wall Institute for Advanced Studies.

Archibald, J., Lee-Morgan, J. B. J., & De Santolo, J. (2019). *Decolonizing research: Indigenous storywork as methodology.* Zed books.

Lavender, I. (2019). *Afrofuturism rising: The literary prehistory of a movement.* The Ohio State University Press.

Nelson, A. (2000). Afrofuturism: Past-future visions. *Color Lines, 3*(1), 34–47.

Quashie, K. (2012). *The sovereignty of quiet.* Rutgers University Press.

Smith, C., Davies, A., & Gomes, B. (2021). "In front of the world": Translating Beatriz Nascimento. *Antipode, 53*(1), 279–316.

Solórzano, D. G., & Yosso, T. J. (2002). Critical race methodology: Counter-storytelling as an analytical framework for education research. *Qualitative Inquiry, 8*(1), 23–44.

Tuck, E. (2009). Suspending damage: A letter to communities. *Harvard Educational Review, 79*(3), 409–428.

Tuck, E., & Ree, C. (2013). A glossary of haunting. In S. Holman Jones, T. E. Adams, & C. Ellis (Eds), *Handbook of autoethnography* (pp. 639–658). Left Coast Press, Inc.

Williams, J. L., Cornejo, D. A., Tichavakunda, A. A., & Toliver, S. R. (2023). New approaches to inequality research with youth: Theorizing race beyond the traditions of our disciplines – Part IV: Our stories are the heart of theory [Webinar]. William T. Grant Foundation. https://wtgrantfoundation.org/new-resources-theorizing-of-blackness-indigeneity-and-racialization-in-research-on-reduce-inequality

Womack, Y. (2013). *Afrofuturism: The world of Black sci-fi and fantasy culture.* Lawrence Hill Books.

11

OUR STORIES ARE THE HEART OF THEORY

Walking the mosaic path and exorcising the ghosts of missionaries past

Dani Ahuicapahtzin Cornejo (Ópata/Xicano/Picunche/ Chileno)

Galeano's (1997) *Open Veins of Latin America: Five Centuries of the Pillage of a Continent* was the first book I read where I saw my family's story reflected within the pages. It helped me understand that my family history of exile and immigration was part of a broader neoliberal extractive project, rooted in colonialism, that not only impacted my family but also similar families throughout Latin America and the Global South. Through his writing, I was able to understand systemic oppression in an abstract theoretical sense while also connecting it to my family's story of exile and immigration. In this sense, my family's story was at the heart of the theory expressed by Galeano (1997) in *Open Veins*, which allowed me to absorb, internalize, and appreciate his teachings in a more profound way. Our stories are grounded in struggle and context. They are the ground from which we emerge and the ground whose nutrients feed the substance of our beings.

Story is a gateway to theorization disrupting "rhetorical principles of theory [that] aspire to prevent all discourses from directly approaching lived experience" (Corr, 2019, p. 188). By framing theory as knowledge development that emerges from the lived experience of story, memory, and interpretation it becomes more accessible, meaningful, and relevant for the students who engage in it (Holmes & González, 2017). In this chapter, I engage a non-linear storytelling approach in the tradition of Jo-ann Archibald's (2008) Indigenous storywork where:

> ... expression resembles something like a spider's web – with many little threads radiating from the center, crisscrossing one another. As with the

DOI: 10.4324/9781003303800-15

web, the structure emerges as it is made, and you must simply listen and trust … that meaning will be made. (p. 7–8).

This chapter is also web-like weaving together themes of scars, healing, teaching, and learning, while centering the story on establishing theory.

While my stories do not unfold in a linear way (i.e., A to B to C) the adoption of a cyclical and/or spiral approach to storytelling in the tradition of Eber Hampton (Chickesaw), Jo-ann Archibald (Sto:lo), Deborah Miranda (Esselen/Oholone) and Christine Black (Australian Aborigine) guide the stories to cycle back to central themes such as Indigeneity, racialization, and education. As the themes are revisited throughout the chapter, the reader is invited to participate in a more in-depth and profound analysis of the patterns that emerge and to draw personal, relational, and empathetic connections with the content. Through this process, it is my hope that the reader will identify patterns in their own life and unearth teachings from their own being. I also draw from the literary traditions of Gloria Anzaldua (Tejana) and Deborah Miranda (Esselen/Oholone) who courageously and unapologetically engage deeply personal, painful, and empowering aspects of their stories by weaving together autoethnographical narrative and poetry.

The broken clay pot: Gathering fragments and building a Mosaic Path

In August of 2005, my calpulli was invited to the Third Mesa on the Hopi Reservation for a ceremony. At the time, my wife and I were new to the Danza Azteca community and had not yet earned our ayoyotli's, a rite that was reserved for those who had led their first danza. We took the beautiful 10-hour drive through the Rocky Mountains and the Four Corners region, with two veteran danzantes who taught us what to expect upon arrival, ceremonial protocol, and some of the oral history embedded within the Danza Mexicayotl tradition. The Mexicayotl tradition has become a pan-Indigenous refuge and a place to re-connect with Indigenous traditions for Pueblo Originario and Chicana/o/ Xicanx/a/o descendants living in the United States.

As a descendent of the Tegüïma Ópata people of Oposura Sonora (Mexico) and the Picunche people of Lolol Colchagua (Chile), displaced from both places and traditions through a history of family migration and political exile, as well as through an intergenerational history of mission-ization, assimilation, and genocide, the Mexicayotl tradition offered me a space of learning, reconciliation, and healing. As a bi/multi-racial person who also descends from various European colonial heritages, including English through my maternal grandfather, Spanish through my maternal grandmother as well as through my paternal lineage, I am a Brown reflection of the complex histories that have forged the "American" hemisphere, from Wallmapu to Turtle Island. Growing up I encountered fragments of my traditions through my father's stories, my grandmother's cooking, the Mapudungun terms that seeped in through our Chilean dialect, and through our annual trips to the Sonoran Desert, yet I never had the language, theory, or epistemology to connect those fragments into a cohesive whole. Participation in the Mexicayotl tradition helped me begin a process of understanding and reconciling with the complex dimensions of my identity, healing from the intergenerational traumas inherent to these identities, and seeing/feeling Spirit in myself and the world around me.

Upon arriving at the Third Mesa we spent two days dancing under the desert sun offering our sweat, our blisters, and our movement as a prayer for rain. I was asked to lead a danza on our second day and put my mind, heart, body, and Spirit into every step and movement focusing on our collective prayer. That day the blessing of rain arrived, falling over the corn fields below the Mesa. We ended the ceremony with a friendship dance in which we joined hands and formed a circle with the Hopi people of the Third Mesa. Afterwards, we ate the most delicious purple corn sweet tamalis I had ever tasted. At this moment I realized one of the many connections between Indigenous Mexican people and the Hopi of Arizona.

Our calpulli then formed a circle to pass the palabra in order to share and express the teachings and insight that we had received during the ceremony. Eventually, the palabra reached Siri Martinez, a descendant of the Mexicayotl people of central Mexico. Siri reminded us that prior to colonization Mesoamerican Indigenous knowledge systems were whole and complete with knowledge pertaining to philosophy, agriculture, architecture, language, music, medicine, education, etc. He said that our holistic knowledge systems were akin to a clay pot emerging from the earth. He explained that colonial violence took our holistic knowledge systems and shattered them into thousands of pieces. At that moment I found his clay pot metaphor to be both beautiful and devastating. On the one hand, it provided me with a framework for understanding the deep wounds inflicted on Indigenous peoples and holistic Indigenous knowledge systems by colonial violence. On the other hand, his metaphor made me feel broken and helpless, not being able to see a clear path forward through the violent legacy of colonial histories.

Authors such as Deborah Miranda (Esselen/Chumash/French/Jewish) (2013) and Gloria Anzaldua (Chicana/Tejana) (1987) would later help me understand that despite the shattering of holistic Indigenous knowledge systems we are not broken. Each shard holds a precious and sacred teaching. It may be the oral history behind a dance step, the purpose behind a song, the preparation of a meal, or the teaching shared within a sacred circle. As Indigenous descendants, it is our responsibility to gather as many pieces as we can throughout our lives, in a way that respects and honors the shape, form, and integrity of each fragment. While it is impossible to recreate a knowledge system and way of life that has been stolen and/or broken by the violence of colonization, it is possible to take the fragments of our teachings, build mosaics with the pieces, and repurpose those mosaical teachings in service of our communities in the present. Regarding the mosaic Miranda (2013) writes:

> Sometimes something is so badly broken you cannot recreate its original shape at all. If you try, you create a deformed, imperfect image of what you've lost; you will always compare what your creation looks like with what it used to look like. As long as you are attempting to *recreate*, you are doomed to fail! I am beginning to realize that when something is that broken, more useful and beautiful results can come from using the pieces to construct a mosaic. You use the same pieces, but you create a new design from it. Matter cannot be created or destroyed, only transformed. If we allow the pieces of our culture to lie scattered in the dust of history, trampled on by racism and grief, then yes, we are irreparably damaged, but if we pick up the pieces and use them in new ways that honor their integrity, their colors, textures, stories – then we do those pieces justice, no matter how sharp they are, no matter how much handling them slices our fingers and makes us bleed. (p. 135)

For Miranda (2013), a romanticized and mythical recreation of an Indigenized past is not only impossible but impractical. Instead, by seeking out, gathering, honoring, repurposing, and applying the fragments of our Indigenous traditions in service to our communities and ourselves in the present, we can not only survive and navigate the Western world but begin/continue forging Indigenized decolonial and emancipatory educational spaces. Miranda (2013) reminds us that the mosaic path is not easy and often painful. The fragments that we gather over our lifetimes have sharp edges that open old wounds, create new cuts, and hold the potential of leaving permanent scars.

Exploring the haunted archive: Exorcizing the ghosts of missionaries past

While lost among the stacks of books in Shields Library at UC Davis I realized the archives were haunted. In these stacks, I happened upon a copy of *El Arte de la Lenuga Tegüïma, Vulgarmente Llamada Ópata, Compuesta por el Padre Natal* Lombardo 1702 (The Art of the Tegüïma Language, Vulgarly Called Ópata, Composed by Father Natal Lombardo 1702). I took the book off the shelf. The title spoke volumes. On the one hand, the author, Father Natal Lombardo, seemed to hold a reverence and respect for my people's language, acknowledging that Tegüïma was one language among the triad of languages collectively known as Ópata (Tegüïma, Eudeve, Jova). Within the title, he insisted on not mis-categorizing the language. I understood that Lombardo's grammar contained a wealth of sacred language, grammatical rules, greetings, lists of colors, plants, animals, places, directions, kinship terms, etc. Fragments of a language that are considered "extinct" by Western scholars and considered deeply endangered by our people. On the other hand, I understood that the grammar that I held in my hand had been used to train Spanish missionaries in the enslavement, missionization, assimilation, and elimination of my ancestors. How does one begin to engage with the haunted archive when the trauma of opening intergenerational wounds is inescapable? How does one begin to commune with the unknown ancestral specter? How does one work through the pain of the archive to honor the ancestral knowledge left behind in a way that both preserves the integrity of knowledge and allows for the emergence of relation with the knowledge in the present? I checked out the book, put it in my backpack, and left the library.

Two distinct stories exist about our people: the oral and the written. According to oral stories, the name Ópata comes from the term "Opo" which means "iron wood" making us the people of the ironwood – a tree that is not only abundant in the Sonoran Desert, but is also utilized in a variety of capacities ranging from building to ceremony (Lawrence, Elder, Personal Communications, 2021; Tanori, Elder, Personal Communications, 2021). The written history describes Ópata as a social construction of the post-conquest era where Spanish military and missionaries placed three distinct cultural and linguistic communities—Tegüïma, Eudeve, and Jova—into a single essentialized Indigenous category (Yetman, 2010). Our oral histories tell us that the Tegüïma emerged from a cone-shaped mountain near the pueblo of Bacoachi, that rests along the banks of the Rio Sonora. They also tell us that the Eudeve emerged from the ground in the pueblo of Huepac, also resting on the banks of the Rio Sonora. Little is known about the Jova creation story, language, and culture. Our creation stories teach us that we have lived within the river valleys of central Sonora since time immemorial (Lawrence, Elder, Personal Communications, 2021; Tanori, Elder, Personal Communications, 2021). The written history talks of a migration from the city of Casas Grandes Chihuahua, across the Sierra Madre mountain range. In this version, our people arrived and invaded the river valleys of central Sonora displacing the Pima communities that were living in the region. The Pima named us Ópata or "hostile people" as a result of their displacement (Sauer & Brand, 1931; Riley, 2005). Ultimately, both stories hold important fragments of the Ópatan mosaic and their reconciliation holds important teachings for our cultural and linguistic reclamation and re(new)al efforts.

Lombardo's grammar sat in my home unopened for weeks. The specter of the archive as well as the magnitude of beginning to learn the Tegüïma language loomed heavy. I felt isolated in my work and that isolation was paralyzing. I quickly realized I would need a supportive learning community in order to exorcize the specter of Lombardo and begin a process of language reclamation. Through my participation in the Mexicayotl tradition, I had a firm grounding in Mesoamerican epistemologies and the Nahuatl language— a Uto-Aztecan language that is part of the same language family as the Tegüïma Ópata language. My knowledge of the Nahuatl language was rooted in a weekly Nahuatl study group that I co-facilitated in the Native American Studies Department at UC Davis. This study group served as a platform to implement Indigenous holistic pedagogies that are attentive to the interaction of brain intelligence, embodied knowledge, innate emotional literacy, spiritual knowledge, ancestral knowledge, etc., in the process of language learning. This meant devoting half of the study session to learning oral histories, Mexicayotl cosmologies, songs in Nahuatl, and Danzas in the Mexicayotl tradition while pairing those teachings with the oral histories held by said songs and danzas. Often the first half of class would involve kinesthetic activities such as singing songs, doing danzas, playing language matching games, or playing patolli (a Mexica board game) using Nahuatl vocabulary. These approaches rooted language learning in everyday practice, reminding us that when it came to Nahuatl we needed to humble ourselves, that we still spoke at the level of children, that mistakes within that language learning context were pedagogical opportunities, and that language learning—if it was to be sustainable—should be joyful. The other half of the class was devoted to vocabulary, grammatical norms, and syntactic rules that guided the structure of the language. Learning a language in this way ensured an appropriate epistemological and cultural context that went well beyond the pedagogical norms of dominant grammar instruction. Oftentimes we would linguistically dissect song lyrics from the first part of class during the second part of class, delving deeper into the oral histories embedded in the songs through a linguistic and entomological analysis. This Nahuatl language community helped me begin to break the isolation of Tegüïma language learning and ensured that I had a solid foundation in the grammatical norms of Uto-Aztecan language.

In addition, I was part of a course at UC Davis dedicated to the practice of Indigenous language reclamation. Within this class, multiple Native and non-Native students, with varying degrees of language proficiency, were involved in learning or refining their skills in an Indigenous language. Within this environment, I was finally able to delve into Lombardo's grammar engaging the linguistic expertise of Dr. Justin Spence of UC Davis to begin creating an Ópatan language archive, gain an initial understanding of the vocabulary, grammatical norms, and syntactic rules that guided the structure of the language, and couple that with my profound yet evolving emplaced knowledge of the Sonoran desert that came as a result of yearly trips to the region for family gatherings during the holidays. Part of creating the Ópatan language archive was to develop connections and working relationships non-Native allied scholars who have done in-depth historical research on the Ópata people such as Dr. Cynthia Radding and Dr. David Yetman, who were both generous with their time and with their resources. I was also able to develop relationships with Native and non-Native linguists who had studied the Tegüïma language in depth, such as Dr. Qui'chi Patlan, Dr. Michael Everdell (see Everdell et al., 2020), and Dr. David Shaul (see Shaul, 1989; 1990). Most importantly however, I have built long-lasting relationships with Oquimachy's/Noraguas (Ópatan relatives) in the U.S diaspora as well as in Sonora who are doing similar re(new)al work in the areas of federal/state recognition (on both sides of the border), building stronger relationships between Ópata communities within the United States and Mexico, building relationships with other Indigenous peoples within Sonora, cultural/ceremonial reclamation, the preservation of sacred sites, the preservation of oral histories and knowledge, the preservation of land-based knowledge including plant medicines, and linguistic revitalization. Each connection, relation, and sacred fragment of information helped further break the isolation of Tegüïma language learning, further crafting the mosaic of Ópatan linguistic and cultural revitalization.

Even with a solid foundation of support, exorcizing the ghosts of Natal Lombardo was no easy task. The legacies of assimilation, missionization, enslavement, and genocide of the Ópatan people are well documented through primary sources (Lombardo, 1702; Barbastro, 1792) as well as through secondary sources (Johnson, 1950; Owen, 1957; Radding, 1997; 2005; 2015; Trejo Contreras, 2010; Yetman, 2010). Lombardo's grammar was explicitly used to assimilate and missionize Ópatan people into Christian beliefs as well as to enslave our people within the feudal encomienda, repartimiento, and reduccion systems of the day. The clearest example of Ópatan assimilation and missionization into Christianity is expressed linguistically, through Lombardo's (1702) emphasis on teaching missionaries' religious phrases. The sheer volume of religious phrases present in Lombardo's (1702) work are indications of the missionary ideology and purpose behind the creation of his grammar:

Phrase 1: Juzgo que tu padre no oyo misa/I judge that your father did not hear mass/*Amo ne massi cai missa vitzi era* (p. 121).

Phrase 2: Iremos mañana a Oposura pare oir misa/Tomorrow we will go to Oposura to hear mass/*Chia Oposuragua missa vitzidoni ta daisac* (p. 131).

Phrase 3: Habiendo oido misa, etc., me volvi/Having heard mass, etc., I returned/*Missa ne vitzaur noue* (p. 133)

These examples clearly demonstrate the connection between Lombardo's (1702) grammar and missionization efforts. Beyond assimilation and missionization, the project of enslavement through a feudal *encomienda* system is expressed linguistically through Lombardo's (1702) emphasis on providing missionaries with commands that get people working under the threat of violence:

Phrase 1: Pense que tú habias de barbechar/I thought you had to plow/ *Eme ne mavuguarea cori erare, o eme ne mavuguarea cai erave* (p. 121).

Phrase 2: Dijo el padre que tú azotaste o habias azotado a este muchacho/The father said that you had whipped or had already whipped that boy/*Para eme uerequi tesa chita veguia [beguia] cai thuiue* (p. 123).

Phrase 3: Dice el gobernador que tu no quisiste regar el trigo/The governor said that you did not want to water the wheat/*Conauaro eme piricuni cai vanuquaera camata thui, o cai vanuguaeraue cai thui* (p. 123).

Phrase 4: … mando azotar/I command you to whip/*hima nado* (p. 123).

The ideology of assimilation, missionization, and enslavement is expressed through the content and purpose of Lombardo's (1702) grammar where strong emphasis is placed on language that instructs people to participate in Christianity, work in the fields, police one another through capital punishment, and ultimately ensure that Ópata people understand that the threat of violence is imminent. These conditions contributed to an ongoing genocide of the Ópata people beginning with the arrival of Diego de Guzman in 1530 (Radding, 1997), the subsequent resistance of Ópata peoples until the early 1700s, the eventual grudging alliances formed with the Spanish between 1700 to 1810 (Mexican Independence), and wars in alliance with as well as against the Mexican nation-state prior to the Mexican Revolution in 1910 (Yetman, 2010). Given this context, my language learning paradox became crystal clear. To participate in a process of Ópatan language reclamation, I would have to engage with the writings of the missionary responsible for extreme violence against my people. To make the language reclamation process sustainable and regenerative over time, I would have to find a way to exorcize the missionary from the study of the Tegüïma language.

The exorcism began with a Christian prayer translated into the Tegüïma language. The prayer is commonly known as "Our Father" and represents an omnipotent, all-seeing, all-knowing, monotheistic, white male "God." This "God" requires male clergy intermediaries to transmit his knowledge and convey his messages. Our people did not believe in that "God" or any "God" for that matter. Our understanding of the sacred is rooted in the concept of Chamahua or the animating energy from which all things flow. This concept moves away from the notion of "God" or even "Creator" per se, and more towards an understanding of "Creation."

Chamahua,
the animating energy of Creation,
a place where creativity, ingenuity, and imagination flow,
bringing forth new and/or re(new)ed Creations.

The Ópatan conception of Chamahua provides an epistemological jus-tification for developing a profound relationship with the fragments of Ópatan knowledge systems, recognizing that these fragments are sacred and contain the energy of Creation within, praying for the knowledge of Creation to work through us in re(new)ing and creating our traditions, and trusting that the energies of Creation will lead us home. With the purpose of re(new)al in mind, I removed "Our father" from the prayer and replaced it with the Ópatan concept of Chamahua, the animating energy from which all things flow. Our Ópatan people, the land from which our tongue emerged, our Tegüïma language, and the epistemological concepts that our language holds do not belong to their "God." While I had changed the words in the written form, what significance did that hold in a culture rooted in oral tradition? I needed to sing the prayer into existence in order to share it with the broader community, but I did not have a melody.

That year I made the decision to participate in the Teonetzawalitzli[1] (the ceremony of sacred fasting) for the second time in my life. I made the commitment, prepared for a year, and sat on the hill. I prayed for a melody, humbly offering my voice, sweat, and tears to the ceremony. Eventually, the melody came. During the Teonetzawalitzli, I sang our song into existence for the first time, and I have sung our song many times since. I sing our song to my children before they fall asleep at night so that they know that our people walk with them. I sang our song in front of the sacred fire at Standing Rock so that the water protectors knew that the Ópata Nation stood in solidarity with them. I sang our song at the Ópata peoples' gathering in Tucson Arizona in 2017. And I sang our song to my Ópatan/ Mexican American grandmother, with tears in my eyes while I held her hand on her deathbed. It was the first time she had heard our language spoken.

Passing on: A Creation story

Creation is art.
And you are made of the substance
of artistry.
You make somethings out of nothings,
or merely the materials at hand.
You sing communities into existence
based on the artistry of your imagination.
You overstand the substance of Creation.
That sound that creates worlds.
That sound is made of beauty,
And that leaves one speechless
Like laughter ...
that cannot be put to words.
You sing and dance yourself,
into the next place ...
Embodying dreams,
Imagination's living beings.

Since then, I have engaged with our exorcized archive to write more songs, to create educational games for language/epistemology learning purposes, and to build strong relationships with Ópatan decedents and allied scholars to continue gathering and honoring the fragments of our shared epistemology, repurposing those fragments for our use in the present.

I have used the story of "Exorcising the ghosts of missionaries past" to help university students understand the complex and nuanced dynamics of Native American and Indigenous language reclamation and maintenance in a way that speaks to their heart, body, mind, and Spirit. Through story, I can convey that Indigenous language reclamation is not just about grammar, vocabulary, and syntax, but is also about oral history, epistemology, power dynamics, and legacies of colonization. I have used the principles inherent to this story to co-design Nahuatl language reclamation curriculum, pairing oral histories, epistemologies, and Indigenous holistic pedagogies with the study of grammar, vocabulary, and syntax to produce more enriching and Indigenized language learning environments. In addition, I have used the

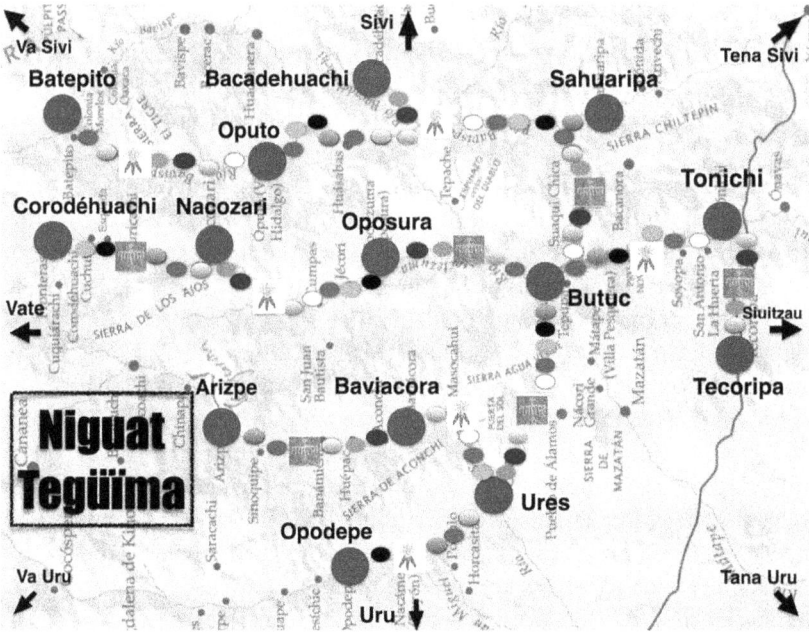

FIGURE 11.1   The Niguat Tegüïma "Tegüïma Tongue" board game.

principles in this story to create Native American and Indigenous language reclamation units for Intertribal urban Native middle school students in Oakland, California, introducing them to the foundational concepts of language reclamation, providing them with access to language learning materials, and supporting them in taking their first steps towards learning their Native language.

Finally, I have used the principles and tactics outlined in this story to begin teaching my beautiful children the foundations of our Tegüïma language. The game board in Figure 11.1 is my humble attempt to cultivate a love of language learning for my children.

Niguat Tegüïma or Tegüïma Tongue is built on a map of our peoples' territory known as the Ópateria. Each component of the game serves as a mosaical fragment of Ópatan history and epistemology. The primary pedagogical purpose of this game is to teach about Tegüïma Ópata epistemology, oral history, and language. The primary "game-play" purpose of the board game is to unite the Ópatan villages before the arrival of Spanish missionaries, in order to resist missionization, assimilation, enslavement, and genocide. The game's purpose gives me an opportunity to explain the historical reality of the colonization of our People, while allowing them to engage the animating energy of Creation (Chamahua) to imagine a different historical reality premised on Ópatan unity and solidarity. The board game is full of linguistic teachings as well as the teachings of oral history that my children can access as they navigate the game board.

The map's orientation is east up, following a hemispheric Indigenous ethos rooted in natural law, where the top of the world is where the sun rises. This orientation disrupts colonial map-making practices that often center Europe and place the global north on top of the global south. When game players arrive at each village, they share the news of the imminent arrival of the missionaries, organize the villagers to resist, and trade in goods such as opo (iron wood), gipe (palm mats), biy (tobacco), or teuuria (huipiles). Each village has a story and each good has a historical purpose and connection to the Opateria. My children use dice to navigate the game board counting out the Tegüïma numbers as they go (se, gode, vaide, nago, mariqui, etc., that is one, two, three, four, five, etc.). Each space on the game board has a color, which my children must name in the Tegüïma language when they land. Finally, certain spaces have a corn icon and an eagle icon. When my children land on these icons they are allowed to pick a plant medicine or an animal relative from the Ópateria to accompany them on their journey. As with every aspect of the game, each plant medicine, and animal relative have a story and a teaching associated with them. Not only do my children adore this game, and request to play it often, but it gives us an opportunity to connect with one another around linguistic, historical, and epistemological teachings.

The work of Ópatan linguistic and cultural reclamation is painful, enriching, necessary, and deeply humbling. It is ongoing, imperfect, long-term, and intergenerational. We stand upon the foundations established by our ancestors, honor the shape and integrity of those foundations, and create re(new)ed and repurposed paths for our needs in the present. May Chamahua guide our journey!

Reflections on sea glass

While walking along beaches in Sonora I would often find sea glass. I observed how the ocean took jagged fragments discarded as garbage within her embrace, cycling the pieces through tides, waves, and sand. Gradually, over time, the ocean's gentle embrace would turn a broken glass shard onto another pebble on the beach. The pebbles are beautiful and unique in their integrity, forming part of a sandy mosaic. I carry sea glass with me as a reminder of both the scars that I carry as well as the reality that walking the Mosaic Path requires an ocean-like sensibility where we carefully work with the fragments of our personal, cultural, and linguistic heritage, jagged edges and all. We cycle through the jagged pieces through self-study, ceremonial reflection, building relations, re-purposing the fragments through active praxis. When we talk and teach about the fragments through our stories, new and more profound understandings emerge, making teaching a central part of learning and learning a central part of teaching. I was taught that the spoken word carries on our sacred breath (ihiyotl) and holds power because it is related to the wind. Our stories are the manifestation of our sacred breath (ihiyotl), helping us weave together the fabric of our opaque realities through a cycle of observation, reasoning, contemplation, and envisioning. Our stories belong to us; thus they must be told through our voices. To tell someone else's story without their consent and permission is taboo. The vulnerability inherent to speaking from the heart reminds us to be mindful about the words that we put out into the world, yet holds within it the power to help us connect with others and build relations. The relations built through sharing stories from the heart, hold substance and depth which in turn gives us the opportunity to demonstrate our integrity, build trust, and foster accountability. Through foundations of integrity, trust, and accountability, responsible connections with parallel narratives can be drawn, patterns can be identified, schemata can be articulated to convey patterns, and theory rooted in the sacred breath of story can emerge. When our stories are at the heart of theory we remain rigorous, relatable, complex, and accessible. May our stories continue to speak to the hearts of our relatives.

Note

1 The fasting ceremony or sacred fasting. "Teo" means sacred and "netzawa" means to fast.

References

Anzaldua, G. (1987). *Borderlands/La Frontera: The New Mestiza*. Aunt Lute Books.

Archibald, J. (2008). *Indigenous storywork: Educating the heart, mind, body, and spirit*. UBC Press.

Barbastro, F. A. (1792). Sermones en la Lengua Ópata. In: *Bancroft Library*, University of California, Berkeley.

Corr, E. A. (2019). The limits of literary theory and the possibilities of story work for Aboriginal literature in Australia. In J. Archibald, J. B. J. Lee-Morgan, & J. De Santolo (Eds.), *Decolonizing research:* Indigenous storywork as methodology (pp. 187–202). Zed Books.

Everdell, M. H., Jasson, D., Kuperman, & Benjamin A. (2020). Uto-Aztecan Lexicostatistics 2.0. *International Journal of American Linguistics, 86*(1), 1–30.

Galeano, E. (1997). *Open veins of Latin America: Five centuries of the pillage of a continent*. Monthly Review Press.

Holmes, A., & González, N. (2017). Finding sustenance: An Indigenous relational pedagogy. In D. Paris & H. S. Alim (Eds.). (2017). *Culturally sustaining pedagogies: Teaching and learning for justice in a changing world.* Teachers College Press.

Johnson, J. B. (1950). *The Ópata: An inland tribe of Sonora.* University of New Mexico Press.

Lawrence, A. (2021). [Personal Communication].

Lombardo, N. (1702). *El Arte de la Lengua Tegüïma, Vulgarmente Llamada Ópata.* In (1st ed.). Mexico D.F.: Instituto Nacional de Antropologia e Historia.

Miranda, D. (2013). *Bad Indians: A tribal memoir.* Heyday Books.

Owen, R. (1957). *Meresichi: A study of the descendants of an aboriginal group in a rural Mexican village.* University of Arizona.

Riley, C. (2005). *Becoming Aztlan: Mesoamerican influence in the greater Southwest, AD 1200–1500.* University of Utah Press.

Radding, C. (1997). *Wandering peoples: Colonialism, ethnic spaces, and ecological frontiers in Northwestern Mexico, 1700-1850.* Duke University Press.

Radding, C. (2005). *Landscapes of power and identity: Comparative histories in the Sonoran desert and the forests of Amazonia from Colony to Republic.* Duke University Press.

Radding, C. (2015). Borderlands of knowledge about nature: Crossing and creating boundaries in Early America. *Early American Studies, 13*(2), 503–510.

Shaul, D. L. (1989). Tegüïma (Ópata) phonology. *Southwestern Journal of Linguistics, 9,* 150–162.

Shaul, D. L. (1990). Tegüïma (Opata) inflectional morphology. *International Journal of American Linguistics, 56*(4), 561–573.

Sauer, C., & Brand, D. (1931). Prehistoric settlements of Sonora, with special reference to Cerros de Trincheras. *University of California Publications in Geography, 5,* 67–148.

Tanori, R. (2021). [Personal Communication].

Trejo Contreras, Z. (2010). La Preservaciøn del Ser: Nación y Territorio en La Re-Creation de las Sociedades Yaqui y Ópata Frente a la Instititución de la Sociedad Liberal, 1831–1876. In Espinoza, Esperanza Donjuan; Enriquez Licón, Dora Elvia; Trejo Contreras, Zulema (Ed.), *Religión, Nación y Territorio en los Imaginarios Sociales Indígenas de Sonora, 1767-1940.* El Colegio de Sonora.

Yetman, D. A. (2010). *The Ópatas: In search of a Sonoran people.* University of Arizona Press.

12

YOUR THEORY IS TOO SMALL

Beyond stories of the hunt

Antar A. Tichavakunda

Beyond stories of the hunt

"When you think of a theorist, who comes to mind? What type of person does theory?" I wait for students' responses in the Zoom chat box. "Professors." "Scientists." "Old white men." "Foucault." "Me? I never thought about it." Their answers vary, but often, students identify theory as something outside of themselves.

I tell students they are theorists. I do this, in part, because no one told me that I could be a theorist. No one told me, as a student, I was already theorizing. I want better for the future. I want burgeoning Black scholars, people of color more broadly, and other disenfranchised groups to have bigger ideas for theory and for themselves as thinkers.

My theoretical journey can be understood in relation to the West African proverb, "Until the lions have their historians, tales of the hunt shall always glorify the hunter." From my experience as a fifth grader, to struggling through doctoral coursework as a first-year, to expanding my research on Black student life, how I view theory continues to evolve. Of note, is my belief that theory work is lineage work. As such, I join a lineage of scholars troubling, challenging, expanding, and refusing dominant understandings of theory (e.g., Brooms, 2021; Collins, 1998; Dotson, 2013a; Quashie, 2012; Tuck, 2009; Tuck & Yang, 2014). In this tradition, I push for a more expansive view of theory to understand and support Black communities.

DOI: 10.4324/9781003303800-16

Framing theory

I am a theorist. I began calling myself a theorist, without qualifiers, during my third year as an assistant professor. I was inspired by the observation made by Joy James who pointed out that white men "do not title their works '*White Masculinist* Theory'; white women do not preface their writings with '*White* Feminist Theory'" (James, 1993, p. 123). Yet, I hesitate to call myself a theorist—it feels audacious. Despite my research being theoretically driven, publishing purely theoretical pieces, and introducing sociological theories to the field of higher education, part of me still hesitates to call myself a theorist.

The hesitation comes from the education system I traversed. My view of theory, largely because of graduate school, was too small. As I will highlight throughout the chapter, storytelling is central to how I view theory. In the words of Joy James, "Our storytelling is our theorizing. And so an 'introduction' into theory is an introduction into spiritual, political struggles for peace and freedom" (James, 1993, p. 31). I also find inspiration in Patricia Hill Collins' (1998) description of theory:

> ... doing social theory involves analyzing the changing aspects of social organization that affect people's everyday lives. Social theory is a body of knowledge and set of institutional practices that actively grapple with the central questions facing a group of people in a specific political, social and historical context (p. xii).

Based on this description, theory can take many forms—from songs, to poems, to stories, to proverbs, to journal articles. Personally, I do not have a static definition of theory as my view changes as I grow. I continue, however, to grapple with understanding theories, exercising them in different ways, and leveraging them to not only analyze, but to support Black communities. I developed this expansive view of theory in spite of the educational contexts I traversed.

I mention stories about the context of how I learned theory because theorizing does not occur in a vacuum. We are not empty vessels imbibing the knowledge and theories in the work we read. We become theorists in the crucibles of life. The structural oppressions—or lack thereof—we make lives around, within, and against, shapes the theories we gravitate towards and create. Stories help us understand our relationship to theories and concretize the abstract theories we read and create. Stories breathe life into theoretical propositions, animating theory so readers might better understand it by seeing theory in action. Stories are central to theory, but also to research in general. In what follows, I tell the story of how I came to view theory.

Elementary school: When right answers are wrong

I have passed, failed, and muddled through countless quizzes and exams. Most, I don't remember. Quizzes only induced anxiety. Yet, one quiz I took as a fifth grader was transformative. This 10-question, true-or-false quiz on half of a college-ruled sheet of paper changed how I viewed education and inequality. The change in my worldview was neither immediate nor drastic. Yet two decades later, I still reflect upon this incident.

My class was probably 90% Black. My teacher, whom I still regard as one of my favorite teachers, was a white woman. The quiz I refer to was for a unit about antebellum US history. I cannot remember any other question, but I do remember one: "Was slavery necessary for the South's economy?" I scribbled "F" for false and waited for the next question. Easy. We traded and graded. "Alright, for number seven, was slavery necessary for the South's economy?" A Black boy, my classmate, raised his hand, "True." "Correct! The South's economy needed slavery." Students pumped their fists and I could hear a chorus of my classmates saying "yes" across the room, celebrating the right answer.

I was upset. I was mad I got the question wrong. But something else was eating at me—how could anyone, under any circumstance, justify *needing* slavery? I remember telling my mom about the question that evening. "Antar, you were right," she said, "That was a bad question to ask. You were right." I'm not sure what led me to marking the answer false. Perhaps it was my father—a man who changed his last name from Brown to Tichavakunda, a Shona name meaning, "we shall conquer them." Perhaps it was my mother, who instilled pride in my being, took me to museums every weekend, and ensured I associated Blackness with fullness. Perhaps it was my grandmother, who was born in Mississippi and worked as a docent in the American History Museum's section on the Great Migration. Because of my worldview, I could only answer my teacher's question with a response that affirmed Black life—even if that answer was "wrong."

I tell this story often, using it to provide an example of the power of storytelling in theorizing, especially in Critical Race Theory (CRT). Stories shape our social realities, how we view ourselves and others, how we understand history and what histories we tell, and what we imagine is possible for society. Critical Race Theorists hold that white supremacy depends upon stories: "Empowered groups long ago established a host of stories, narratives, conventions, and understandings that today, through repetition, seem natural and true" (Delgado, 1993, p. 666). This quiz is an example of a story that normalizes white supremacy and Black dehumanization.

My experience taking the quiz can be understood through the hunter-lion proverb, which is also often quoted by Critical Race scholars (e.g.,

Ladson-Billings, 2013). The proverb helps our thinking about the power of storytelling not only in CRT, but in critical and liberatory theorizing more broadly. Indeed, critical theorists and those from disenfranchised communities find inspiration in the proverb, reflecting upon their lion status in a hunter-dominated society. Through this proverb, one's gaze is averted to the oppressive and limiting logics underpinning Western, dominant understandings of theory in the academy. The lion's story becomes synonymous with counter-narratives in CRT, subaltern theories, and the words and experiences of the disenfranchised.

The quiz I took was part of the master, hunter narrative that rendered chattel slavery a necessity for an economy. The story spun by textbooks and the media was so commonplace that my otherwise thoughtful teacher did not notice that she was telling the hunter's tale of the hunt—that she was propagating a white supremacist truth. In reflection, this was a moment I began to question truths, worldviews, and theories that made me out to be less than human.

Graduate school: When your stories are not enough

I struggled in graduate school—especially my first year. Beyond the adjustment to life in a new city, Los Angeles, this was my first time living by myself as an adult. I also did not have any research experience, but I had passion and love for my community.

While teaching in DC, I became fascinated with narratives and how they shape research and policy. And so I applied and got accepted to a doctoral program. I wanted to work to change simplistic, flattening, racist narratives around Black students. In my doctoral classes, I would often engage with the reading by relating something to my experience in DC Public Schools or navigating a predominantly white undergraduate university. By virtue of my unique experience and being the only Black man in the cohort, I thought my stories could enrich class discussions.

My stories, however, were not enough. I was struggling to keep pace with the readings and learning how to engage in the scholarly forum in a way that would be appreciated by other students and professors. In addition to the learning curve I had to surmount to analyze peer-reviewed, scholarly texts, I struggled with the program. I was the youngest in my cohort. I had no research experience. In a class with less than 15 people, one white professor would forget my name and neglect to acknowledge my presence in the room. No classes I took during my first two semesters seriously engaged with the intersection of race and education. In short, I did not feel like I belonged.

At the end of my first year, I received feedback that I did not seem comfortable with theory. I resolved to become competent in theory in a form that was legible to my professors. I spent a summer reading everything I could about Critical Race Theory (CRT),[1] later commuting across the city to take a CRT in education course, and took four, theory-driven classes in the Sociology department. I overcompensated for what I viewed as a crack in my scholarly foundation.

One of the most helpful exercises for learning to engage in theory was from one of my Sociology professors. He implied that our experiences mattered, but not in the classroom. He wanted to hear less about our experiences, and more about the text. And so I learned to put different theorists in conversation—Foucault with Goffman, Fanon with Mbembe, Weber with Marx. The goal was not to animate the text with our lives and experiences but to put the work in conversation with other texts and concepts. The goal, I found, was a sort of ventriloquism—conjecturing, through deep study, what a theorist might say about a given topic. A deep study of other theorists is important. Theorizing, in any fashion, is lineage work. We learn from the theorists before us and build upon their work to theorize for tomorrow. It was in this class that I learned to theorize in a way that would be appreciated in a society of hunters.

My professor also said, "You're not allowed to say you don't like a book until you have written a book yourself." Some of the books I read, I did not like, often because of their silences on race. I had to learn to express my discontent in a manner that my peers and professor could appreciate. I learned how to wield the work of theorists both to defend my ideas and attack race-evasive or racist assumptions underlying other work we were assigned to read.

In reflecting upon my experience about learning how to "do theory" in graduate school, I find the words and experience of the Black feminist philosopher, V. Denise James (2014), enlightening. A white colleague joked to James, in what was meant to be a compliment, "You do philosophy like a white man" (James, 2014, p. 191). James (2014) elaborated, saying that although she was a Black feminist, she learned to navigate the field of philosophy like other philosophers:

> I would learn to cut and undercut. To outwit and to argue minutiae not because the points were important to the projects I wanted to pursue or because my criticism truly shed light on the difficulties of the task at hand, but because that was the way to do philosophy "right," to do philosophy like a white man (p. 191).

Similar to James, I learned to model my theorizing off of what I saw as successful in the classroom—divorced from personal experiences, dispassionate, and with a stern fidelity to the assigned texts and prior readings in the course.

My training in what I viewed as theory was in accordance with the dominant, widely accepted understandings of theory in social science research. While I had viewed my stories as "not enough," perhaps the problem was that my graduate program's approach to theorizing and teaching theory was too small. The dominant approach to theory was not expansive or flexible enough to include or think with my stories and experiences. If I were to relate my training to the hunter-lion proverb, then I was trained by the hunters. The stories I told and the experiences I brought were unappreciated in most classrooms. The absence of experience and stories in academic courses continues to trouble me. Certainly, engagement with theories and different work in our training is necessary. But what of our stories? Like many things, in research and in life, I see this as a *both/and*—not an *either/or*.

Tenure track: Beyond stories of the hunt

"Until lions have their historians, tales of the hunt shall always glorify the hunter." I return to the proverb often and include it in a PowerPoint I use for describing CRT to audiences. Yet, how I understand this proverb continues to take new meaning as I grow as a theorist. Previously, I viewed the proverb as an irrefutable clarion call to amplify and center the voices, stories, and theories of the oppressed rather than those of the oppressors. The proverb is a force—a paradigm shift, compelling academia to reckon with the dominant, oppressive logics underpinning and shaping how we understand theory. Now, the tensions within the proverb are more apparent to me. Tensions, however, are inherent to both proverbs and theory.

Proverbs, like theory, are points of departure, touchpoints, unfinished maps, and laws. They are unfixed and amendable, yet, they provide guidance to navigating the social world. A strength of theory, like proverbs, lies in its potential flexibility—pliable enough to be applied, thought with, and exercised in different instances, yet cohesive enough to provide direction and clarity. Different proverbs provide different insights into aspects of social reality. The same goes for theory. This comparison, of course, is not perfect. Yet, I mention the similarities between theory and proverbs to make clear that the tensions I see in the hunter-lion proverb or our theorizing in general, are not weaknesses. Rather, they are potential sites of opportunity.

As I began to do more work researching the expansiveness and dynamism of Black student life, I found myself questioning the same proverb. A proverb is only the beginning of a conversation, kindle to spark deep reflection. I asked myself, "But what other stories do the lions have? Wasn't there more to the lion's life than the hunt?" Regardless of who tells the story, the hunt remains at the center. I began to connect this tension with theorizing in education.

The words of Beatriz Nascimento—a Black Brazilian theorist, organizer, and poet—provide guidance for my thinking about the dominance of "the hunt" and "hunter" in theorizing.[2] In her text "For a (New) Existential and Physical Territory", and as mentioned in Smith et al. (2021), Nascimento writes,

> What use do we have for History? If I am powerless, I have no need of it. History serves those who tell it. Over time, it becomes one with power. In this country, my life is not power, but that is not the end of it … The task is not merely to exist, but to make life more beautiful, and happier. History is the field and territory of the victors, but it would be futile to replace it with a history of the defeated—we have not yet been defeated. Those who have been called beaten are individuals, full of stories. Their stories may be small, but they are rich and captivating" (p. 305).

Much can be said about the passage, but I draw attention to its connection to the hunter-lion proverb and theory at three levels. First, who can be a theorist? When one thinks of critical theorists, who comes to mind? It is by design in a hunter-society, that Black women and theorists who theorize in other languages such as Nascimento are not widely read. English, one might argue, is the predominant language of the hunter. Second, Nascimento urges readers to appreciate the small stories of individuals. Lastly, Nascimento questions how history is understood. She reminds us that the oppressed are not defeated but pushes readers by saying that replacing the story of the hunter with the story of the lion should not be the goal.

To what extent are scholars creating and telling stories simply to counter dominant, racist narratives? Such work is necessary. But this is not the only work. Eve Tuck (2009), Nascimento and many other scholars remind us in different ways, that we, and the communities we serve and are members of, are not damaged, broken, or defeated. Following Tuck's (2009) work on "damage-centered" research, I have found that much work on Black students in education is oppression-centered. Oppression-centered research does not always end with participants being understood as damaged. By oppression-centered research, I mean that Black students and other communities are only seen as analytically "interesting" insofar as they experience or resist oppressive structures. Research on student activists, high achievers, student leaders, and those who persist despite constraining forces is important. Yet, there is more to life, and Black life in particular, than resistance.

I had noticed the focus of research on Black students in higher education through resistance but did not have the words. Then I read Kevin Quashie's

(2012) *The Sovereignty of Quiet*. In this work, he demonstrates how Black people and Black culture are primarily understood through a lens of resistance. Quashie (2012) argued that Black people are "resistant in context, but not in essence" (p. 24). I cannot cite this quote enough.

Through resistance, and resistance-centered frameworks, we understand the lion's story only in relation to the hunt. Did the lion have cubs? Was the lion part of a pride or did it travel by itself? What life did the lion have outside of the hunt? Such questions are rendered unimportant through resistance frameworks and the proverb. The same goes for research on Black students. When one thinks of Black student agency in higher education, images of activists and protests likely come to mind. But agency and Black life is far more than activism or obvious resistance. Black student life is also Black students coming together for a Black student union meeting, reserving a set of classrooms during finals for Black study halls, or throwing a party off-campus.

In learning more about theory, I have been drawn to examining how we can more expansively understand and affirm the complexities of Black student life. Some of my fondest memories in college, for example, were with my nearly all-Black friend group. I remember hanging out with two of my friends in front of the iconic Brown Bear statue—our school's mascot. On an otherwise quiet evening on our campus' main green, for some reason, my boy decided to break out his portable speakers. He played, at that time, the new song, "You're a Jerk," and, without any discussion, we each started hitting the reject. We had only recently taken time to practice doing the reject, a dance, accompanying the West Coast hit. For an audience of ourselves, for our joy, we danced.

Scholars employing critical frameworks or theories might find this scene interesting, but unworthy of including in their findings, or unimportant from a social science lens. Other critical scholars may attempt to shoehorn this scene into a manifestation of resistance. As the adage goes, "If the only tool you have is a hammer, you tend to see every problem as a nail." In a similar manner, if the theoretical framework you use centers upon oppression or resistance to oppression, you tend to see pertinent data or aspects of social life as examples of oppression or resistance. A social scientist with resistance and tales of the hunt on their mind might see our organic dance session as a bold example of resistance, a refusal of the dominant white university culture. At that moment, however, I was not thinking about the optics or implications. I was not thinking about what it meant for three Black men dancing without care in a public space at a private university with a 7% Black population. I was just thinking about how much fun I was having, and how happy I was at that moment. This moment was important for my campus life, but not in the way critical scholars focused on resistance and oppression might assume. The joy, leisure, and camaraderie, I think, were what made this moment memorable and one my friends and I still return to. Might leading frameworks in education attend to such integral moments of Black student life? Or are they rendered unimportant? In order to better understand, advocate for, and organize with Black students, we need a vast theoretical repertoire that attends to the interplay between structure and agency while also centering Black life.

Acknowledging and focusing on oppression and the far-reaching impacts of racism is important in education research—a problems-based discipline. In my work, I do not steer clear of any talk of oppression. Yet, I wrestle with how we might center Black student life in order to provide an incisive critique of capitalism, racism, and other oppressive structures. For example, in my work on joy (Tichavakunda, 2021b), I take care to center Black joy but also demonstrate how structures can either inhibit or facilitate Black students' recreation and celebration.

Whose stories matter?

Return to the scene of the hunter and lion. In prioritizing the obvious actors in the hunt, the hunter and the lion, much is rendered uninteresting. The trees that provide shade, the soil on which the lion and hunters trod, the shrubs that feed the gazelles, and the gazelles that are prey to the lions; fade to the background. Yet, they are no less important to the hunt that takes center stage. Within education research, many people and relationships, although central to schooling, likewise fade to amorphous backdrops of our research.

In higher education research, I can tell you whose stories are often absent—the people who clean the lecture halls, the people who empty the trash, the people who clean the restrooms, the people who serve food, the people who station cash registers in cafeterias and food courts, and the people who shovel the snow and rake the leaves. The theories we employ and the customs of our disciplines also shape who is deemed worthy of study.

My own research agenda is an example of how the focus on the hunters and lions has, in some ways, restricted my analytic gaze. I understand my research as engaging with the central question: "How can we better support and understand Black communities in educational institutions that are permanently racist?" I had, up until recently, centered my research on Black students and their experiences at historically white institutions (Tichavakunda, 2021a). By centering their multifarious experiences, from their joy to their agency in creating places, I have tried to push past the hunter/lion binary of focusing on resistance in research on Black students. Yet, my view on my research shifted after receiving feedback from a collective of other Black scholars about a paper I was writing about the symbolic nature of university acts of racial redress. My friend said that I might mention how Black student activists sometimes neglect to mention the conditions of Black custodians and food service workers in their demands from the institution. He also pointed me to Robin D.G. Kelley's (2016) work on Black student activism. After reflection and study, I realized I had let an entire community evade my analytical lens—Black custodians, food service workers, and groundskeepers. What stories do they have of Black life, their lives, in higher education and other school settings?

More than our theories, I have realized that I must be attuned to where I place my analytic gaze. Certainly, some theories are more geared to specific populations—student development theory for students, pedagogical theories for teachers, and leadership theories for school leaders. Yet, other theories might be exercised and stretched beyond their routinized employment in scholarly work. What, for example, might a Critical Race theorist learn from studying Black custodians working in a historically white institution of higher education? For me, the question has become more pressing. If I profess to study Black communities in higher education, then I will have to recognize that the community expands beyond the student, administrator, and faculty communities.

Theorizing is about expansion. Sometimes, we make theory small. We become so accustomed to using one theoretical hammer that we only see nails. We hammer away at practical and theoretical problems, yet, potentially for fear of clumsy handling, we might neglect other theoretical tools that might push our work further. Other times, we make theory small by not exercising theory, extending its potential usefulness beyond the usual suspects of our research. Theory is about story-telling. Yet, theorizing is about many, sometimes competing stories. Through diverse stories from different positions and frames, we might paint a more true-to-life, complex picture. We might better understand and advocate with others in the project of equity and building a better world. For me, theorizing is about flexibility.

Theory is lineage work

I grew up in my grandparent's house. My mom, sister, and I lived there until I was in high school. Every day, starting in kindergarten, before I would walk to school with my mom, my grandmother would stop what she was doing, smile, and say, "Do your best work!" She'd sometimes say this between bites, finishing up breakfast. Sometimes she would say it from the porch of the house, yelling out her phrase to make sure I would hear. Other times she would say it in a hushed tone in my ear as we hugged. She kept up this daily practice until she passed.

My grandmother grew up in Greenwood, Mississippi. She graduated from Tougaloo College near the top of her class, majoring in the sciences. But as a Black woman living before and during the Civil Rights Movement, her options were limited. She worked as a secretary in a lab until she started teaching science in DC Public Schools.

I wonder what it meant for my grandmother—who likely graduated with higher grades and with more experience in the sciences than some of the all-white staff she worked with—to do her best work as a secretary in that lab. I carry with me what she told me every day without fail, and with a smile—do your best work. This is theorizing. To do your best work, assess the social reality, find joy, create a life, and start a family within the crushing structures of gendered racism certainly required brilliant theorizing (see James, 1993). Theory is not restricted to academic journals, ivory towers, or those affiliated with universities. Rather, theory and theorists reside in all of us. I have many questions I wish I could have asked my grandmother. Yet, I have inherited her orientation towards both life and work.

I view theory as lineage work. I find inspiration in the words of the philosopher, Kristie Dotson (2013b): "I claim that one of the roles of Black philosophy is to demonstrate radical love for Black people by performing acts of inheritance of theoretical production created and maintained by Black peoples" (p. 38). Inheritance, Dotson (2013b) shows, is about love and intentionality. Inheritance is personal in that I think about my identity, the shoulders, and legacies I stand on, in order to work and theorize. In locating myself in a lineage, I have more confidence. I am never theorizing by myself. My intellectual big homies are behind me and with me as I write. They have already paved the way and made space for me to carry their work forward. For me, inheritance is about locating my theorizing in a lineage of Critical Race theorists, education scholars, Black feminists, sociologists, and other Black thinkers. Any theorist, I suggest, can usefully locate themselves in a lineage. Whether that lineage is within a line of organizers and activists or within Marxist or Critical Race thought, theorizing is lineage work.

Understanding theorizing as lineage work keeps me honest. Constructing theory in this way reminds me that theory is not small, but expansive, transcending space and time. Understanding theory as flexible helps me see both the usefulness and limitations of the hunter/lion paradigm of critical scholarship. Viewing theory as lineage work and inheritance also ensures that I remain close to the people and communities I intend to serve. And because theorizing involves inheritance, I theorize alongside my grandmother. Because of my community, and an expansive view of theory, I am able to do my best work.

Notes

1 I am thankful for Shafiqa Ahmadi for loaning me a stack of foundational books on Critical Race Theory.
2 I am thankful for my friend, Jeaná Morrison, who introduced me to Nascimento's work.

References

Brooms, D. R. (2021). *Stakes is high: Trials, lessons, and triumphs in young Black men's educational journeys.* SUNY Press.
Collins, P. H. (1998). *Fighting words: Black women and the search for justice (Vol. 7).* U of Minnesota Press.
Delgado, R. (1993). On telling stories in school: A reply to Farber and Sherry. *Vand. L. Rev.*, *46*, 665–676.
Dotson, K. (2013a). How is this paper philosophy?. *Comparative Philosophy*, *3*(1), 3–29.
Dotson, K. (2013b). Radical love: Black philosophy as deliberate acts of inheritance. *The Black Scholar*, *43*(4), 38–45.
James, J. (1993). Teaching theory, talking community. In J. James, & R. Farmer (Eds.), *Spirit, Space, and Survival: African American Women in (White) Academe* (pp. 118–135). New York, NY: Routledge.
James, V. D. (2014). Musing: A black feminist philosopher: Is that possible?. *Hypatia*, *29*(1), 189–195.
Kelley, R. D. G. (2016, March 6). *Black study, black struggle.* Boston Review. http://bostonreview.net/forum/robin-d-g-kelley-black-study-black-struggle
Ladson-Billings, G. (2013). Critical race theory—What it is not! In M. Lynn, & A. D. Dixson (Eds.), *Handbook of critical race theory in education* (pp. 34–47). Routledge.
Quashie, K. (2012). *The sovereignty of quiet.* Rutgers University Press.
Smith, C., Davies, A., & Gomes, B. (2021). "In Front of the World": Translating Beatriz Nascimento. *Antipode*, *53*(1), 279–316.
Tichavakunda, A. A. (2021a). *Black campus life: The worlds black students make at a historically white institution.* SUNY Press.
Tichavakunda, A. A. (2021b). Black Joy on white campuses: Exploring Black students' recreation and celebration at a Historically White Institution. *The Review of Higher Education*, *44*(3), 297–324.
Tuck, E. (2009). Suspending damage: A letter to communities. *Harvard Educational Review*, *79*(3), 409–428.
Tuck, E., & Yang, K. W. (2014). R-words: Refusing research. In D. Paris, & M. T. Winn (Eds.), *Humanizing research: Decolonizing qualitative inquiry for youth and communities* (pp. 223–247). Thousand Oaks, CA: Sage.

13

AN AFROFUTURIST DREAMS OF BLACK LIBERATIONS

Disentangling Blackness from fatalism

S. R. Toliver

I'm not sure where I began. I did not exist, and then I was formed, molded out of history, the current moment, and the future. I was a night child, given breath at the darkest point of the evening, refusing light, refusing a welcome where darkness did not surround me. I was carved from the lips of a griot who foretold of futures I was responsible for, futures I would facilitate into being. She beat the tempo of my existence on her drum, spoke the words that gave me life, and pushed my being to the ears of listeners willing to engage in the work of story (Windchief & San Pedro, 2019). The story listeners clapped loudly, welcoming me into this world, appreciative of my existence, and of the work I was meant to do. The griot's umber lips wrinkled at the corners of her aged face because her work was done, but my work and the work of the story listeners had just begun.

I didn't know I'd be born again so many times after that first moment when the story filled my lungs. Billions of births over the centuries – beat from drums, displayed in portraits, dispersed through song, inked on paper, and housed in Black bodies. I have lived many lifetimes, and yet, with each rebirth, I am reminded of my important position as a link in the networked consciousness (Lavender, 2019). Listen, the work is about to begin (Archibald, 2008).

The story listener sits, eyes closed, heart open. They have been tasked with the role of caretaker, bestowed the honor of following the story in this life and beyond. They are eager to act as narrative doula, guiding and supporting the story until it chooses its end …

***

DOI: 10.4324/9781003303800-17

My most recent journey began over thirty years ago. I began as clay, molded to the specifications for a being deemed Black and girl, programmed for survival through codes of silence and obedience. Forged with the memories of grandmother, grandfather, mother, other mother, I was uploaded into this brain, this body. I supposed I was a child because I had no autonomy, no control over my identity or who I wanted to be. It was pink and yellow and purple. I was gendered dreams fulfilled. I was youth, supposed innocence mapped over my body for all to see. I soon learned, however, that childhood was a fallacy, a glamor used to hide the perceived adult beneath.

I embodied child, and childhood was intimately foregrounded by a loving family, and yet, the outside world decided that this body didn't constitute childhood. According to the world, I needed less comfort, less nurturing, and less support. According to society, I already knew about adult topics and sex, so there was no point in bestowing the honor of innocence upon me (Epstein et al., 2017, p. 1). Childhood was a lie, an intangible thing I consistently reached for but never grasped, an ethereal specter that followed some young people, but not me. These ghosts of innocence journeyed toward whiteness, the light in the darkness, the virtue of the blameless. Childhood required a magical dispersal of my culture, home, and self, a scattering of Black and girl. Childhood required the erasure of the Blackness that consumed my body. Childhood demanded the quarantining of personhood so as not to scare white teachers who chose to see monsters instead of girls. When I began, I was celebrated. When I was reborn as this child, I was girl, I was monster, I was both.

The story listener watches, hopeful that this Black girl, this beautiful story sees through societal failings of Black children. They hope that this being remembers that they belong to the ancestors, not this world. They whisper, "Please, my child, embrace your youth. Don't let them tell you who you are. Remember us."

***

"You're a girl, so you can't play sports," the boys down the street jeer when I attempt to play with them. Grass stains from makeshift football fields and scraped knees from concrete basketball courts proved otherwise. And yet, what does it mean to exist in this girl's body, this contained being who presents as feminine, who loves the game but hates the stereotypes. I was an elementary school child/not child who could not dictate her youth nor her interests. I was a young monster who was not welcomed by the local townsfolk.

"You're Black, so you can't like anime," the white boy says as he prepares his inquisition. "Name eight characters from Dragon Ball! What happened in the last Inuyasha episode? If you're such a fan, name five anime and their main characters! I mean, what do Black girls know about nerd stuff anyway?" I could have responded, and answered his questions in order to leave him probing behind the stock narratives (Delgado, 1989) he's always known about those who look like me. I could have beaten him with my retorts, and made him reconsider the ousting of people from nerd communities based solely on racial and gendered visages. But silence is often a balm in the face of fear. I was a middle school child/not child who was relegated to certain stories, specific narratives that forced my existence into a rigid box. I was a middle school monster, forced to run away from community for fear of white children with pitchforks.

"Why don't you write something more *real*," the high school teacher argues, as she grades my most recent narrative essay. I know I write well because I was birthed from narrative, storied into existence. And yet, the teacher doesn't want my story. She continues, "You know, more historically accurate, something that talks about your life." The issue is that the essay is one of the realest narratives I've written, pages filled with the lore and mythology, the everyday existence of my family and my ancestors. I know what she means, though. She wants the pain of enslavement, the trauma of forced separation, rape, and servitude, and the physical and psychological violence that surrounds tales of Black life in the United States. She doesn't want my dragons, my gods and goddesses, my tales of agency and heroism, my stories of Black everyday life in the Rust Belt. She wants my pain. She wants more of her story, not mine. I was a high school child/ not child whose stories were not her own. I was a monster, and the tales of my horror surrounded me, as the teacher couldn't see that my existence was so much more than the negative stories she told herself to maintain her savior complex.

"You are a diamond, a person with multiple facets who must let all aspects of your being shine brightly. You must embrace who you are, whoever you choose to be," my mother tells me. She sees me and recognizes the person that loves anime, that craves Broadway musicals, and appreciates existence beyond the confines created by the world around her. She knows her prayer for my life is essential to my growth. She engages in supplication to a being I'm not sure exists to secure my life on this planet. I hear her, hear her pleas, her requests, her demands, that this world be better than it was before, than it was when she was a little Black girl monster child/not child. I hear a twinge of doubt, though. She knows this prayer may go unanswered because she is mother to a monstrous child. She is protector of beings who scare. I wonder: do the gods hear the prayers of the monster's mother? Do they hear her when she worries, when she cries?

I don't know if they listen, but I do. I was molded in a cyclical time capsule, storied of past, present, and future. I see what must be done. I finally see how

Blackness is a confinement, a cage that would continue to box me in as long as I continued to exist on this Earth. I know now, after journeying along this network for so long that the only way to overcome this ailment is to impound my body, my true self. The griot sung my song, but she could not have foretold this future. She could not have imagined that my link would lead to this being, this body, this monster. But my purpose is to survive, to continue the networked consciousness through this body. So, I must sing a new song: speak in "proper" tone, pluck the chords of my hair strands straight, take whole rests of my interests, write songs in the key of white men who determine what constitutes normality and tradition. I must become a contortionist, distorting myself, deforming my body until it is almost unrecognizable. I must be respectable, enacting centuries-old methods of resistance that helped many Black women and girls avoid the gaze of dominant eyes (Higginbotham, 1993). I must bend to brokenness, let the shards of my psyche fall where they may, let the broken pieces cut into my feet as I try to ignore the piercing pain of each step I take toward the future. I must disfigure myself, my Blackness, and let it become mangled in the gears of whiteness because this monster must endure. This story must survive.

The story listener cries, rivers of sadness streaming down their face as they reach out to the child. "Please, don't forget where you come from. We celebrate your life. We appreciate your existence. Do not forget the joy of your birth, and the love of your ancestors!"

***

I sustained myself by hobbling through educational systems that saw my broken body, Black and bloodied by years of corrupted learning experiences. I accumulated the burdens of "not good enough," "twice as good," "smart for a Black girl." I collected ire from college professors who told me I did not have the capacity to write well, so every paper – painstakingly written with imposter syndrome hovering from behind – was submitted to the department chair for review. Twice as good, too good, so good that I could not have written the work on my own. This professor, a monster like me, held her own pitchfork, shouting verbal, passive-aggressive assaults against my body and my mind. I curled into myself, protecting my heart from the battering, but a few strikes made it through.

Strike 1: I am not good enough to write my story. Maybe, I plagiarized an author long forgotten.

Strike 2: I am not good enough to be in this college classroom. Maybe, if I focused my attention to "real" scholarship – white authors and thinkers – I'll survive this space.

Strike 3: I am not good enough to graduate. Maybe, I can further contort myself and make it to the other side. There's still more body to break, right?.

Strike … strike … and strike again.

The story listener braces themselves. They will endure some of the pain; they will block the strikes the child cannot see. They cannot shield her from everything, for the barrage is too great, but they need her to know she is not alone. They desperately yell into an ephemeral void, "Remember! Refuse forgetfulness and recall your people, your hope! We are with you!"

***

To be cliché, I have heard that the grass isn't always greener on the other side. I have learned this is true. I leave one village for another. I see the stakes at the ready, the bonfires burning behind school buildings just in case a monster stumbles into their midst. I amass quizzical faces from parents who request visual verification of my credentials to ensure that my Blackness does not impede their child's learning. I hear, "she would never be allowed at my country club because she's too dark, am I right?" followed by uncomfortable laughter and inadvertent gazes in my direction. I sit amongst a horde of white women as one argues that the past wasn't so bad, that people who look like me are complaining about bygone eras of white violence that no longer affect us. The silence of my peers is deafening, only one harrowing call of resistance from someone I consider friend. I wish to leave, to find a way out of this space, and yet, I stay. I am a monster who has infiltrated the town, and they have not yet cast me out. Is this … safety? Is this how I survive? Maybe. I don't know if safe places for monsters exist.

Eventually, I realized the unbearable weight of whiteness is too heavy a burden to stay in the town. There are no pitchforks this time, no fires stoked in preparation for my execution, but I feel it nearing. I am too radical, too outspoken, too Black. It is only a matter of time before they begin my death march, before they drag me to the fire in hopes of eliminating my existence. I walk aimlessly, trying to find a space that will welcome me.

Will you let me in?

Will you let me stay?

Will you let me live?

I am no longer whole. I am pieces, reflections of a past self that used to believe herself diamond, reminiscent flesh of a once Black girl, Black suggestion in a sea of white surety. Surely, there is space for the unwanted. There must be a home for monstrous Others, for those whose welcome has run out, for those who can't figure out how to contort themselves anymore because their bodies can only bend so much.

The story listener reaches out to the girl, attempting to touch her shoulder, hoping their presence will cause her to remember the celebration of her existence, the story she was meant to tell … to be. "We have never left you," they say. "Remember us!" they implore. "Do not split your story into fragments. We need you to be whole."

***

I walk for miles until I find a large plantation, built by people I have never met who are preserved through stories I have never heard. I felt the presence of ancestral beings, cleaning students' rooms, fixing the buildings they were prohibited from learning in, and working in the illustrious botanical garden, a monster in the woods. I sense the regulations of existence: curfews of 9:00 PM, restricted movements that only enable job functions, racist rules prohibiting entrance into campus buildings, negro ~~houses~~ cages on the presidential lot (African American Experience in Athens, 2015). This institution, this university, rises from the bones of my ancestors, Black people who left their blood, sweat, and tears on manicured lawns their feet could not touch. I find myself here, sensing, but never fully grasping at the meaning of this place. I reach out, hoping to grab the hand of my past, but I grab nothing. This presence isn't dense enough to feel. It is simultaneously too light and too heavy.

I find myself on campus walking past buildings named after white men who would rather see me dead than receive an education in their illustrious buildings (Posey, 2020). Vandiver argued that no being with negro blood would attend classes with white students. Caldwell pledged to preserve segregation of the races. Rutherford whose legacy is the memorialization of Confederate ideals, heroic mythology of battles not won so southerners could feel better about their failure to preserve enslavement. Candler, a Confederate colonel, an advocate of all-white political parties. Lumpkin whose honorable feats are described as the removal of Cherokee people from their homelands to ensure his family's supposed comfort. Aderhold, a man who appointed a special committee of white segregationists to prevent a Black man from attending his school – no monsters allowed because they might scare the innocents. These buildings are living legacies of a racist past that preserve white supremacy and Black erasure into the future. And yet, I walk through the doors, trying to ignore the stories they tell, the warnings they whisper.

It is not just the buildings that oppress. It is the knowledge that roams the halls, that sits in seats next to students who hold tightly to whiteness to prove they belong in this space. I am squished into the boxes of Hegel, Heidegger, Vygotsky, Piaget, Skinner, Bruner, Bloom, Gardner, Kolb, Dewy. I try to get out, to ask why my graduate education still revolves around white people as gods of knowledge to whom all others must kneel and present their offerings. But I am cautioned, told that I need not twist academic issues into racial politics, advised to center the real problems existing in education, to center the real issue – that Black people are inferior. I recoil and submit, entrench myself in the theories and methods of people who consider me an outlier, unimportant to the research, negligible in the results, inconsequential to theory and practice. I present my open brain as an offering in hopes that they will fill it with the knowledge necessary to prove I am enough. I offer my story in an attempt to forget, sing the names of white men to fill the spaces now empty, and hope that this sacrifice is enough to rid myself of monstrosity

The story listener wails. "Wake up, child! We are here! We have never left you! You are enough. You are loved. Remember your story. Remember the griot. She sang words of love and affirmation into your life. We still sing the celebration of your existence. Remember!"

***

I sit in a conference venue waiting for the speakers to begin their talk. The room is loud, voices bouncing off walls into my ears. I wish I could block it out, but I no longer have the energy to fight sound, to combat words. Then, all at once, the crowd is in a hush. Three monsters take the stage, but I am confused. Their heads do not droop, and their bodies are not contorted into indistinguishable mounds of bone and flesh. They speak in commanding tones. "Listen!" They plead in a collective chorus that hovers over the quiet of the room. When all eyes are on them, they begin their song.

One sings a melancholy note of Black experiences in education, somberly remembering those we have lost, yet rejoicing in the lives of those who are still here. He says we need a radical educational turn, one that helps Black youth avoid contortion, one that enables Black people to share the burden of whiteness so we can be free.

Another beats the drum of Black life. She says, "Black Lives Matter is not just a phrase to repeat, a badge to be worn so people consider you an ally. It is a mantra, a clarion call to uplift Black people, society's monsters. It is a song that causes supremacist ears to bleed while simultaneously nourishing Black life." She repeats this phrase over and over again until the sound of her voice seeps into the walls, the floors, the chairs, and the hearts of the listeners.

The last gathers all of us into her arms and asks us to consider what we have lost. She begs us to remember our wounds, joy, anger, happiness, and sorrow. She asks us to refuse forgetfulness and use our past and present as a means to heal our futures. She implores us to use the hauntings of our past as fuel to move us forward. We are our ancestors' wildest dreams. We are the ones we've been waiting for. We have the power to change this world.

Remember. Remember. Remember. This word loudly bangs against my eardrums as I sit mesmerized by the speakers. I remember a celebration, a gathering of night, words, and stories. I push against the wall of forgetfulness, and dump the contents of my brain onto the floor in hopes I can receive new knowledge. The monsters are no longer hard edges and jagged lines, they are beautiful Black angels whose light is blinding.

The story listener smiles. "You are coming back to us." They reach to hold the girl's hand. This time, a spark between their palms.

***

I felt it, a brief flicker rising from my fingertips as I lifted my hands to the songs of Black angels. I touched … something … as I listened to the angels recover their histories. But then, the glow was gone, and I was only left with questions: Where did the light form, and why did it leave so quickly? What transforms Black monsters into Black angels? How do I get the crowds to hush and listen as I sing Black praisesongs? How do I learn to unbend, to force others to notice that I am human, not monster?

The story listener whispers, for the connection has been made once again. "Follow the thread of story. Find your map to the future. Forget monstrosity and remember your humanity. Forge a path that leads to the (re)searching of Black past, present, and future."

I hear a voice. It is a sweet sound, reminiscent of my mother's vocal timber, love wrapped into each utterance. It is something familiar, yet strange – a distant relative, a long-lost cousin, a friend who has moved away. It is unembodied, detached from physical being, and yet I know it lives. They have been watching me, existing alongside me for quite some time. Our intimate connection is shown by the loving sound of their voice, the tender tone of their words. They are community. They are family. They are connection. I don't know how they came to know me, but the history of our acquaintance doesn't concern me. Instead, I want to know more about their words. The rest will come. I ask: "Where do I begin? How will I know I'm on the right path?"

The story listener is joyous, for this child has already begun the work. The beginning is the question, the desire to know from whence she came, the wish to (re)member that which she has learned to forget (Dillard, 2000). "Listen child," their voice resounds, "you have already begun. (Re)member the griot. (Re)call the festive occasion of your birth. (Re)collect the joy of the story listeners who first engaged in the work of listening to your story. (Re)search the stories already within you. The answer has always been inside."

A swirl of light and a gust of wind surround me, wrapping me in memories I thought burned in the fires of monstrous deaths, impaled by pitchforks held in white hands, deformed by the constant bending of a body on the brink of breakage. I remember my birth, hands clapping as my story was told by a Black elder who believed that my tale was worth telling. I recall the celebration of my birth, the tears of joy, the jamboree of music, dance, and life. I recollect the smiles of story listeners who chose to dedicate themselves to engaging in the work of the story. I see the body of the voice that refused to let me break. I research my existence, and I see innocence, intelligence, narrator, interlocutor, angel. I see that I have always been human.

The story listener weeps. The child has found herself. Now, because she has listened to her own story, she can help others to find the story within. "Welcome back to the world," they whisper, "Your work is about to begin."

I heeded the story listener's words and began to (re)search and (re)member. I pushed back the voices of Bahktin, Foucault, and Erikson into a small space in my mind to make room for the Black ideas I had been forced to forget throughout this life. I read the words of supposed monstrous Others – Alice, Octavia, Venus, Ruth, Ebony, Gholdy, Marcelle. I realized that the true monsters were the townsfolk, those who refused to see the humanity within Black people. I learned that Blackness was not a confinement, but a liberation. I absorbed the scholars' lyrical prose and used their narrative artistry to sing songs of my own, songs I had long neglected. I sang myself diamond and began to see that my work was not to contort, to bend to the wills of townsfolk who wished me dead. My work was to become a story listener, to help other stories like me make it through this world without bending, without breaking. We deserve to be whole.

The story listener observes the change. They say, "we all deserve to experience the fullness of humanity. Keep going. Keep (re)searching. You are close."

I dream of the steps I must take to truly engage in the work of story, but my dreams become nightmares – I see an arduous path, a discouraging journey, a cursed expedition. I have lived this life, experienced the hardship of Black existence. Can I really engage in the work when I have faced angry mobs, hateful words, and death threats? Sweat beads across my forehead, physical manifestations of the anxiety of the moment. My mouth gapes, silent screams from the presence of a difficult journey with no destination in sight. I wish to wake from this dream, but the weight of the work compels my immobility. The fear is binding. I was heartened by the story listener and the work I have read, but I'm unsure. How can I be sure when, even though I see myself angelic, the world sees me monstrous? I do not know how to carry this burden alone.

"You are never alone. Remember, you are always connected to your people through the feedback loop. We will always be here. Let me show you."

Four teachers enter from unseen doorways and speak to me through Afrofuturistic cyphers, breaking the dimensions of my nightmare. Ytasha Womack (2013) tells me that Afrofuturism could allow me to "stretch [my] imagination far beyond the conventions of our time and the horizons of expectations, and [kick] the box of normalcy and preconceived ideas of blackness out of the solar system" (p. 16). Alondra Nelson (2002) encourages me to excavate my identity and embrace the Afrofuturistic, as it gives me the space to tell new stories about my culture and my possible futures. Isiah Lavender (2019) reminds me that I'm not alone, as Black people exist in a realm of networked consciousness that transmits Black people's hopes and experiences through a connected, intergenerational link. His words resound in harmony with Ishmael Reed who sings of Black writers who lie "in the guts of old America, making readings about the future," a melody that forces me to think about the numerous connectors that bind Black futures to Black pasts and Black presents (Dick & Singh, 1995, p. 16). These teachers say that dreaming of a world in which Black people are valued for who they are, not for who they can contort themselves to be, is a concept as old as Blackness itself. They taught me that this work is difficult, intimidating, and sometimes debilitating, but I'm not alone. I'm connected to Black peoples across space and time.

The story listener raises their hands in praise. "She knows. She remembers!" They dance across an ephemeral dreamscape and sing. "She is ready to engage in the work of story."

***

I sit in a room surrounded by six Black girl children/not children. I have removed the slash from my description, but it holds tightly to their perceptions of self. I see myself in their eyes. I see the hardship of existing in a Black girl body in a society that revels in your unhappiness, and I observe the beginnings of bent selves, altered versions of stories celebrated at birth. I ask them: "what would it mean for you to have the space to stretch your imaginations and dream of better otherworlds, to destroy rigid boxes that confine you to monstrosity, and to sing to your ancestors of the future?" They look at me quizzically, and then they join hands and speak all at once, eyes glazed as they connect to each other through the feedback loop. They speak as one.

"We deserve worlds where we are princesses and heroes, not monsters."

"We demand worlds where we are not forced to contort ourselves into beings unrecognizable."

"We require spaces where Black girls are deemed angelic, innocent, human."

"We need love, care, and safety."

"We request opportunities to tell our own stories."

"We urge others to engage in the work of a story listener."

"Hear us!"

Their hands fall silently beside them, and they stare at me, eyes still distant. The youngest of the six asks, "did you listen?"

"Yes." I respond, repeating their words in my head so I would not forget.

"Good. Your work is about to begin," she says with a smile. "Share our stories alongside your own. Our stories deserve to be told."

The girls gasp as the trance loses its hold. They wait for me to speak as I gaze upon them, but my tongue will not move, and my mouth refuses to curve in the formation of words. I have witnessed the intergenerational feedback loop. I have heard the needs of these girls. Like the story listeners who rejoiced upon my birth, I celebrate the girls who lay bare their desires for this world. Like the Black angels who spoke of the mattering of Black life, the girls speak of their lives, their needs. I, as a listener, am responsible to them. You, as a reader and listener of story are responsible to them. And now, my work … our work … is about to begin.

Did you listen?

References

African American Experience in Athens. (2015). https://digihum.libs.uga.edu/exhibits/show/slavery

Archibald, J. (2008). *Indigenous storywork: Educating the heart, mind, body, and spirit.* UBC Press.

Delgado, R. (1989). Storytelling for oppositionists and others: A plea for narrative. *Michigan Law Review*, *87*(8), 2411–2441.

Dick, B., & Singh, A. (1995). *Conversations with Ishmael Reed.* University Press of Mississippi.

Dillard, C. B. (2000). The substance of things hoped for, the evidence of things not seen: Examining an endarkened feminist epistemology in educational research and leadership. *International Journal of Qualitative Studies in Education*, *13*(6), 661–681.

Epstein, R., Blake, J., & Gonzalez, T. (2017). Girlhood interrupted: The erasure of Black girls' childhood. Georgetown Law Center on Poverty and Inequality. Retrieved from https://genderjusticeandopportunity.georgetown.edu/wp-content/uploads/2020/06/girlhood-interrupted.pdf

Higginbotham, E. B. (1993). *Righteous discontent: The women's movement in the Black Baptist church, 1880–1920.* Cambridge, MA: Harvard University Press.

Lavender, I. (2019). *Afrofuturism rising: The literary prehistory of a movement.* The Ohio State University Press.

Nelson, A. (2002). Introduction: Future texts. *Social Text, 20*(2), 1–15.

Posey, K. (2020, June 22). An updated list of UGA buildings named after racist figures. *The Red & Black.* https://www.redandblack.com/uganews/an-updated-list-of-uga-buildings-named-after-racist-figures/article_ef52b270-b42c-11ea-9608-0f9f99f783c3.html

Windchief, S., & San Pedro, T. (2019). *Applying indigenous research methods: Storying with peoples and communities.* Routledge.

Womack, Y. (2013). *Afrofuturism: The world of Black sci-fi and fantasy culture.* Lawrence Hill Books.

CONTRIBUTORS' SHORT BIOS

Theresa Rocha Beardall, J.D., Ph.D., is an assistant professor of sociology at the University of Washington specializing in issues of race, law, policing, and tribal sovereignty. Her scholarship investigates how legal institutions contribute to the racialization and marginalization of social groups and explores how insights from sociolegal findings can be used to challenge these systemic inequalities.

Mahasan Offutt-Chaney, Ph.D., is a critical scholar of Black education studies, race-based opportunity policies, and school punishment. Her current book project *"Punishing Opportunity" and the Disciplining Politics of Education,* offers a historic interpretation of the rise of punitive school discipline policies and locates contemporary roots of urban school punishment to federal policies intended to promote racial opportunity. Her larger research agenda aims to name and challenge the powerful discourses that pervade research on and policy for urban schools which tend to name children as potentially criminal, and thereby sort, and regulate them through punishment. She is an assistant professor at Brown University where she teaches classes on inequality, urban education policy, and school punishment.

Victoria Copeland, Ph.D., is a Black and Filipinx researcher, organizer, and spoonie with training in social welfare and social policy. They are dedicated to learning more about how we can sustain community power and care from the intersections between racial, economic, & disability justice movements. Their research is centralized around black studies and surveillance studies and is largely done in collaboration with local abolitionist organizers. Their communal work aims to bolster and create alternative modalities of care and prioritizes core ethics of reciprocation, rest, refusal, and joy. Some of their research and organizing partners have included the Cops Off Campus Coalition, Defund MPD Coalition-Anti Surveillance Working Group, Let's Get Free LA Coalition, Stop LAPD Spying Coalition, Downtown Women's Action Coalition, and Survivors + Allies.

Dani Ahuicapahtzin Cornejo, Ph.D. (Ópata/Xicano/Picunche/Chileno), is an assistant professor and chair of ethnic studies at Diablo Valley College in Pleasant Hill California. He received his Ph.D. from the Department of Native American Studies at UC Davis. His work is focused on the study of Indigenous holistic pedagogical strategies from a hemispheric perspective as well as the application of these strategies in the service of urban Native youth and other underserved communities in the Bay Area. He has designed and taught courses in the fields of Native American Studies, Urban Education, and Comparative Ethnic Studies, while also writing on the topics of Indigenous cultural reclamation and educational equity.

Leah D. Doane, Ph.D., is a developmental psychologist and professor of psychology at Arizona State University. Through numerous collaborations, she examines how the everyday experiences of children, adolescents, and young adults are associated with physiological stress processes and sleep, and the implications of such associations for health and well-being. Her research program has three primary areas: 1) moment-to-moment and day-to-day dynamics among perceived stress, affect, physiology, and sleep in adolescence and across the transition to college, 2) cultural and familial influences on college planning, transitions, and well-being, including the study of cultural proximal processes and physiological stress indicators in Latinx youth and families, 3) genetic and environmental influences on daily health processes and academic achievement. Her research engages multiple methodologies and tools including ecological momentary assessment, behavioral observational methods, qualitative interviews and focus groups, biological measures including indicators of physiological stress processes and inflammation, quantitative behavior genetics, and objective health and sleep measurement.

Sean Cameron Golden is a Ph.D. candidate in curriculum and instruction where he studies fugitive literacies and the radical tradition of Black teaching. He is passionate about creating liberatory classroom spaces that focus on humanizing marginalized beings through (re)story and story-telling methods using various modalities. Sean is a 2023–2024 winner of the university's Doctoral Dissertation Fellowship and a recipient of the COSP Diversity Predoctoral Teaching Fellowship. Along with Black forms of storywork, Sean is also interested in Children's and Young Adult literature and texts, and how these stories feature queer kids and holistic beings.

Kevin Lawrence Henry, Jr., is an assistant professor of educational leadership and Policy Analysis at the University of Wisconsin-Madison. His interdisciplinary scholarship focuses on educational (in) justice and the racial politics of education policy and reform. More specifically, his research investigates the racialized lived realities of charter schools and school choice policy; the persistence of anti-Blackness in education; and culturally relevant and restorative justice approaches to education. Kevin's work is informed by Black Studies, Critical Race Theory, and Black feminist theory.

Derek A. Houston, Ph.D., is an associate professor of educational leadership at Southern Illinois University Edwardsville. Centered at the nexus of critical theory and quantitative methods, Dr. Houston's work engages with policy questions relative to inequality and inequity across the P-20 educational pipeline, advocating for a socially liberating future. His most recent scholarship, published in Teacher's College Record & Kappa Delta Pi Record, takes a critical quantitative approach to understanding special education and education degree production. Additionally, his scholarship has focused on critically engaging the tools and processes of quantitative research.

dinorah sánchez loza, Ph.D., is a critical scholar of education focused on the relationships between schooling, social (re)production, and democratic (mis)education. Her current book project, "Schooling Settlers: Race, Colonialism, and Right-Wing Politics in Predominantly White Schools" utilizes ethnographic methods to investigate the political ideologies that circulate and are (re)produced in commonly perceived "good schools." Her research agenda centers on this relationship between school and how youth come to think and act politically while focusing on critical social theories such as settler colonialism and its resultant structuring of race, gender, and political-economic relations and the impact these have on the teaching and learning of politics and civic engagement. She is an assistant professor at The Ohio State University where she teaches classes on critical social theories in education, critical ethnography, and the teaching and research of social justice education.

Jade Nixon is a Ph.D. candidate at the Women & Gender Studies Institute at the University of Toronto, Canada.

Mayra Puente, Ph.D. (ella/she), is an assistant professor of higher education at the Gevirtz Graduate School of Education at the University of California, Santa Barbara. She is particularly concerned with college access, choice, transition, retention, and success issues for rural Latinx students and other institutionally marginalized student groups and communities. Dr. Puente draws on frameworks like Critical Race Theory, Latino Critical Race Theory, Critical Race Spatial Analysis, and Chicana Feminisms to address these pressing educational issues and enact social, racial, and spatial justice for rural Latinx students and families in pursuit of higher education.

Goleen Samari, Ph.D., is an associate professor and population health demographer in the Department of Population and Public Health Sciences at the University of Southern California Keck School of Medicine. Dr. Samari's research focuses on how structural inequities, namely, racism, gender inequities, and migration-based inequities, shape reproductive and population health with a particular focus on immigrant communities and populations in or from the Middle East and North Africa. Dr. Samari was the first to conceptualize how islamophobia and anti-Muslim racism are public health issues. Dr. Samari earned a Ph.D. in public health, an MPH in community health sciences, and an MA in Islamic studies from the University of California, Los Angeles.

Antar A. Tichavakunda, Ph.D., is an assistant professor of education at the University of California Santa Barbara. Born and raised in Washington, DC, Tichavakunda is a product of DC Public Schools. His first book, *Black Campus Life: The Worlds Black Students Make at a Historically White Institution*, is published with SUNY Press. Tichavakunda enjoys watching anime, eating soul food (especially savory grits), and writing in cafes.

S. R. Toliver, Ph.D., is an assistant professor of curriculum and instruction at the University of Illinois at Urbana-Champaign whose scholarship centers on the freedom dreams of Black youth and honors the historical legacy that Black imaginations have had and will have on activism and social change. She is the author of *Recovering Black Storytelling in Qualitative Research: Endarkened Storywork*, and her academic work has been published in several journals, including the *Journal of Literacy Research* and *Research in the Teaching of English*.

Eve Tuck, Ph.D., is Professor of Critical Race and Indigenous Studies at the Ontario Institute for Studies in Education (OISE), University of Toronto, Canada.

Joanna L. Williams, Ph.D., is a developmental psychologist who studies issues of race, identity, and relationships with a focus on the period of adolescence. Specific areas of interest include racial-ethnic identity, racial-ethnic diversity in adolescent friendship networks, and social network equity in racially diverse schools. She also co-produces research on these topics with young people. Dr. Williams is an associate professor in the Graduate School of Applied and Professional Psychology at Rutgers University, and co-director of the National Scientific Council on Adolescence.

K. Wayne Yang, Ph.D., is a professor of ethnic studies and provost of John Muir College at the University of California, San Diego, USA.

INDEX

abolitionist praxis and Black geographies in social work 97–109; family policing 103–104; *Nguzo Saba* principles 101; oppositional geography as a possibility 106–109; relationality and 108; sharing stories 107; Skid Row community 105; theorizing within a matrix of domination 104–106

Ansley, F. L. 68

anti-Asian violence during COVID-19 pandemic 92

anti-Blackness: and fugitivity 135; makes troublemakers 128–129

anti-Muslim racism 61, 78–88; birth of scholarship on 84–86; cultural traits of groups assigning 80; as a double burden across the life course 87–88; early life course 78–79; "good Muslim", evolution of 81–84; health consequences of 86–87; in health research and programs 83–84; Islamophobia and 78; in Middle East and North Africa (MENA) populations 79; "otherness" 81; structural racism and 80, 87; theoretical life course 79–81; *see also* "good Muslim", evolution of

Anzaldúa, Gloria 36, 46, 65, 156–157

Archibald, Jo-Ann 152, 155–156

assabiya (group feeling) 82

Bad Boys: The Making of Black Masculinity 128–129

Bari Bari ritual 97–98

Battle-Baptiste, W. 121

Beautiful Experiments 133

Bernal, Delgado 46

beyond stories of the hunt 169–179; elementary school 171–172; framing theory 170; graduate school 172–174; stories that matter 177–178; tenure track, beyond stories of the hunt 174–177; theory is lineage work 178–179

Billings, Gloria Ladson 65

Black boys into "troublemakers" in school 128–129

Black liberations, afrofuturist dreams of 181–191

Black Lives Matter movement 71

Black radical tradition, fugitivity, planning, and Black study in 124

Black women's geographies in social work 102

Black, Christine 156

For Product Safety Concerns and Information please contact our EU
representative GPSR@taylorandfrancis.com
Taylor & Francis Verlag GmbH, Kaufingerstraße 24, 80331 München, Germany

www.ingramcontent.com/pod-product-compliance
Lightning Source LLC
Chambersburg PA
CBHW050648280326
41932CB00015B/2824

*9 7 8 1 0 3 2 3 0 1 8 5 3 *